The Politics of Human Rights in East Asia

D1694824

The Politics of Human Rights in East Asia

Kenneth Christie and Denny Roy

Pluto Press

LONDON • STERLING, VIRGINIA

First published 2001 by Pluto Press
345 Archway Road, London N6 5AA
and 22883 Quicksilver Drive,
Sterling, VA 20166–2012, USA

www.plutobooks.com

British Library Cataloguing in Publication Data
A catalogue record for this book is available from
the British Library

Library of Congress Cataloging in Publication Data
Christie, Kenneth.
  The politics of human rights in East Asia / Kenneth Christie and Denny
Roy.
    p. cm.
  ISBN 0–7453–1419–8
  1. Human rights—East Asia. 2. Human rights—Asia, Southeastern. I.
Roy, Denny, 1960– II. Title.
  JC599.E18 C48 2001
  323'.095—dc21

                                                          00–009420

ISBN 0 7453 1419 8 hardback
ISBN 0 7453 1414 7 paperback

10   09   08   07   06   05   04   03   02   01
10   9   8   7   6   5   4   3   2   1

Designed and produced for Pluto Press by
Chase Publishing Services, Fortescue, Sidmouth EX10 9QG
Typeset from disk by Stanford DTP Services, Northampton
Printed in the European Union by Antony Rowe, Chippenham, England

Contents

Note

The views expressed in this book by Denny Roy are his and not necessarily those of the US government.

For Marianne from Kenneth
For Brittney from Denny

Acknowledgements

Kenneth Christie

Many people and institutions have helped to shape my thinking about Southeast Asia over the years. I am grateful to the Institute of Southeast Asian Studies (ISEAS) in Singapore for allowing me to use their very valuable library from time to time, and to their excellent library staff for providing me with such good information. I have also benefited from a visit to the Nordic Institute for Asian Studies in Copenhagen, where I had access to a wonderful library and very conscientious library staff. I would like to thank Erik Skaaning, Jens-Christian Sørensen and Per Hansen for making my stay very comfortable above and beyond the call of duty. Special mention must be made of Inga-Lill Blomkvist and Eva Nielsen who provided me with a wealth of information on my topic and really went out of their way to ensure I was getting all the material I needed. Thank you also to Anne Schlanbusch, Birgit Klintebach and Per Ronnås for the warm welcome they gave me.

I would like to thank some people for reading portions of the manuscript and commenting on it, including Gary Risser on Thailand, and Hari Singh on Malaysia. I am grateful to Thammassat University and in particular to Dr Corrine Phuangkasem for allowing me to give a seminar on human rights at a symposium they organised. I would also like to thank my students in Singapore, South Africa and Norway for the insights they have generously shared with me over the years on these kinds of issues.

I would like to thank the people at Lichado, the Cambodian human rights NGO, for making me very comfortable during my stay in Cambodia in 1998 and for the support they gave me. In particular, Dr Pung Chhiv Kek Galabru and Eva Galabru were extremely helpful under very difficult circumstances and they have my utmost admiration for the tremendous work they do to further the cause and practice of human rights in Cambodia. Finally, I would like to thank Roger Van Zwanenberg, Robert Webb and Ray Addicott for seeing this project through. Thanks are also due to Therese Zeil and Marianne Bruvik for technical assistance.

Needless to say, any mistakes incurred throughout the book are our own.

1
Introduction

Consider the following statements made by East Asian elites at various times in the 1990s.

> The Confucianist view of order between subject and ruler helps in the rapid transformation of society ... in other words, you fit yourself into society – the exact opposite of the American rights of the individual.
>
> I believe that what a country needs to develop is discipline more than democracy. Democracy leads to undisciplined and disorderly conditions.[1]

> Lee Kuan Yew (Senior Minister, Singapore)

> The West tells us that democratic freedom and human rights are fundamental to the achievement of economic and social development. We in ASEAN never disputed that democracy for the people and opportunity for the individual to develop his or her own potential are indeed important principles ... [however] the norms and precepts for the observation of human rights vary from society to society ... Nobody can claim to have a monopoly of wisdom to determine what is right and proper for all countries and peoples. It would be condescending, to say the least, and suspect for the West to preach human rights to us in the East.[2]

> Mohammed Mahathir (Prime Minister of Malaysia)

> Human rights are interrelated and indivisible comprising civil, political, economic, social and cultural rights. These rights are of equal importance. They should be addressed in a balanced and integrated manner and protected and promoted with due regard for specific cultural, social, economic and political circumstances ... the promotion of human rights should not be politicised.[3]

> ASEAN Foreign Ministers (July 1993)

1

These comments were fairly typical of the mood of leaders of highly successful East Asian economies in the early to mid-1990s. They do not represent everyone – Thailand and the Philippines, for instance, clearly had different ideas – but they do represent some consensus among elites in the East Asian region about the virtues of promoting authoritarianism and disregarding democracy and universal ideas of human rights. These constructs and their relationship with each other have returned to the limelight of many studies of politics, modernization and globalization in the 1990s. While authoritarian models of central planning collapsed in the Soviet Union and Eastern Europe, the liberal democratic, free market model appeared to have emerged triumphant. However, the political version of this formula was called into question by the success of East Asian countries, which sought to argue that their economic ascendancy was predicated on a different set of values and concerns from those of western democracies. The values proclaimed here are broadly illiberal and undemocratic, and question whether economic development ultimately leads to political liberalization. They are also uninterested in universal notions of human rights and what they constitute. Freedom, a central element of a human rights culture, for instance, has been a widely debated subject. As David Kelly has argued: 'nowhere are reports about freedom – its perilous ascendancy in Taiwan or its suppression in Rangoon, its exuberance in Manila or its mediocrity in Singapore – in greater currency than in this Asian region'.[4]

Liberal democracy and individual human rights, some East Asian elites argued, are inappropriate to the political and social culture in Asia, a culture that promotes 'order', consensus and harmony over confrontation and adversarial forms of politics. Moreover, given the remarkable economic success of Southeast Asia (until the currency meltdown of 1997), many felt they were in a position to resist such intrusions. For those with democratic instincts who hoped that democracy and human rights norms would gain a foothold in the region, the record was disappointing as authoritarian regimes bucked the trend of the 'third wave' of democratization.[5] The region opposed and displayed antipathy towards individual human rights. Furthermore, these regimes seemed to offer an alternative form and mode of governance. Table 1.1 illustrates their reluctance to embrace the third wave of democratization.

Table 1.1 Southeast Asia: Freedom and economic growth

Southeast Asia	Freedom Score			GNP 1996 per capita (US$)	Average Annual Growth (%) 1995–96
	1994	1996	1998		
Singapore	5	4	5	30,550	5.6
Malaysia	4.5	4	5	4,370	5.8
Brunei	6.5	6			
Indonesia	6.5	6	6	1,080	5.8
Thailand	4	3	2.5	2,960	4.4
Myanmar (formerly Burma)	7	7	7		
Vietnam	7	7	7	290	7.3
Cambodia	4.5	6	6	300	3.9
Laos	6.5			400	4.0
Philippines	3.5	2.5	2.5	1,160	4.5

Sources: GNP per capita and annual average growth rates are from the World Bank (1998) *World Development Indicators*. Freedom scores are from *Freedom in the World: The Annual Survey of Political Rights and Civil Liberties* (1994), (1997) and (1999): Freedom House Survey Team. The figures given for the scores are the mean of the combination of political rights and civil liberties scores. The scale proceeds from 1.0 (most free) to 7.0 (least free).

Moreover, some critics of modernization theory and its implications also argue that those forms of liberal democratic values and universal human rights are highly problematic if considered universal. A liberal democratic system (which is shaped by 'cultural particularity')[6] is also 'informed and justified by the ideas of equality and freedom as well as by a recognition and accommodation of "the fact of pluralism", [and it] is a culturally distinct, historically contingent artefact, not readily transferable to East and Southeast Asian societies with different traditions, needs and conceptions of human flourishing'.[7] As Bauer and Bell assert: 'The new human rights discourse is also a reaction to the increasing pressure on East Asian Governments to comply with international human rights norms. This pressure comes from an international community that has heightened expectations for a part of the world that has become irrevocably integrated into global markets.'[8] In order to underpin and provide roots for their economic freedom and equality, democracy in Southeast Asia requires the problematic juxtaposition of different sets of alien values and needs to suit their particular context. The contention here is that the liberal democratic project (with its cultural particularity), its individualism and rights constructs appear alien in such a context.

It is well known that the term 'human rights' was originally a western concept originating from the experience and political philosophy of Western Europe. One of the dominant themes of Western European history has been the struggle of citizens to limit the powers and intrusiveness of their rulers. Many western political thinkers have characterized government as a necessary evil, ideally given the task only of providing the protection and minimal supervision that allow the people to achieve prosperity and self-fulfilment. When the phrase 'human rights' came into popular usage after the Second World War, it referred to laws protecting citizens from being abused or suppressed by their governments – what are now more specifically called civil and political human rights. The need to distinguish this class of human rights, also known as 'first generation human rights', arose from the assertion of Third World commentators that social and economic rights ('second generation human rights'), which are guarantees that basic needs (food, shelter, employment, medical care, etc.) will be met, are desired by the majority of the world's population at least as deeply as civil liberties. As we shall see, many of the authoritarian regimes in Asia have couched their human rights agendas in reference to national security concerns. These usually include some or all of the following: maintaining a country's survival and prosperity; protecting against attack or molestation of one's citizens, territory or assets; and the preservation of 'core values', which may include a particular political system or way of life. More often than not, national security and regime security mean the same thing for authoritarian states determined to maintain power.

AN OVERVIEW OF HUMAN RIGHTS IN ASIA

A few observations help to establish a context for talking about human rights in Asia. First, it could be argued that in Asia there is no history of 'human rights' as understood in its western context.

Human rights in their original sense (to which Asians have been obliged to react) not only apply to all groups of people in all societies, regardless of their socioeconomic status, but are also conceived of as fundamental entitlements that 'trump' all other considerations which may stem from an individual's relationship to social networks or to the state. In Asia and other Third World societies there is no tradition of such entitlements. People are believed to have basic duties, not basic rights, and these duties arise from a person's status or group affiliation. Thus, a ruler may have a duty to rule justly and the rich a duty to give to the poor, but this does not mean that the people have a right to be ruled justly or that the poor have a right to receive charity.

Most Asian countries are anxious eradicate poverty and catch up economically with the long-industrialized North. As a result, development has assumed cult-like status. As suggested by Abraham Maslow's 'hierarchy of needs', essentials such as food and shelter *seem* less important, in the sense that less thought and effort are devoted to procuring them when they are plentiful, and more important when they are scarce. In the relatively wealthy West, by contrast, more attention is devoted to secondary and tertiary aspirations, such as control over one's destiny. This is why there is less emphasis on economic development in richer countries than in poorer countries, and why Asians are willing to make great sacrifices for economic development. This opens the door for the controversial argument, put forward by many Asian government officials, that some civil and political liberties must be given up to achieve prosperity.

While processes of democratization may appear universal to western theorists, something very different was happening in the East. This book examines the context of the debate on human rights that has emerged in Southeast Asia, its relation to globalization and the assumptions that are made surrounding it, in the light of these states' concerns about regime security. These are, of course, cultural caricatures, a juxtaposition of Asia's strengths to the West's weaknesses in a kind of reverse Orientalism. Critics have made several other trenchant counterpoints. First, most of the impetus for the Asian values movement seems to have originated with officials serving in 'soft authoritarian' regimes fighting off both internal and external pressures for political liberalization: leaders such as Malaysia's Mohammed Mahathir, Singapore's Lee Kuan Yew and

Kishore Mahbubani, and a number of representatives of China's Deng and Jiang Zemin regimes.[9] Many other Asians – including opposition politicians such as Korea's Kim Dae Jung (prior to his election as President in 1997) and Burma's Nobel Prize-winning pro-democracy activist Aung San Suu Kyi, Asian human rights non-governmental organizations, and even a number of officials such as President Fidel Ramos of the Philippines – have questioned the notion that civil liberties are inherently 'western' and inappropriate for Asia. This gives rise to the suspicion that the views of the Asian values spokespeople are not truly representative of the region, and that their campaign is a tactic to help dominant but threatened political parties maintain their monopolies on power.

Today, what are characterized as 'Asian' values were once prevalent in the West, and indeed are still strongly espoused by many conservatives in Western Europe and the United States. The old western values have been eroded by industrialization, economic development and capitalism in general. In Asia many societies are undergoing a similar transformation as they achieve new levels of wealth and industrialization, leading in turn to the anxiety that has generated the Asian values rhetoric. Thus, the debate may be miscast; it is not Asian versus western values, but rather tradition versus modernity. The whole purpose of the Asian values movement is to maintain the high rates of economic growth to which the region has become accustomed without developing the social pathology that has followed affluence in the West; or, to put it another way, to enjoy the positive aspects of modernization without its problems. Unfortunately for the champions of Asian values, this may not be possible.

HUMAN RIGHTS AND SECURITY IN ASIA

Although the size and diversity of the region suggest caution in making generalizations, it seems defensible to assert that Asian states – in comparison with their western counterparts – have tended to view human rights as a threat to national security. Indeed, the contrast in attitudes towards human rights and national security between East and West is stark. The US government is committed to the proposition that extending (civil and political) human rights makes the state and its people more secure. Believing that it has largely accomplished this task domestically, the US government has sought to enhance US state and individual security by promoting human rights abroad. The Clinton administration has been particularly acquiescent to the logic explained here by Madeleine Albright:

> Because we live in a country that is democratic, trade-oriented, respectful of the law and possessed of a powerful military whose personnel are precious to us, we will do better and feel safer in an environment where our values are widely shared, markets are open, military clashes are constrained and those who run roughshod over the rights of others are brought to heel.

John Shattuck, Assistant Secretary of State for Democracy, Human Rights and Labor, adds, 'human rights are and will remain a key element in our foreign policy' because 'When human rights standards are observed ... Americans are safer, and we are more likely to find good partners with whom to pursue shared economic, diplomatic, and security goals.'[10] The United States may be the state most active in the promotion of human rights internationally, but other western states generally accept that democracy and the observance of human rights 'are the foundation of justice and peace in the world'.[11]

There is no comparable view in Asian officialdom. Asian states have been more inclined to believe, as the West once did, that how a government treats its citizens is a matter of sovereign prerogative and is no foreigner's business. Officials in the People's Republic of China speak for many when they contend that human rights pressure, whether from domestic sources or from overseas, is an affront to the authority of the ruling party. Pressure from foreigners, in particular, is alleged to be fraught with ulterior motives that have direct ramifications for national security. In a typical response to the US State Department's annual report on human rights in countries around the world, the Chinese charged, 'the authors of the "Reports" don't really want China to be strong, stable, and developing, nor do they want to see any improvement and development in the human rights conditions for all the Chinese people. What they really want to do is to use human rights as a tool with which to vilify China in the international community and sabotage China's stability and development.'

We would like to point out that there are tremendous variations in how human rights are perceived and levels of democratization throughout this vast region we cover. Heterogeneity is far more apparent than homogeneity and our effort is not to reduce these states to any neat, formulistic categories. China is clearly quite different from Thailand, Vietnam from Taiwan, and so on. We have attempted to assess the human rights records to illustrate the differences and the similarities of this complex area and to show their interesting variations. Despite the differences, we will argue that many of the states in the region have sought to promote values and ideas that defend their forms of cultural relativism and actively attempt to deflect criticism of what is essentially an authoritarian mode of government. But before we can proceed to examine some of these assumptions, we need to state the arguments presented by some East Asian states in defence of their political systems and constructed values. It is these values and views that appear at the core of the rationales for illiberal democracy and the denial of the applicability of universal human rights to their particular systems.

COMMUNITARIANISM VERSUS INDIVIDUALISM

In East Asia it is often asserted that their cultures protect the community at the expense of restricting the freedoms of the individual, while the West takes the opposite approach. According to James Hsiung: 'pressing for one's own interests without regard to the interests of others is seen as no more than the pursuit of individual self-interest, not the pursuit of human rights defined as rights of fellow humans'.[12] In this sense, empirically based assertions are prominent: the high rates of violent crime, divorce, drug abuse, homelessness and family disintegration in much of the West, particularly the United States, appear to confirm the belief that the western model has failed and that Asia in many ways represents a more stable and virtuous alternative. The over-protection of criminals and deviants has made life miserable for all society, according to the guardians of moral virtue in authoritarian regimes in Asia, and the editorials in newspapers confirm this. Newspapers in various Southeast Asian regimes frequently publish accounts of the 'decline' of the West, contrasting explicitly and implicitly their own thriving, efficient and crime-free states with the decadent, recession-hit, chaotic West. To avoid this social decline, these writers argue, the rights of the community as a whole must come before those of the individual.

The question of imprisonment provides a concrete illustration of the different approaches to the community versus individual rights problem. In the US judicial system, the plaintiffs carry the burden of proof, and safeguards against a wrongful conviction are so rigorous that obviously guilty defendants are sometimes acquitted. In Southeast Asia, imprisonment without a fair, public trial is common. An *Asiaweek* editorial defended governments that 'have weighed the risks of jailing the wrong man and concluded that more innocent people are put in danger by letting criminals go for lack of evidence. Critics of preventive detention ought to consider whether the common good should be endangered to protect the civil liberties of a few.'[13] Clearly in the case of Anwar Ibrahim, the former Deputy Prime Minister of Malaysia, currently in jail for corruption and sexual deviancy, the risks proved too great for the authoritarian, anti-individual human rights leadership of Mohammed Mahathir – a stark case of attempting to remain in power whatever the costs to civil liberties. Moreover, an intrinsic element of the western conception is that rights belong to individual human beings; that the struggle for these rights has been in part defined by a struggle against a reluctant state; and that notions of free speech, free assembly and fair trials have all embodied the idea that the right of the individual against the state has to be protected.

Southeast Asian societies, by contrast, are more inclined to assert the rights of the group; thus the group, not the individual, is the starting point in any analysis. This view maintains that obligations to the community are more important than rights procured from it. As one of ASEAN's senior statesmen has argued on the question of individualism, Asia has a totally different conception from that of western societies:

> Whether in periods of golden prosperity or in the depths of disorder, Asia has never valued the individual over society. The society has always been more important than the individual. I think that is what has saved Asia from greater misery ... I believe that human-rights standards, as distinct from democracy as a form of government, will become universal. It will not be western standards, because the West is but a minority in this world.[14]

While rights were often won from the state in western societies over time through processes of democratization, the argument seems to be in Southeast Asia that rights are either duties that the citizen owes to the state, or privileges that the state distributes when it feels it appropriate to do so. The defenders of rights standards in this region also argue for their own cultures to be taken into consideration; a communitarian basis to its society, which is distinct from the western individualistic ethos. This communitarian tradition seeks consensus, in contrast to the western adversarial tradition. In April 1993, many Asian states signed the Bangkok Declaration, to the effect that while reaffirming the basic principle of universal human rights, one should bear in mind the importance and significance of various national and regional particularities:

> While human rights are universal in nature, they must be considered in the context of a dynamic and evolving process of international norm-setting, bearing in mind the significance of national and regional particularities and various historical, cultural and religious backgrounds.[15]

It was an indication that 'cultural relativism' had made inroads into the working of their policies and that human rights were regarded as an evolving and not a fixed set of norms and values. This debate became more and more vigorous and, as Freeman notes, it is only a 'manifestation of the general problem of the relation between the ethical universalism presupposed by the human rights doctrine and the claims of ethical particularism, best known to human rights scholars as the problem of "cultural relativism"'.[16]

PRIVILEGES VERSUS ENTITLEMENTS

In the western liberal tradition, there is a general feeling that abuse of power by political elites is a constant threat. Wise and selfless autocrats are considered the exception rather than the rule. The history of western politics has largely concerned the struggle of private citizens to win their freedoms, viewed as natural or God-given rights, from reluctant governments and to preserve these liberties through their institutionalization.

  East Asian regimes posit a completely different view of the relationship between state and society. Here, leaders are traditionally believed to be morally and intellectually superior to the common people. In ancient China, for example, the quality of rulers was supposed to be guaranteed by the government's civil service examination system, which assessed knowledge of classical Confucian writings. Scoring well in the examination would indicate both scholastic acumen and familiarity with the codes of virtuous behaviour – appropriate preparation for state officials. Rulers in Southeast Asia (at least until recently) consequently are far more trusted than their western counterparts. People may grumble in private about autocratic leaders, but they still defer to them and often vote them back into office or acquiesce in their continued tenure of office. In a typical Southeast Asian society there has traditionally been little public criticism of the ruler, who may often be perceived to have the mandate of heaven. Compared to Western Europeans and North Americans, East Asians are more likely to accept that individual liberties must be sacrificed if the state is to carry out its role of maintaining the security, stability and prosperity of society as a whole. What political rights the people do enjoy are viewed as privileges, gifts from a benevolent leadership, rather than entitlements. This is in line with Confucian ideals regarding government and society.

Malaysia is one of the countries that appear most vociferous in its attacks on the West. Its leader, Dr Mohammed Mahathir, regularly denounces the West, claiming that it is hypocritical and has double standards on human rights. Regular barrages fill Malaysian newspapers and international conferences when Mahathir issues statements about the West's hypocrisy on such matters as the Gulf War and the crisis in the Balkans. In many cases the language of development, human rights and democracy and their implications has become inseparable for East Asian leaders, a set of issues and problems to be addressed. This gives these regimes ammunition in human rights debates with the West. If the western understanding of human rights is closely bound up with the West's culture and historical experience, some Asian theorists assert, it cannot serve as a guide for regions with a vastly different cultural and historical backgrounds. As Hsiung argues, 'For an East Asian not to know the rules above – that is, to avoid ostentatious confrontation and to observe the need for balancing "freedom of" with "freedoms from" – would be almost incredible.'[17] Many regional commentators increasingly assert that 'Asian' and 'western' values are fundamentally different. Asians, they say, value family obligations, chastity and hard work, while westerners are obsessed with personal gratification and are prone to laziness, drug abuse and promiscuity. This 'cultural' issue has a political dimension as well.[18] Clearly, the claim of a local perspective on human rights based on 'Asian values' is often a self-serving ploy by leaders seeking to gain prestige in the region by criticizing powerful countries such as the United States or to rally domestic support by playing up the threat of foreign imperialism, currency speculators and other perceived 'threats'.[19]

GLOBALIZATION, HUMAN RIGHTS AND DEVELOPMENT

It is difficult to talk about the development of human rights in East Asia without reference to the phenomenon of globalization, which has played its part not only in the region's dramatic economic growth, but also in its rapid downfall in the Asian economic crisis which erupted in mid-1997. Part of East Asia's resistance to human rights criticisms from the West has been made on the claim to *status parity*, that is that this region was a major player in the global economy and therefore there was less room for conditionality and sanctions to force compliance with international human rights regimes. Globalization has made national state borders increasingly porous with the result that economies and populations have become increasingly interdependent. What hurts East Asia also hurts the West, particularly when returns on investment fall. Studying the role of multinational corporations in the movement of capital, goods, services and labour around the world has become a mini-growth industry in itself.

One of the many effects of globalization has been the growth of poverty and disparities on an economic and social scale; globalization is at once, paradoxically, a blessing and a curse. It helps to promote economic growth, but much of that growth is unbalanced and uneven. Financial crises appear more often and have severe impacts on local populations, causing social disintegration and maldevelopment.[20] Despite the promotion of liberal market economies and economic development as the answer to poverty, more often than not the gulf between development and individual rights has deepened and the tensions have been sharpened. The East Asian 'miracle' might have been a miracle for the World Bank and development economists, but it always masked real underlying disparities and social problems. The financial crash and the currency meltdown have simply brought these into dramatic focus. There are serious questions involved in globalization; questions of illegal (and legal) migration, labour standards, prostitution, child labour and child prostitution and discrimination against ethnic minorities, to name just a few. However, globalization has also had positive effects in that these debates have started to take place and a 'rights' consciousness has developed which allows us to look at different perspectives more clearly. Jusuf Wanandi, an Indonesian intellectual, has captured some of the problem:

> The globalization of the economy means that individual communities can no longer remain isolated. Our communal approach is definitely changing as a result of the influence of international values. What we need to find now is an appropriate mixture of individualism with continued respect for authority.[21]

The notions of multiculturalism or its opposite, the homogenization of cultures, which appears as a by-product of globalization, has generated identity problems, asserted a politics of difference and fostered struggles for recognition (by various minority groups among others). Indigenous groups have now become more assertive in their claims to political and economic rights. The tension between economic development, rapid growth and the state of governance is an important one. The protracted conflict in East Timor testifies to this; in part, globalization has helped to highlight the case of appalling human rights abuses here.[22]

Empirically and theoretically, most East Asian states are – or have recently been – authoritarian rather than democratic, and developing rather than developed. Regional commentators, theorists and politicians argue that their countries should focus on economic progress first, with the expectation that some degree of political liberalization will follow later. Built into this position are the assumptions that economic/social rights are more important than civil/political rights, and that the latter hinder economic development. This is one of the key arguments of Asian authoritarian elites, a practical reason why they cannot afford liberal democracy.

These societies in general have formulated two major views when it comes to development. First, development is a collective activity primarily supplied by state agencies and other groups in society. Second, it is an economic and social process perhaps requiring in the short term the infraction of classical civil and political rights. Choice, for instance, might not be as important in employment as in the state directing labour towards certain development projects. The formation of trade unions to protect workers' rights is clearly less important than development goals, which in turn might infringe human rights in the process. There is no promise or even proof that once such development goals have been attained, civil and political rights will be extended to citizens; no social contract is carved in stone in this process. In the end, the fulfilment of collective rights requires the postponement of individual political rights until the perceived level of development is reached in which the latter become less of a comparative luxury. Implicit here is the assumption of a trade-off between basic needs and luxuries, with human rights (in the western sense) falling into the latter category. Otherwise, there would be no need to set aside human rights until development was consolidated. Thus the concept of collective rights will necessarily entail the postponement of individual political rights until the perceived level of development is reached in which the latter become less of a comparative luxury. Hsiung argues that the cultural difference in this regard is clear:

> A labor strike may be considered an exercise of a union's right of collective bargaining in the Western adversarial tradition. But often, especially during a sanitation or transit strike, it may victimize many members of the public. The principle of human rights as wholeness is, in the East Asian consensual tradition considered to have been violated. This is why labor strikes are not popular with the public, even in Japan ... [there is] public aversion to labor strikes as an extreme form of selfishness (because they abridge the rights of a larger number of third parties).[23]

This leads us into the hotly debated issue of whether or not authoritarian government is necessary for successful economic and social development. Those who posit this view argue that nation-building requires discipline, austerity and obedience to measures that may be unpopular in the short run, but will yield great dividends in the future. In such circumstances – in effect, a national emergency – governments cannot ensure the successful prosecution of their policies without limiting civil liberties (freedom of speech and of the press, the right of accused criminals to a fair trial, freedom from physical abuse by the police, and so on). As a society becomes wealthier, more orderly and better educated, civil and political privileges will naturally increase. But if the basic goals of development are not achieved, all subsequent aspirations, including human rights, are doomed. It is therefore unfair for the West, whose sense of human rights developed within its political and historical context, to demand that poor, politically unstable underdeveloped countries guarantee as broad a range of individual freedoms as exists in the developed world. The problem with this is, at what stage does a society determine that human rights are not expedient and are elevated to a different plane in terms of priority? As we can see in Tables 1.2 and 1.3, the region of East Asia and the Pacific, which contains the subset most reluctant to democratization and individual human rights notions, also showed the most progress in several indicators of social and economic development.

Table 1.2 Population living on less than $1 a day in developing regions, 1987 and 1993

Region	1987 millions	1993 millions	1987 per cent	1993 per cent
East Asia and the Pacific	464.0	445.0	28.8	26.0
Europe and Central Asia	2.2	14.5	0.6	3.5
Latin America and Caribbean	91.2	109.6	22.0	23.5
Middle East and North Africa	10.3	10.7	4.7	4.1
South Asia	479.9	514.7	45.4	43.1
Sub-Saharan Africa	179.6	218.6	38.5	39.1

Source: World Bank (1998) *World Development Report: World Development Indicators*.

In contrast to this sequential approach to democracy and human rights, others (mainly liberals and advocates of the western liberal democracy) argue for concurrency: human rights, particularly civil liberties, do not threaten economic and social development, and therefore can and should be implemented immediately, even by Third World countries. These theorists question the logic of the argument that civil liberties undermine nation-building. Allowing fair, constructive political debate of major policy issues, protecting citizens from torture at the hands of state authorities and from imprisonment without a fair trial, and permitting freedom of worship are not incompatible with economic development. Indeed,

Table 1.3 Progress in social indicators

Region	Infant mortality per 1,000 live births 1970	Infant mortality per 1,000 live births 1996	Under-5 mortality 1980	Under-5 mortality 1996	Gross primary school enrolment (per cent) 1980	Gross primary school enrolment (per cent) 1995
East Asia and Pacific	79	39	74	47	88	115
Europe and Central Asia	—	24	—	30	—	100
Latin America and Caribbean	84	33	82	41	—	111
Middle East and North Africa	134	50	141	63	68	97
South Asia	139	73	174	93	67	99
Sub-Saharan Africa	137	91	193	147	80	75

Source: World Bank (1998) *World Development Report: Word Development Indicators*.

implementation of these rights is likely to increase a government's legitimacy and encourage hard work and sacrifice for national goals. In this light, western-style human rights are seen as a benefit, even a necessity, for the poor. They are not a luxury for the rich. As empirical support for this argument, proponents could point to many cases in which restrictions on civil liberties coincided with economic stagnation rather than economic progress – the Philippines under Ferdinand Marcos, India during Indira Gandhi's 'Emergency', and the Soviet Union and Eastern Europe under communist rule.

Another debate stemming from this is whether the different variations should be implemented concurrently or sequentially by developing countries. Many of the non-western theorists who promote socioeconomic rights argue that these must precede civil and political rights. Indeed, the fact that the western conception of human rights overlooks problems such as starvation and homelessness is taken as evidence for how removed rich countries are from the challenges faced by the underdeveloped world. A second, corollary argument emanating from Southeast Asia is that western individualistic tendencies which push for human rights and democracy are inconsistent with – perhaps even inimical to – the drive for economic development, which is, after all, their society's primary economic and social goal. Again, this is based on a misleading argument. Recent research has reasserted the ideas of modernization theory that socioeconomic development is one of the most important factors in democratization. Countries in East Asia (such as Taiwan and South Korea) and Latin America were all prompted to turn towards increasing democracy by high levels of economic growth in the 1980s. So the case is made for correlation being the opposite of Southeast Asian claims. It is not individualism and democracy that undermine economic growth, but economic growth that undermines authoritarianism and leads to democracy and increasing respect for human rights.[24] Several of the states in East Asia that have adopted forms of democracy and increased respect for individual human rights – Japan, South Korea, Taiwan and, more recently, the Philippines – have experienced as high rates of economic growth and development as the Southeast Asian states which have decried so-called western individualism, such as Singapore, Malaysia and Indonesia. These countries are on the defensive; of the 31 countries that experienced democratization or became more liberalized between 1974 and 1989, 27 were in the middle-income range. Countries that were previously classified as non-democratic, once they have progressed to middle-income status, appear to proceed through a 'transition' stage in which pressures for democratization, greater pluralism and human rights concerns gain more credibility. It would be hard to attribute the reluctance of Southeast Asian states to embrace more openness to differences of 'culture' and 'Asian values' given the democratization of Taiwan and South Korea.

Once socioeconomic development replaces economic development as an indicator, the correlation with democracy strongly increases. Huntington has argued that with increasing modernization and prosperity a 'zone of choice' emerges in which more democratization is required to deal with the new complexity of societal relationships. For example, greater plurality is illustrated by more complex interest groups and a greater degree of cosmopolitanism.[25] Furthermore, recent literature has stressed the positive correlation between development and democracy when more than GNP and GDP figures were taken into consideration. Prospects for democracy increased, in other words, when there were broad improvements in quality of life. Such improvements would include among others lower infant mortality, increased adult literacy and increased life expectancy.

The debate is not simply about one category of human rights versus the other. In essence, the argument concerns whether the term 'human rights' ought to be understood in the narrower, western sense of civil/political rights only, or in the broader, Third World sense of civil/political *and* socioeconomic rights. It is not difficult to see the respective political agenda underlying the two positions. Western commentators use the concept of human rights to criticize authoritarian regimes for stalling or resisting political liberalization. Broadening the concept of human rights is a defensive tactic by Third World countries, all of which sustain regimes that are authoritarian in one degree or another. The expanded concept of human rights diverts attention away from the specific areas most embarrassing to Third World governments and creates a bigger picture, which may include areas in which these regimes can point to successes, such as improved overall living standards. Some governments have even used the broader conception of human rights as a basis for counterattack, saying that the West may permit a wide range of individual liberties, but fails to protect people's socioeconomic rights as well as some of the countries westerners accuse of 'oppression'. An article in *Asiaweek* claims:

> Singapore opposition parties do not get equal time on television, but disadvantaged minorities do not riot, loot and burn. Malaysia detains dissidents without trial, but children are not gunned down at school. Taiwan does not allow free speech advocating communism, but its inner-city youth do not dissipate their energies on drugs. In South Korea one can be arrested just for publicly harbouring affection for Kim Il Sung but may walk the streets without fear of muggers.

In addition, there are problems with assuming (as Hsiung does) that East Asian workers will resist striking to avoid offending public sentiment or making the public victims of their action. For elites substitute public as in other categories. It is clearly not in the interests of the elites who wish to stay in power, for labour to go on strike. Their interests lie in preserving the status quo in order to prevent regime change; strikes reflect discontent with the distributive function of government. And arguments that the public in East Asia do not like strikes merely serve to belie the fact that the ruling powers have more to lose.

The relativist, anti-liberal argument continues that the industrialized democracies themselves showed little interest in human rights until they became affluent and politically stable. Only then did they abolish slavery and exploitative child labour, enfranchise more than a small minority of their own citizens and abandon imperialism. It is therefore unfair for the West to demand that poor, politically unstable Third World countries act as they do. East Asian commentators often make the case for the superiority of economic/social rights over civil/political rights by dramatically juxtaposing immediate survival needs with some of the less inspiring civil liberties. The argument could be justifiably rephrased, losing much of its effect, as follows: 'Which would developing peoples rather have? A commitment from their governments to sacrifice civil liberties in the hope of increasing the availability of food, or a guarantee that they will not be tortured or extra-legally imprisoned by the state?' The trade-off logic is questionable; curtailing civil liberties does not necessarily hasten economic development, nor does protecting them necessarily stifle prosperity.

Human rights, democracy and economic development are not separate and distinct categories, but rather are increasingly inter-linked. What is interesting is the use of these linkages by various authoritarian regimes to justify, promote and continue policies of control and repression within such a geopolitical framework. Governments' arguments are frequently couched in anti-western rhetoric and a degree of defensiveness, which suggests that a fair amount of insecurity prevails at the elite level. More often than not, these are pragmatic decisions which belie the fact that this is a ploy by elites to maintain and preserve neo-authoritarian forms of governance. How to produce a 'subject' political culture in the face of 'economic' transformation is the dilemma that Singapore faces in its nation-building process. Even the terminology of 'soft authoritarianism' is problematic in its relationship to political meaning. For 'consensus' we can substitute 'coercion'; for 'harmony' it means 'order and control'; and for 'participation' substitute 'submission'. Many Asian regimes are not as immune to the effects of rapid economic development as their governments would like us to believe. Asian, or shared 'values' have always had a distinctly synthetic air. Globalization and modernization in most rapidly developing countries undermine traditional values, forcing elites to manufacture and invent values to enhance their regime's survival while couching them in terms of national survival. The effects of this can be seen quite clearly at different levels in modern Singapore. Emigration among professionals is high; ordinary citizens are turning in their droves to religion (particularly evangelical Christianity) to fill the spiritual vacuum in their lives and there are high levels of social alienation from political and intellectual life.

It is not, however, the individualistic tendency of western democracy and human rights that undermines traditional, family oriented societies in Southeast Asia, but the processes of industrial-ization and urbanization, which in turn produce an increasing individualization of society.[26] Even the People's Action Party of Singapore, noted for its high-level profile in defending its authori-tarian version of 'Asian' democracy in a Government White Paper released in 1991, stated that 'Traditional Asian ideas of morality, duty and society, which have sustained and guided us in the past, are giving way to a more Westernised, individualistic and self-centred outlook on life.'[27] Consequently, when Asian values spokespersons cite the moral disintegration and decay of western societies as a man-ifestation of too much liberal allowance for individual rights and democracy, they ignore the argument that individualism is the consequence not of democracy and human rights, but of industrialization, increasing literacy rates and other changes at the societal level that transcend culture. Asian habits of industriousness, selflessness, filial piety and community before self are continually emphasized in juxtaposition to the former.[28]

The day-to-day reality of an individual, materialist culture as represented in East Asia bears little resemblance to rhetorical versions of shared values. In another analysis of political change in Southeast Asia, Michael Vatkiosis has argued that 'modern urban existence and the capitalist system has begun to erode the traditional collective values which the ruling elite claim lie at the core of their values'.[29]

CRITIQUING THE DEBATE ON DEMOCRACY AND HUMAN RIGHTS

The most important argument advanced by East Asian societies is that the individualist tendency of western human rights and democracy will undermine the social cohesion that derives from their more collectivist tradition. In 1990, the Singaporean government warned 'their' people about the western vice of individualism and its harmful and 'esoteric' concern with human rights. Some political scientists have also been engaged in critiquing these debates and their relationships. They argue that the state in modernizing East Asian economies is engaged in appropriating democratic practices as a strategy for managing forms of socioeconomic change. The notion that the state acts in a managerial capacity to prevent regime-threatening change is synonymous with a view of the middle classes as beneficiaries not adversaries of authoritarian forms of governance. Why should the middle classes revolt and demand more openness, political liberalism and the development of civic society simply because that has been asserted as a dominant theory to explain the relationship between development and democracy in western societies? From the perspective of those who promote democracy based on the value of autonomy (central to *liberal* democracies), Daniel Bell argues that it is 'far from obvious that most East Asians want to be free and equal with respect to political decisions even in principle – on the bottom, the traditional political culture of the east Asian commoner continues to be one of passivity and dependence on one's betters'.[30] Where were the new

Chinese middle classes during the Tiananmen Square incident, for instance? 'What then explains the growing presence of liberal social groups clamouring for more freedom and equality, and what is the likely shape of illiberal democracy that may emerge in Asia?' In contrast to liberal democracy, East Asian elites believe that the state fulfils both tutelary and disciplinary purposes. Particularly important is the notion of the paternalistic, 'interventionist' state, which can justifiably intrude to maintain order, stability and harmony. This has also been widely cited as one of the major factors in explaining their economic success. In this sense the rule of law means nothing more than preparing citizens for the requirements of a national plan formulated by a wise and virtuous bureaucratic elite than as a mechanism for the protection of individual rights. The notion of *law* in China and Singapore is devoid of meaning for the protection of individual rights; instead it is often wielded as the coercive instrument of state power. Asian values and the national plan are attuned to one another in the politics of 'soft' authoritarianism. These values are concerned with asserting the cultural and political 'difference' between East and West. Moreover, according to Jones and Brown, by 'strengthening the traditional virtues of consensual conformism, the centrifugal egoism of libertarianism might be avoided'.[31] If western, middle-class liberal values are responsible for democracy, 'Asian' values stressing conformity and communal loyalties over pluralism and individualism can equally be responsible for a version based on 'soft authoritarianism'.

Other characteristics of 'illiberal' or 'Asian' democracy that have come under scrutiny include, patron–client communitarianism, personalism, authority, dominant political party and strong state politics. These typically are contrasted with the western liberal versions of free and fair elections, political participation, multi-party systems and recognition of political and civil liberties, among others. In sum, there are three central features of an East Asian 'illiberal' democracy. These are (1) a non-neutral understanding of the state; (2) the evolution of a rationalistic and legalistic technocracy that manages the developing state as a corporate enterprise; and (3) the development of a managed rather than a critical public space and civil society. This view holds that while western societies appropriated democratic processes to serve the ends of liberal ideals such as freedom and equality, democracy (at least in its liberal variant) in East Asia requires the problematic juxtaposition of values and needs best suited to that particular context. While processes of democratization may appear universal to western theorists, the processes are seen very differently in Asia.

THE ASIAN CURRENCY CRISIS AND THE STATE OF DEMOCRACY

There can be little denial that economic and social rights are important in developing countries; indeed, these rights are set out in the UN Declaration of Human Rights and the subsequent documents and Conventions that have followed. We are not attempting to prioritize rights in this manner; the notion that one set of rights is more important than another is, we feel, a disingenuous claim by some Third World and (in our case) East Asian leaders to justify widespread abuses of human rights. Massive and prolonged economic growth (in double digits, sustained over the past two to three decades), social transformation, rapid industrialization and high savings have helped to fuel these economies within a framework of strict social order and control. However, this has not been achieved without costs to human rights and dignity. There have been several critiques of the development thesis and the notion of growth within and without Southeast Asia.

While the argument in East Asia was characterized as one over unchanging principles, this theoretical debate (like many others) clearly reflects contemporary historical developments. With the relative decline of once overwhelming US economic and military strength and the impressive recent growth posed by Japan, China and the East Asian newly industrializing countries (NICs) until 1997, many Asians concluded that the West was in decline and their own region would be the next centre of global power. The Asian currency crisis of 1997 dispelled these ideas. In July of that year, an economic and financial crisis emerged in Southeast Asia, which has broadened and deepened in scope and in nature since, and the effects of which have been and remain devastating. It has not bottomed out and the effects have been devastating. There were various internal and external reasons for the crisis. In the first instance these countries were too successful in their economic growth: they became victims of their own success and this led investors to underestimate some of the weaknesses in their economies. The financial sector could not keep pace with the demands being placed on it. The result was that their economies overheated, they maintained pegged exchange rate mechanisms for too long, they had weak management, poor control of risk and weak enforcement of prudential rules and supervision. Moreover, according to an IMF report, they had real data problems, including lack of transparency, creating uncertainty, and problems of governance and political uncertainties created a crisis of confidence. Externally, international investors underestimated risks and large capital flows to these countries were driven by this under-estimation. In short, the Asian system(s) displayed all the characteristics of an economic nervous breakdown.[32] The crunch came in May 1997 when the Thai baht came under attack from currency speculators. The Philippines also went into crisis and Thailand called on the IMF to help on 2 July 1998. As a result, the currency was devalued by 15–20 per cent. By the end of July we had what has since been termed the Asian currency meltdown. From the beginning of November 1997, there were indications that the crisis has deepened. The Indonesian rupiah had declined in value against the US dollar by more than 60 per cent. In fact, the crisis was felt in Indonesia more than anywhere and with devastating results. By March 1998 the value of the rupiah had decreased by 80 per cent, causing a crisis in private sector foreign debt.

In some of the chapters that follow, particularly those on Southeast Asia, we will be assessing the implications of this social crisis for the different countries involved. Now Asian commentators are much more circumspect about their region's prospects in the global political economy. The argument for community over individual loses much of its credence in the region if GNPs in the West were growing faster than those in East Asia. And the fact that these countries are facing an economic crisis and have not yet expe-rienced its full implications, can be seen in the movement towards political liberalization as consumers, having now been denied continued economic growth and success, look for other political goods to claim from the erstwhile paternalistic state. Arguing for an Asian 'Way' and an Asian-style democracy based on illiberal, undemocratic values was a mainstay of Southeast Asian politics as long as these countries were riding the wave of a miracle economy. When they started to fail, many were at a loss for words. Modern-ization, which many of the states throughout the region seemed to have been accepted without question, appeared to have stopped dead in its tracks. After experiencing almost double-digit growth for several decades, these economies now found themselves in the grips of a regional and global crisis.

CONCLUSION

The volume of human rights discourse in East Asia approached deafening levels in the 1990s following the end of the Cold War and collapse of authoritarianism in the Soviet bloc. The debate in itself was a result of the globalizing tendencies of appeals to liberal democracy and human rights, with Asian authoritarians who were economically successful assuming defensive postures to protect their vested interests. Asian values in that sense were an attempt to deflect external criticism of the lack of human rights policies and democratization projects in Southeast Asia, a region which should have been at the forefront of democratic expansion. In claiming to be different, these regimes were disingenuously papering over the cracks of authoritarianism. The question then became, for how long would this maintain itself?

The damage inflicted by the currency crisis on the Asian values thesis and on the political legitimacy of leaders there has forced them again into defensive postures. In Indonesia, Suharto stepped down and was replaced by Habibie, who lasted 16 months before falling victim to a new 'democratic dispensation'. In Malaysia, Mahathir was besieged with calls to resign and allow other parties to take over. As a result he has decided to take an even more authoritarian stance, subverting the rule of law, manipulating the judiciary and threatening to demolish any progress in human rights made in contemporary Malaysia. In the crucial elections in Malaysia in late 1999, he won a major victory, retaining power in the face of accusations of corruption and authoritarian leadership. It is a telling story of leaders who have for too long clung to power and are now unable to recognize the changes that have come about as a result of globalization have, in fact, undermined their positions. Globalization and rapid development, in other words, have brought with them demands for liberal democracy and respect for a human rights culture, on a universal basis. Part of the problem is related to the notion of modernization and political order, a theme running throughout our text. It is a question in part of how one organizes one's society in the global economy; how to provide a balance between sometimes competing issues of freedom and order, between individual and state responsibilities and duties. In theory, human rights as a global force might either enhance or undermine regime security. Extending human rights enhances regime and national security to the degree that the two sets of interests are seen as parallel; that is, threats to national security are also threats to the well-being of individuals.

How can human rights strengthen national security? We can conceive of at least three ways.

First, maximizing the rights of citizens may increase their loyalty to the state. People with many rights appreciate their privileges and develop a desire to preserve their political system, realizing that an alternative system may grant them fewer rights. Such citizens are therefore willing to make comparatively large sacrifices to defend the state when this becomes necessary.

Second, promoting and protecting human rights may improve a country's relative power, often synonymous with the most common usage of the term 'national security', by hastening its economic development. It is often argued (more commonly in the West than in Asia) that free information flow and the rule of law, which are consequences of expanded civil and political liberties, will facilitate innovation, efficiency and entrepreneurship. Similarly, a government that does its best to implement socioeconomic rights (guaranteed access to adequate food, housing and education, for example) would see a corollary increase in its people's productivity.

Third, by promoting human rights abroad, a state may make itself more secure. Lack of protection of human rights by foreign governments can create domestic turmoil with consequences that may spill over into one's own territory, including outflows of political or economic refugees, arms trafficking spurred by a civil war, or uncontrolled degradation of the environment.

If human rights abuses overseas can lead to national security threats at home, it could be claimed that the national interest justifies encouraging or pressuring foreign governments to clean up their acts. The 'peaceful democracies' argument is also relevant here. War between countries with democratic political systems is virtually unknown, giving rise to the theory that democracies enter a 'zone of peace' among whose constituents warfare becomes obsolete as a means of settling disputes or furthering national agendas. A democratic state that accepts the peaceful democracies theory may conclude that promoting democratization abroad improves its own military security, since every authoritarian foreign country that converts to democracy reduces the pool of prospective enemies. Indeed, this is the stated position of the Clinton administration. Democratization is indistinguishable from the expansion of civil and political human rights, again suggesting that one's own national interest (in the democratic states, at least) supports a policy of prodding authoritarian regimes to liberalize.

On the other side of the issue, there are at least three ways in which individual and national security might come into conflict, and in which the interests of the state or regime would dictate dishonouring human rights.[33]

The first is the case of an authoritarian regime lacking popular legitimacy. If the leadership upholds the full range of civil and political human rights, including the right of dissent, free discussion of political issues and polices, assembly, peaceful protest and participation in the selection of officials, the power of the regime would be weakened, and in some cases the regime – and perhaps even the political system – would be overthrown. Narrow self-interest, therefore, gives the regime a powerful incentive for restricting civil liberties.

Second, the argument is made (more commonly in Asia than the West, in this case) that human rights cause chaos. Granting civil and political rights, particularly in a society that does not have a well developed tradition of responsible exercise of such rights, may lead to a proliferation of activities that hinder progress towards achieving national goals such as unity, public order and economic development. The state could claim that national security calls for the prevention of strikes, demonstrations, incitement of hostility towards minority groups, and even the undermining of public confidence in national officials, institutions or policies. Hence, restrictions on civil liberties would be characterized as necessary for the state to fulfil its obligation as promoter and protector of national progress.

The notion that the East Asian model represents a viable alternative to liberal democracy and individual freedom is undermined by what McPherson[34] discussed in the politics of choice. That is that underdeveloped countries cannot afford a liberal democracy because there are far too few political goods on sale. However, as we have seen, these states are now highly developed and form the most dynamic regional economy on a global scale. Modernization theorists have also argued that there are other factors apart from economic development related to modernization. These include the 'force of historical incidents in domestic politics, cultural factors, events in neighbouring countries ... leadership and movement behaviour ... and particular historical experiences',[35] among others. There is little doubt that globalization and modernization have transformed the human landscape of Southeast Asia in an extra-ordinarily dramatic and probably irreversible way. The fact that the Asian currency crisis has illustrated that economic performance can no longer be relied on to maintain leadership credibility in Southeast Asia is but one factor in the increasing movement towards democracy here. However, the disastrous effects of the Asian economic crisis from 1997 onwards is just one effect (albeit a negative one) of the wider patterns of globalization and inter-dependence that increasingly shape patterns of international relations. It has had widespread social and economic ramifications and will make inroads into the authoritarian nature of governance which has characterized many Southeast Asian states. As consumers in Asia increasingly turn away from material goods, observers will find the range and choice of political goods expands rapidly as witnessed by the rapid growth of non-governmental organizations (NGOs) and civic society throughout Southeast Asia, campaigning on everything from the environment to human rights. As Bauer and Bell note: 'East Asian activists, opposition political parties, and intel-lectuals are challenging the human rights claims of their own governments (if given the opportunity) and fighting for government transparency, economic and social justice, and democratic rights.'[36] Such groups, their supporters and their indigenous, critical arguments against authoritarian rule are in a good position to be the harbingers of a new human rights culture and liberal democratic values which support such cultures.

Part 1
Southeast Asia

Kenneth Christie

2
Malaysia, Singapore and ASEAN

Before I write about Southeast Asia, one must bear in mind that it is a remarkably diverse and heterogeneous region in terms of government, social and economic systems. Brunei has an absolute monarchy; Vietnam and Laos have post-socialist authoritarian regimes; Singapore and Malaysia have one-party authoritarian regimes with the façade of parliamentary democracy; Thailand and the Philippines have elected representative democratic systems; Burma (Myanmar) is a military dictatorship which appears fascist in nature; Indonesia's system seems in a state of transition from authoritarianism to a more representative form of regime; and Cambodia continues to defy definition – it is a mixed bag, difficult to define and impossible to quantify. In this chapter Malaysia and Singapore will be discussed, two states which have experienced a great deal of political and economic stability over the last 30 years. Both countries share the reputation of being the champions of the 'Asian' way of democracy and attitudes towards human rights. Their respective statesmen, Dr Mohammed Mahathir and Lee Kuan Yew (former Prime Minister, now Senior Minister) have become self-appointed spokesmen for East Asian values in general, regularly appearing at international conferences, meetings and in the media to denounce western interference, western value systems, liberal versions of democracy and human rights. Both hold high-profile positions in the debate of Asian values versus western democratic and liberal rights, although clearly they emphasize different aspects of the debate. These are the defensive mechanisms of two enormously successful leaders who fear that their personal and regime legitimacy is in decline and have decided to deflect this by promoting 'Asian values' and their personal styles of democracy. Despite beliefs that there is a global trend towards democracy and human rights, such leaders have rejected such models for their own societies. Moreover, they have become more and more assertive at attempting to define what they see as legitimate, alternative forms of governance, which has come to mean their own brand of 'soft' authoritarianism.

MALAYSIA

Malaysia is regarded as one of the most successful Muslim countries of the Third World, although lines of political power and economic influence have traditionally been divided along racial lines, with the Malays in charge of the political structures and the ethnic Chinese controlling a great deal of the material wealth and commerce. Malaysia has always sought to establish a fairly high profile in terms of how it presents its relationship to the West and what it regards as the dangers of cultural imperialism and economic hegemony. Its leader, Mohammed Mahathir, has maintained a tight grip on power, by authoritarian means. His recent struggle with his erstwhile deputy, Anwar Ibrahim, which resulted in the latter being brought to trial and convicted on flimsy evidence, has seen him further increase the anti-human rights, lack of procedure, political culture that his leadership appears to have embraced. The Asian currency crisis has hardened the position of soft authoritarians like Mahathir. He appears determined not to follow the route that President Suharto of Indonesia once pursued and appears willing to bend any rules in Malaysia's electoral democracy.

Historical Overview

Malaysia, like many of the states of Southeast Asia, has a long social and cultural history, fragmented by various periods of migration and colonization. It has moved with some success to a pluralistic culture reflected in the diversity of the three main population groups, Malay, Chinese and Indian, which again reflects its historical background. In the fifteenth century, Malacca, an enormously powerful political, economic and religious influence in the Southeast Asian region, dominated what we now know as Malaysia. The Portuguese reached the height of their influence here between 1511 and 1641; thereafter the Dutch, followed by the British, were the imperial influences on Malaysian social and economic development. By the end of the eighteenth century the Straits Settlement, comprising Singapore, Penang and Malacca, had been formed. And in 1896, the four states of Perak, Selangor, Negri Sembilan and Pahang came together in a Federation with the capital based in Kuala Lumpur. Many of the other states maintained the British as 'advisers' and established large rubber plantations. The British in fact had some of their most interesting colonial adventures in East Malaysia when the adventurer

Charles Brooke was made the 'white' Rajah of Sarawak in 1841, after putting down a revolt against the Sultan of Brunei. The North Borneo Company was established and administered by Sabah from 1882. After the Second World War, they assumed formal control of these areas. With the dawn of the twentieth century, the development of ports, roads and railways, and large-scale influxes of workers from China and India, accelerated the expansion of the rubber and tin industries, again promoted by the British.

At this point the country was divided into two distinct parts: Peninsular Malaysia comprising the most important centres of power and economics with 40 per cent of the land mass, and the Eastern Malaysian Provinces of Sabah and Sarawak in North Borneo comprising enormous swathes of rainforest, which are now suffering from steady depletion through large-scale logging projects. During the Second World War, the Japanese army overran Malaysia and, following the end of the hostilities, the communist guerrillas, who had been waging an armed struggle against the Japanese, focused their energies on ending British rule. Malaysia finally gained its independence on 31 August 1957. Like many of the colonies, resistance to imperial rule formed its sense of nationhood. In 1963, the Federation of Malaysia was formed; it appended the former parts of British Borneo, Sabah and Sarawak in East Malaysia along with Singapore. (Two years later, on 9 August, Singapore was expelled from the Federation, much to its disappointment. It was widely believed at the time that Singapore could not survive on its own.)

The establishment of the Federation saw the opening up of a period of confrontation between Indonesia and Malaysia, which provoked bitter Cold War-type hostility to one another. Malaysia, like Indonesia, has suffered from more than its fair share of ethnic problems. In May 1969, it was devastated by an explosion of racial riots, incited in part by envy at the success of the Chinese minority; this engendered savage inter-communal and ethnic street fighting. A State of Emergency was declared with the government coming under the control of a National Operations Council. The Malay-dominated government came under pressure from industrial unrest, strikes and sabotage and initiated various repressive responses, legislated as the Internal Security Act 1960 and various banishment laws, which served only to reinforce the ethnic resentment, especially among the Chinese minority. Ethnic issues in that sense have always ensured a weakening rather than a strengthening of civil society. When this ended, the 'rules of the game' were revised to ensure that the ethnic Malay predominance in politics and economics would be guaranteed and, despite the 'return to normal' in 1971, when parliament was convened after a 21-month lapse, the emergency laws were not repealed.

The government now introduced the New Economic Policy, which ensured that Malay political control was based on corporate ownership; Malays were given quotas in education, the civil service and business affairs. Twenty years later the National Development Policy was to repeat these aims. In the 1970s, planned economic development saw five-year national plans attempt to manage long-range growth which increased rapidly in the 1980s, when the government promoted private investment, the export of manufactures and the abandonment of many tariffs on imports. It is clear, however, that inter-communal tensions remain. In times of economic downturn, the Chinese community always appear apprehensive. For while their ability to generate wealth is welcomed, they are scorned because of social envy.

Malaysia has a federal government with jurisdiction over 13 states. Its parliamentary system of government holds regular multi-party elections. In a similar manner to the People's Action Party in Singapore, one major multi-ethnic coalition, the National Front has maintained power since 1957 with a certain amount of competition between the major coalition partner, United Malays National Organization (UMNO), and opposition parties, who occasionally win state elections. Mohammed Mahathir, who has served as the Prime Minister since 1981, has pursued policies for rapid growth, industrialization and modernization since his accession to power. A non-political monarch is elected from among the nine state hereditary rulers (the sultans) every five years. This guarantees symbolic Malay predominance within the political system. The more practical realities of politics are entrenched in the leading role of UMNO. In conjunction with the strong leadership of Mohammed Mahathir, UMNO is the most important party in the multi-ethnic, National Front coalition and has led the alliance to five consecutive mandates from the electorate. The coalition also includes the Barisan Nasional (National Front), UMNO's main Malay rival. In October 1996, Mohammed Mahathir won the approval of the party to lead UMNO for a further three years, but the continuing tension between Mahathir and his deputy Anwar Ibrahim called into question the underlying political stability which has characterized much of Malaysian politics since independence. Democracy in Malaysia can be seen as defined in strictly procedural terms. The formal rules of the game appear more important than substantive concessions to liberal democracy and human rights. Multi-party elections, the right to vote and majority rule are all seen as 'rules of the game' in which the people give up their right to exercise real choice. Elections merely serve to confirm the power and strength of the ruling coalition. At the end of November 1999, Mahathir and his ruling National Front coalition won a convincing victory. Despite the veiled threats and anxiety this election generated in the wake of Anwar's arrest and imprisonment, the man who has led Malaysia since 1981 retained his grip on power. However, the victory must be seen as a qualified one. The National Front's poll of 56 per cent was a 9 per cent decrease from the previous election. Moreover, large numbers of Malays withheld their vote from UMNO, the dominant member of the coalition, while the opposition Islamic PAS Party drew widespread support. This in some respects is an expression of the resentment felt over Mahathir's treatment of Anwar Ibrahim, and a crucial signal that his power base is in decline.

Political Economy

Malaysia began to enjoy spectacular growth from the late 1960s. However, the economic crash of 1997 has seen rising discontent at the way Malaysia's economy is managed. In part the struggle between Mahathir and Anwar Ibrahim, who at one stage seemed certain to assume the leadership when Mahathir stepped down, is the struggle between an older, authoritarian ruler and a new, political and economic modernizer with different ideas about the role of the state in governance.

The Asian economic crisis affected the Malaysian economy in several ways. Aggregate consumption and investment fell and a greater debt exposure meant there was real depreciation of the Malaysian ringgit against the US dollar. Inflation rose steeply as did costs in terms of foreign technology acquisitions, which are vital to Malaysia's dynamism. The banks found it increasingly difficult to recover loans, and there was an increase in graduate unemployment.

Malaysia's initial response was to adopt the IMF proposals and tried to restructure its banking sector, but this did not improve the markets. Mahathir next decided to abandon these policies and reduce Malaysia's reliance on the international community – growth, he argued, could be restored by insulating the economy from short-term capital movements and pegging the ringgit at the fixed rate of 3.8 to the US dollar while relaxing credit dramatically. In August 1998, Anwar Ibrahim, the Deputy Prime Minister, was sacked. He had supported the IMF, Mahathir had not. While Anwar regarded the solution as restructuring the banks, allowing more foreign capital into the country and investment – in other words, more IMF policies – Mahathir took the other perspective that foreign capital was the problem, not the solution. He chose to reflate the economy, cut interest rates and protect the ringgit by imposing exchange controls on it.

There is a difference between Malaysia economic position and that of its close ASEAN neighbours, Indonesia and Thailand; Malaysia's debt is primarily domestic and although the debt is high, its external short-term debt vis-à-vis GDP is low. This has enabled Malaysia to weather the economic storms slightly better than its neighbours.

Initially Mahathir's policies met with some success in boosting the economy.

Economic Policies

Malaysia has a populaton of 19 million and compared to other NICs, Malaysia has had a relatively higher population growth. Like Thailand, it has sustained an impressive growth rate (over 8 per cent p.a. from the late 1980s to 1997). This growth is mainly export-oriented, particularly in the electronics sector. Unlike South Korea and Taiwan, whose growth was spurred by indigenous developments, Malaysia (like much of Southeast Asia) developed because of foreign investment and multinational finance. In addition, exports of crude oil, mining and construction industries and traditional raw materials such as palm oil, rubber and logs have maintained and fuelled this dynamic growth. Dependency on its two main products has been reduced; at one time these sectors accounted for nearly 70 per cent of Malaysia's export earnings, but diversification has led to a much more broadly based economy and Malaysia's emergence as a newly industrializing country (NIC). When Mahathir took power, agricultural commodities dominated the economy (43.6 per cent of exports) along with minerals (petroleum and gas), which accounted for 33.8 per cent, with manufactures at 21.6 per cent of the total exports. Budget figures in 1994 showed that manufacturing was responsible for 77.5 per cent of exports, a dramatic change, from its beginnings.[1] Manufacturing as a proportion of GDP also rose between 1965 and 1992, up from 9 per cent to 29 per cent.[2] Malaysia is now the world's largest producer of air conditioners and a leading exporter of telephone appliances and televisions. At the same time, the share of primary commodities in exports dropped significantly between 1965 and 1992 from 94 per cent to 39 per cent.[3] Between 1965 and 1980 average GDP growth was 7 per cent p.a.; in the years 1980–85, this momentum slackened with world-wide recession, and growth was reduced to 5.5 per cent.

Problems over inflation and the narrow industrial base (which is still heavily dependent on the electronics sector dominated by foreign multinationals) are combined with the fact that a great deal of Malaysian manufacturing is still in labour-intensive assembly-line work – a policy increasingly outmoded given its labour shortages. The development of capital-intensive industries is hindered by shortages of skilled technicians. These problems are being addressed by massive educational programmes. The drop in foreign investment is also problematic; in 1993 the level of investment dropped to M\$6.1 billion from the average M\$17.1 billion obtained in 1990–92. The government has managed to redistribute wealth fairly effectively with regard to the Malay population; their percentage of share capital has increased dramatically from 1.5 per cent in 1969 to 30 per cent in 1990 as a result of officially sanctioned ethnic discrimination in favour of the Malay population. Moreover, government efforts to create and stabilize a Malay middle class have met with some success.

In his book *Malay Dilemma*, Mahathir argued that Malays lagged behind other races because of their attitude to economics, which was partially due to a feudal mentality – Malays were peasants. The central policy to change this was modernization, which would uplift Malaysia and the Malays through heavy industrialization. With increasing success at the economic level, however, social problems emerged throughout Malaysian society. These include widespread corruption and abuse of power, mismanagement, disputes over the Islamic *hudud* laws in Kelantan, drug addiction and 'loafing' (the term commonly used for loitering) among youths. Official estimates show that there are over 100,000 drug addicts among the Malaysian population.[4] Mahathir has unveiled his vision for Malaysia in the year 2020: a fully industrialized country. But following the dramatic success of his economic programmes, concerns are now shifting to how to deal with the massive social problems engendered by these very policies.

The Asian Economic Crisis

The economic crisis placed a very heavy toll on Malaysia and the processes of democratization at work there. By August 1997, Mahathir's control of the economy had become visibly bruised to the point where observers openly speculated how much longer he could hold on to power. Until 1997 prospects had seemed fairly good. In 1995 and 1996, GDP growth had reached levels of 9.5 and 8.2 per cent respectively. There had been continued foreign investment and full employment had been a mainstay of the economy since 1992. But the fall in the value of the other regional currencies, the Thai baht, the Filipino peso and then the Indonesian ringgit, finally took its toll on the Malaysian ringgit; by early 1998 it had dropped to a four-year low; the share index had declined by nearly 40 per cent and per capita income had fallen by US$1,000.[5] At first, the government tried to intervene to support the currency, but this was disastrous – the power of the market was too much to halt the decline. A weak central banking system and weak policy revealed a crisis in policy-making. Anwar Ibrahim tried in vain to switch direction by cutting expenditures on various projects and efforts to reduce the deficit, but many now believe this only brought him further into conflict with Mahathir, who had lost face. Economic efforts were joined by staged shows of support for the authoritarian leader, who rallied around a nationalist cry, blaming foreigners and external influences for crippling the Malaysian economy. Tens of thousands of foreign migrant workers, the majority of them Indonesian and Bangladeshi, were repatriated, many of whom were arrested and treated harshly by the authorities. Many political refugees were also deported with the migrants. Mahathir continued to blame external foreign influences (again in line with Asian values); he blamed international financiers like George Soros and the Jews for currency speculations, which had weakened the economy; he blamed the processes of globalization for undermining the financial system. In short, he blamed the West for the economic crisis. The paradox, of course, was that Malaysia as much as any Southeast Asian state required the financial investment which globalization brings with it. In short, rather than accept responsibility for his or his government's policies, Mahathir's reaction to the problem was to create scapegoats: George Soros, the West, international financial institutions and finally his deputy, Anwar Ibrahim, who was arrested, beaten up, put on trial and finally jailed in a travesty of justice. The dramatic events which occurred after September 1998 confirmed that the Malaysian government of Mohammed Mahathir was not committed to the rule of law but rather rule by law. As the *International Herald Tribune* put it:

> Malaysian policemen wearing black ski masks and carrying submachine guns smashed their way into the house of Anwar Ibrahim, the country's former deputy Prime Minister, late Sunday night and arrested him, just hours after he had led the largest political demonstration in this city's history.[6]

Anwar was arrested on the basis of his moral character: he was accused of homosexual practices, procuring sex and sodomy, all criminal charges in Malaysia. However, it is very hard to believe any of the charges. Rather, it appears there was a power struggle between Mahathir, who was clinging onto power, and Anwar, an economic modernizer who was sympathetic to foreign investors and the IMF strategies, and was seeking to reform outdated structures and secure Malaysian economic advantage into the twenty-first century. On the anniversary of Anwar's arrest, the security forces once again showed their unwillingness to accept any dissent. Malaysian police, acting under the Police Act, arrested four opposition members for rioting and inciting public disorder ahead of a planned protest, this implied that they were planning to hold illegal demonstrations.[7] Others were detained in the action. Shortly after, on 10 November, Mahathir announced a snap general election, several months ahead of when he needed to call it. The result was a dramatic and sweeping victory, his fifth in 19 years of rule. Mahathir again accused Anwar of threatening the security of the Malaysian state when he argued that he was 'an irresponsible number one agitator'.[8] The arrest of Anwar marked a return to harsh repression in Malaysia, the case of an authoritarian struggling to maintain power in the face of economic decline and this time partially succeeding. The economic crisis had seen a hardening of soft authoritarianism in Malaysia and bodes ill for the maintenance and improvement of human rights.

Internal Order and Security in Malaysia

Malaysia experienced fairly stable and peaceful conditions in the 1980s and 1990s, certainly in comparison to repeated coups in Thailand and this despite the government's constant heightened sensitivity to potential security threats. The Internal Security Act of 1960, however, is still in force despite the end of the communist insurgency, and has been used over time to detain opposition leaders. Section 73 of the Act allows detention 'for up to 60 days on suspicion that [the individual] has acted or is likely to act in any manner prejudicial to the security of Malaysia'.[9] This is a blatant encroachment of collective interests vis-à-vis individual rights. The emergency powers invoked after the racial riots in the 1960s became a major issue during the 1983–84 constitutional crisis and, by early 1984, the government had used these powers – as well as other types of security legislation – to stop any kind of activity that, in the view of the government, was a threat to national security and public order.

At least 25 laws in Malaysia that qualify Article 5 of the Constitution, which provides for the 'right to life and personal integrity'. These include the Essential Security Cases Regulations 1975 and the various Emergency Ordinances.[10] The Federal government in Kuala Lumpur has sweeping powers to curtail personal liberty and impose restrictions on most things that are taken for granted in western democracies, including freedom of speech, assembly and association, and religion. Some have observed that the concentration of power in the executive since Mahathir's accession in 1981 has increased dramatically at the expense of an independent bureaucracy and judiciary. The Official Secrets Act is a deterrent to the use of intentional and unintentional leaks from government sources.

The most important basis for action is threats or perceived threats to national security. Al-Arquam, a Muslim sect which has a Malaysian membership of more than 60,000 and millions of sympathizers world-wide, was banned in early August 1994 by the National Fatwa Council of Malaysia in a bid to support the government's efforts to neutralize the movement. The movement was also banned in late August 1994 by the Home Ministry under section 5(1) of the Societies Act 1966, which allows for anyone associated with the group to be detained for questioning by the police.[11] Nine Al-Arquam members were held in detention under the Internal Security Act, which can be extended from the normal 60 days to two years at the discretion of the Minister for Home Affairs.

Analysts believe Al-Arquam was banned because it represents a threat to the ruling coalition; with a large business empire and sophisticated following, it was argued that the movement could have emerged as a threat to the status quo. National security reasons were given as the rationale for the ban, but clearly this belies the real motivations; again national interests have been used as a ploy to promote party and regime interests.[12]

The Malaysian government portrayed its crackdown on Al-Arquam as a principled effort to keep religion out of politics, yet stated that the sect had deviated from the 'real' teachings of Islam. Moreover the government has repeatedly mentioned the need to infuse Islamic values into the social and political system. Some observers maintain that Al-Arquam was victimized because it has withdrawn its erstwhile electoral and political support from UMNO Baru, the main component of the ruling coalition. Others argue that it is related to the political battles between factions within UMNO Baru itself. Either way, the crackdown represents a fundamental violation of human rights and freedom, including freedom of expression, religion and the right to a livelihood.

Corruption is widespread in Malaysia and despite its figleaf of Westminster-style parliamentary democracy, electoral fraud is endemic. As James Chin has noted:

> In March [1997] the High Court made political history when it declared an election victory by the ruling Barisan Nasional (BN) coalition null and void due to vote buying. The judge ruled that 'vote buying was so extensive [that] it affected the election result' in the Bukit Begunan constituency in the September 1996 Sarawak state election. Although vote buying by the BN is widespread in Malaysia, hitherto it has been almost impossible to prove it in court. In this case however there was clear evidence including photographs showing cash being handed out by BN campaigners to voters just prior to election day.[13]

The way in which voters are bought and the use of money politics to influence elections can be seen as an abrogation of citizen's human rights in any sense of democratic values. However, it is clear that Malaysia does have a fair degree of political stability. The military is generally under the control of the civilian government, unlike in Indonesia; there have been no outbreaks of mass violence of the kind witnessed in Thailand, Indonesia or some other ASEAN states in the 1990s; there are few reports of extra-judicial killings or disappearances. The government has used certain measures, again more recently, in response to fears of communal riots. Since the 1997 Asian economic crisis it has placed a fair degree of emphasis on this, perhaps with good reasons given the precedent set by Indonesia. In September 1998 four people (all ethnic Chinese) were arrested under the penal code for spreading rumours on the internet about communal violence. Given Malaysia's sensibilities and vulnerability, the regime feels strongly about ethnic issues and the threat these pose to regime security.[14]

Institutional Security Measures and Freedom of Speech

In terms of freedom from arbitrary arrest, detention or forcible exile, there are three laws which allow the authorities to hold suspects without judicial review or a formal charge process. These are the ISA (Internal Security Act) 1960, the Emergency Ordinance of 1969 (Public Order and Prevention of Crime) and the Dangerous Drugs Act (1985). The first two pieces of legislation allow the government to detain former communists, religious extremists and others and long-term detention is still in use for perceived threats to national security. In April 1996, it was reported that, between 1986 and 1996, 692 people had been held under the ISA. Moreover, in July 1993 it was reported that 1,947 people were being detained without trial, most of whom were being held under the Dangerous Drugs Act. The ISA is also used against passport and identity card forgers. In July 1993, 37 were being held in detention for this reason. The Malaysian government has also used the ISA to prevent alleged 'secessionist' plots against the federal government. In 1990 and 1991, the authorities detained seven Malaysians from the east Malaysian state of Sabah, including Jeffrey Kitingan, the brother of the Chief Minister at the time, Joseph Pairin Kitingan. Jeffrey Kitingan was held for over two years on suspected involvement in a plot to take Sabah out of Malaysian federation, something that is a constant preoccupation of the Kuala Lumpur government. By 1993 all the detainees had been released, but with restrictions on their movement. After Jeffrey Kitingan was released, he was elected as a Sabah state assemblyman in February 1993 and helped to keep his brother in power, but just a month after his election he abandoned his support and formed his own party. Many analysts suspected him of having cut a deal with

Mahathir for his release and figures of millions of dollars were bandied around as the price of defection. In the end Joseph Pairin was forced to resign after his allies also left to join other parties.[15]

The Police Act of 1967 stipulates that a permit must be obtained for all public assemblies; a law that has been used recently against the supporters of Anwar Ibrahim. Political rallies are also banned, which again leaves little scope for the opposition. The arrest of Anwar drew worldwide attention to Malaysia's ISA but it has not abandoned it. Of 198 people in detention under the Act in 1999, most were there for their role in bringing illegal foreign workers into Malaysia, illustrating again the paranoia felt about external influences that might pose a threat to regime security. In October and November 1987, under the ISA the Malaysian authorities arrested 106 people, including politicians, trade unionists and religious figures among others, during 'Operation Lallang'; the government argued they posed a threat to national security. More than 50 per cent of those arrested were released before the end of the 60-day detention period, but at least 40 of them were given two-year renewable detention orders and sent to Malaysia's main ISA detention centre in Kamuntin, Perak. Detainees told of physical and psychological ill-treatment in order to force sworn testimonies at the time.[16] Anwar Ibrahim was also arrested in 1999 under the ISA for alleged corruption and treason against the state.

There have been five crises which have invoked the use of emergency powers. These are:

1. 1948–1960: The communist threat/insurgency in Malaya
2. 1964: Confrontation with Indonesia
3. 1966: Oust Opposition Chief Minister in Sarawak
4. 1969: May racial riots
5. 1977: Oust Opposition PAS Government in Kelantan

A state of emergency can be proclaimed under Article 150 of the Constitution, which allows the suspension of even the most fundamental rights, including the rights to life and personal safety, freedom from forced labour and discrimination, and freedoms of movement, speech and religion. This article has been amended six times since the 1960s; the 1981 amendment, for instance, made the state of emergency a non-justiciable issue, which cannot be challenged by the courts.[17]

Drug trafficking suspects can be held under the Dangerous Drugs Act for up to 39 days before a detention order is issued. At this point there may be granted a court appearance and the suspect may be released; on the other hand, they may be held without charge for successive two-year periods. There is a review process for these suspects but this does not contain any of the due process rights that a defendant would have in a normal court hearing. In July 1993, nearly 1,750 suspects remained under detention or restrictions that amounted to house arrest under this law. Amnesty International argues that sections of the Dangerous Drugs Act contravene Article 11(1) of the Universal Declaration of Human Rights, which states that a person is presumed innocent until proved guilty. It even appears inconsistent with the basis of Malaysian jurisprudence.[18]

The police frequently use force and other coercive means to extract so-called confessions. The most blatant example we have seen of this was the beating of Anwar Ibrahim following his arrest. Anwar appeared in court with a black eye and a medical report showed that he had traces of arsenic in his blood. One of Malaysia's most outspoken political opposition figures, Lim Guan Eng, was sentenced to to jail for supposedly malicious statements he had made in 1995 when he accused the Attorney General of mishandling a case involving the Chief Minister of Malacca who was accused of raping a schoolgirl. In August 1999, a Malaysian lawyer working for the UN had his case referred to the International Court of Justice after he had been sued in 1997 for the incredible sum of 60 million ringgit for alleging corporate interference in Malaysian judicial politics (not an uncommon accusation). The Malaysian government at the time refused to recognize the immunity granted by his UN position.

Freedom of speech is guaranteed in article 10 of the Malaysian constitution, but this is qualified by the Sedition Act of 1948, the Official Secrets Act of 1972, the Universities and University College Act of 1971 (amended in 1975), the Printing Presses and Publications Act of 1984, the Societies Act of 1966, the Trade Unions Ordinance and the 1967 Police Act.[19] Freedom of speech is also limited under the 1970 Sedition Act amendments which are designed to prevent people from discussing privileges granted to ethnic Malays under the Bumiputra policy, as well as other sensitive issues. Freedom of the press is also limited under the Printing Presses and Publications Act of 1984, as amended in 1987; publication of 'malicious news' thereafter became a punishable offence and the government's power to restrict or even ban publications was greatly expanded. The government can use these powers to shut down newspapers. In fact self-censorship of sensitive issues is widely practised.

In March 1995, Irene Fernandez, who was head of the Tenaganita women's rights group, went on trial on charges of falsely reporting that at least ten illegal immigrants had died in detention centres between January and May 1995. By 1998 this trial had entered its third year with no end in sight and the threat of three years' imprisonment. In April 1994, Malaysia expelled a Filipino news correspondent based in Kuala Lumpur on the grounds that she had written an article that was deemed a threat to national security. Leah Palma Makabenta was given 48 hours to leave Malaysia after her work permit was cancelled.[20] In election campaigns press coverage of the opposition is limited; most of the broadcast media are controlled by people close to the ruling coalition Federal government. In short, the Malaysian government appears acutely sensitive to charges of corruption and misuse of powers. The judiciary in particular seems off limits though, as seen in the trial of Anwar Ibrahim, extremely suspect in its methods and decisions.

Death Penalty and Cruel Punishment

In the 1980s executions in Malaysia increased. In March 1980, seven men were hanged under a 1975 amendment to the ISA which made the death penalty mandatory for the unauthorized possession of firearms, ammunition or explosives. In 1975, the Dangerous Drugs Act (1952) was amended, making the death penalty the maximum sentence for drug trafficking. Later in 1983 it became mandatory.[21] In 1996, some 8,500 people were detained under this Act.

People arrested in possession of drugs are usually presumed to be trafficking in drugs, and if convicted, usually face a mandatory death penalty. In the case of Hassim Escandar, hanged in Sabah on 30 April 1993, Amnesty International believes that his conviction under the Drugs Act contravened international human rights law and that Escandar may have been innocent. He was convicted on the basis of two keys allegedly found in his possession, which fitted the padlock of a bag containing 5 kilograms of cannabis. According to Escandar, the keys to the bag were found on another passenger on the bus on which he was travelling.

Under such legal procedure the accused appear guilty unless they can prove otherwise. According to Amnesty this neglects the principle of due process because it relies on presumption of guilt if drugs are found in any bag, box, home, office, shop or car belonging to the accused. As Amnesty notes, between 1983 and the end of 1991, 142 alleged drug traffickers were hanged under such presumption, so that the odds are loaded against the accused from the start. Amnesty also criticizes Malaysia for punishing 'lesser' offences by caning, as does Singapore. These offences include (among more than 40 crimes listed in the penal code) robbery, rape, kidnapping and causing grievous bodily harm, extended in 1993 to include white-collar crime. The maximum number of strokes for an adult male is 24 and 10 for a youth. Women are not subjected to caning. Amnesty has condemned the practice several times, citing the Conventions against torture and other cruel, inhuman or degrading treatment.[22]

Malaysia's Response to the West

Malaysia is one of the countries most vociferous in its attacks on the West. Mohammed Mahathir regularly denounces the West, claiming that it is hypocritical and has double standards on human rights issues. At the end of May 1993, The Voice of Malaysia radio station stated that Mahathir 'has asked Malaysians not to accept Western-style democracy as it could result in negative effects. The Prime Minister said such an extreme principle had caused moral decay, homosexual activities, single parents and economic slowdown because of poor work ethics.'[23] One Malaysian writer has pointed out that the assumption behind 'Mahathir's argument is that "rights" of any sort always means entitlement. Thus he pits his development rights against human rights.' [24] However, there are nuances to this and domestic politics have played a part here, as Philip Eldridge argues:

> Dr Mahathir's often strident anti-Western line should be seen within his primary concern to promote Malaysian development, regional relations and associated domestic political and cultural agendas, with vigorous counter-attack and pre-emptive strikes against potential human rights critics representing the least costly and time-consuming way of dealing with unwelcome intrusions.

At the same time, the Prime Minister plays the role of stern disciplinarian both towards his own people and moral 'backsliders' in the West who would divert them form the path of hard work. At times, his thinking seems to be driven by a 'domino theory' outlook in which initially moderate demands for freedom of expression, workers and women's rights are replaced by increasingly extreme demands, resulting in homosexual marriages, family breakdown and social disorders. While sharing many of the Prime Ministers concerns, Anwar Ibrahim warns against denouncing human rights as Western, since they represent the common values of mankind.[25]

It is now clear that the differences between Mahathir and Anwar came to a head in 1998 and brought many of these issues to the fore of the domestic political agenda. Who should control power? Mahathir has also accused the West of manipulating human rights agendas to foster a dependency relationship with the underdeveloped nations and reduce the threat of competition from the East Asian region. He talks about how they, the West, 'create friction and instability so that if we are unstable they can compete with us'.[26] The key figures in this 'conspiracy' have recently been identified as international currency speculators, such as George Soros, who appear to have engineered the Asian economic crisis to benefit themselves according to this logic. Mahamad Jawhar Hassan, of the of the Malaysian Institute of Strategic and International Studies, has argued that these western ideas are alien values derived from 'post-Renaissance liberal Western traditions'.[27] Moreover, the fact that there is tension between Islamic concepts of human rights and western individualistic conceptions has tended to support Mahathir's version. Muzaffar has argued that rights, responsibilities, relationships and roles should be integrated in accordance with the central Islamic concept of man's 'vice-regency' which is derived from God.[28] Interestingly enough, the non-state discourse vis-à-vis NGOs and opposition figures has come out in favour of balancing domestic and international political, social and economic rights within the Malaysian context with another series of views coming from Chandra Muzaffar, who argues that the West's line on human rights is hypocritical and serves the purpose of maintaining world domination.[29] The notion of individual rights in general has been subject to criticism in Muslim communities in Southeast Asia, particularly when they are fed the state line of the West's hypocrisy over issues such as Bosnia and Kosovo.

Malaysia also supports and has supported some of the more authoritarian rulers in the region, perhaps fearing the knock-on effects if their demise were to become contagious. Malaysia has always been fairly close to Indonesia despite the problems with Konfrontasi in the 1960s. In October 1996, as a measure of obeisance and acceding to the principle of non-interference in members' affairs, the Malaysian government banned the Second Asia-Pacific Conference on East Timor (APCET II). The foreign participants were either deported or refused entry to the country and the police rounded up the local organizers and protesters who were against Indonesia's policies in East Timor.

Mahathir has strongly argued that 'hegemony by democratic powers is no less oppressive than hegemony by totalitarian states'.[30] Only three months after he came to office in 1981, he instituted a 'Buy British Last' policy. This was apparently in retaliation for alleged attempts by the British government to prevent the Malaysian government from gaining control of major Malaysian assets and the steep increase in university fees for overseas students (of whom Malaysians constituted the largest proportion in the UK). The policy lasted two years and only ended with the personal intervention of the British Prime Minister Margaret Thatcher, who concluded a trade and aid deal with Malaysia in 1985. However, the connections between aid, trade and defence were to prove the scenario for renewed acrimony in February 1994 when the British *Sunday Times* revealed that a British construction company involved in the Pergau Dam Project had made special payments at the highest level in Malaysia to secure a contract. These allegations of bribery fuelled enormous resentment in Malaysian elites, but their target of retaliation was, surprisingly, not the British press but British business. In late February 1994, Anwar Ibrahim announced a boycott of all British companies tendering for official contracts. This was lifted in September 1994, when Andrew Neil, the editor of the *Sunday Times* and the chief instigator of the reports, resigned his editorship for an overseas position.

Ironically, despite the ban on government sector contracts, British exports increased substantially in the first half of 1994 (to US$1 billion), an increase of 81 per cent from previous years. The government-controlled newspaper, *The New Straits Times*, gloated in the obeisant attitude of Britain after the ban:

Ministers of the Crown visited Kuala Lumpur with caps in hand, Andrew Neil was booted out as editor of the *Sunday Times*, leading city banks and businesses pooled for advertisements and other exorbitant gestures of contrition, and diplomats bowed low to expiate the British government.[31]

Conditions are expedient for processes of democratization in Malaysia; economic and technological globalization has helped to push Malaysia towards a modern country. The expansion of a middle class and a technically more skilled workforce inevitably will increase the demands for liberalization. The growth of NGOs working at different levels, for instance, is important. These include Voice of Malaysia (Suara Malaysia) and Aliran, a Penang-based group, along with the Malaysian Bar Council among others. Other NGOs have a more international focus. These include three prominent Penang-based groups: Just World Trust, Third World Network and the Consumer Association of Penang (CAP). It is in these kinds of dynamic NGOs where much of the hope for future democratization lies. Despite the fact that conditions in Malaysia are favourable towards liberalization (even though there is limited interest in internal liberal democracy here by some of the NGOs) and there are elites and other NGOs who recognize the need for change, political liberalization is not on the agenda.

Mahathir continually derides such moves as bringing political and social disorder, using what he calls the erosion of values in the West to promote personal and party interests: 'Let us not be slaves to democracy ... If by practising certain aspects of democracy we run the risk of causing chaos in our party and country, we have to choose our party and country above democracy.'[32] Here, more explicitly, national interests are used as a pretext to support personal and regime interests. By blaming everyone but himself and his government, Mahathir has managed to escape the consequences for his regime of the harsh reality of globalization. The pursuit of staying in power has become the measure of how far human rights have suffered in his regime.

Conclusion

Malaysia, along with Singapore, has been at the forefront in attacks on western versions of human rights. Mahathir, like Lee Kuan Yew, has launched blistering attacks on the western press, western institutions and the alleged lifestyles and values of the West. These two men have represented the aggressive ideologues in the Asian values debate, presenting their views in lectures, seminars and interviews in high-profile magazines and journals. To a large extent we can argue that many of these attacks stem from regime insecurity. Opposition and the growth of democratic forces in these societies threaten to undermine the established one-party authoritarian order. Mahathir's rhetoric is in some ways an attempt to deflect criticism from domestic problems. He is particularly vociferous against homosexuals; the trial of Anwar Ibrahim in the late 1990s focused on this issue as one of salience for the values that Mahathir wants to curtail. Despite the outward appearance of Malaysia as a Westminster-style democracy, its security laws and constitutional provisions give the government draconian powers to suppress opposition and deny individual human rights. Mahathir is determined, in the last instance, not to go the way of the other now deposed authoritarian of Southeast Asia, President Suharto. We have noted these problems as clashes between the state and internal groups who appear to pose a threat. The case of Al-Arquam is one example of the regime using the Internal Security Act on the pretext of maintaining religious harmony when it is really a case of violating human rights to undercut any potential political and democratic challenge. Draconian anti-drug laws aimed at curbing social problems have also violated human rights as well as sending home thousands of migrant workers, and have increased the levels of abuse directed against them in Malaysia.The Internal Security Act is still in force long after any communist threat had been lifted. It was used in October and November 1987 to detain at least 106 people without trial in 'Operation Lallang'. Malaysia, like Singapore, has little excuse to maintain these repressive pieces of legislation. Their primary purpose seems to be preventing the growth of democratic opposition and deflecting challenges to their legitimacy as we have seen them employed in the case of politics in Sabah. Francis Loh Kok Wah notes the problematic state of human rights in Malaysia:

In Malaysia, there are a whole series of laws which inhibit and restrict the growth of human rights. There is the pernicious Internal Security Act which denies one the right to a trial. Under The Essential (Security cases amendment) Regulations, one is considered guilty unless proven innocent ... Malaysia has much of the characteristics of a police state.[33]

Bridget Welsh has also argued that Malaysia represents a 'semi-democratic' regime which means that 'Democracy in Malaysia is narrow because it limits the practice of civil and political liberties through restrictions on communication, assembly, the strategic use of detention orders and other legal and emergency powers.'[34] Her results indicate pessimism about any change in the regime in the near future and help to confirm the views represented here that Malaysia will continue to exhibit authoritarian, anti-human rights tendencies; she found that economic growth seemed to have little impact on attitudes towards democratization; many of the respondents in fact supported the undemocratic character of the regime although there were clearly differences in how the various ethnic groups viewed things. Welsh's findings take on an even more pessimistic note when we see that the human rights situation in Malaysia appears to have worsened in terms of the rights to freedom of expression, speech and assembly. Mahathir, embroiled in an obvious leadership struggle with Anwar Ibrahim, clearly decided to pursue a more authoritarian route in his pattern of governance. After several months of severe disagreement with his boss over the handling of the economic crisis, the Deputy Prime Minister was abruptly sacked. Shortly after this he found himself subject to a wide range of police allegations and investigations ranging from being a promiscuous homosexual to leaking state secrets. A series of affidavits, all of which were very suspect in procedural law, were issued, charging Anwar with sodomy, molestation and discussing national politics, among other things. Fifteen human rights organizations issued a statement saying that 'the unsubstantiated affidavits, vague insinuation of treason and other nebulous accusations that have been presented through the media without right of reply are unacceptable'.[35]

There is little room in Malaysia for political rights and civil liberties of the kind enjoyed in the West. Economic development and political stability are the priorities in Malaysia. While law and order seem fairly good and stability prevails at different levels, there are cracks in the system. The Al-Arquam fiasco is one; the more recent arrest and imprisonment of Anwar Ibrahim another. While there seems to be pressures for change vis-à-vis the growth of NGOs and a fairly substantial and educated middle class, the political space still remains closely guarded and any moves to open it are met with strong resistance from the elites. Mahathir's former deputy, a man he groomed for nearly 18 years as his successor, now languishes in jail while his wife carries on the flag of reform, partly in his name, but partly because many Malaysians appear fed up with the style of dictatorial government and the levels of corruption in society. Mahathir has not so far gone the way of Suharto; he has enjoyed resounding electoral success; but there does seem to be a groundswell of opinion which argues that this scenario cannot last for much longer. It remains to be seen how long the ageing autocrat can cling on to power and the repressive strategies he uses to secure it. Malaysia in that sense is not as well equipped for the protection of human rights and processes of democratization as either Thailand or the Philippines.

SINGAPORE

Singapore is one of the richest states in Southeast Asia and has in recent years been elevated to developed status by the international community. It represents a phenomenal economic success story, capitalizing on its entrepot trade hub basis and moving to play a key role in banking and legal services, as well as serving as a major tourist destination for Southeast Asia. It has been seen as containing aspects of the most modern western city and the most exotic eastern fable, a haven for travellers seeking comfort from the less accessible and relatively underdeveloped Southeast Asian countries. It presents itself with stage-managed efficiency in this respect. It is, however, one of the political systems in the region with the most scant regard and undisguised contempt for individual political rights, civil liberties and freedom; it held in captivity the world's longest known political prisoner (longer even than Nelson Mandela of South Africa) and appears to exhibit the greatest pettiness and lack of respect for citizen opinions. In its most recent Presidential 'election', held in 1999, the president was not even elected but chosen from a shortlist compiled by Senior Minister Lee Kuan Yew and approved by the Cabinet. This was despite a poll in the national (government-controlled newspaper) that over 80 per cent of Singaporeans wanted a contest for the position. In many respects Singapore contains only elements of a democratic political culture; it is clear that the explicit require-ments of political and social order, a theme developed by the

American political scientist Samuel Huntington in the 1960s and 1970s, are placed ahead of those of the protection and exercise of individual freedom and rights.

Historical Overview

Singapore has accepted migration from other countries for many years, it lies at the end of the Malay Peninsula, an ideal stopping place and strategic channel for ships heading to the South China seas. Its strategic importance is often seen as vital because of the control of the sea-lanes. Mainly Malays inhabited Singapore in 1819, when Sir Stamford Raffles of the British East India Company arrived to colonize the island, arguing that the British needed an increased presence in the region to curb the dangers of Dutch expansionism. At that time the island was scarcely populated and covered in jungle and marshland, and an Anglo-Dutch Treaty of 1824 gave Singapore, Penang and Malacca over to the British, which soon saw the beginnings of a thriving trading and colonial settlement. The result was the development of the Straits Settlements and, in 1867, a Crown Colony. Half a century later, with the opening of new sea routes, the Suez Canal in 1869 and the introduction of the steamship, the strategic significance of Singapore and its location on major shipping lanes ensured that it would develop a thriving trade, particularly after the development of the tin and rubber industries in Malaysia and Sumatra in the early twentieth century. In the initial decades of the twentieth century, large numbers of immigrants came from China to take part in this growing economic boom, largely working in the clerical, shipping and government services. By the 1930s the ethnic proportions that exist today were already in place. The Second World War exposed the weaknesses of the British Empire and the surrender of Singapore to the Japanese in 1941 highlighted the inability to protect their colonies. At the end of the war, any claim the British might have had to rule was severely dented by their mistakes.

With the expulsion of Japanese troops, the island resumed the status of Crown Colony until 1959, when it was granted independence. Several indigenous nationalist movements, including the People's Action Party under the tutelage of a Cambridge-educated lawyer, Lee Kuan Yew, had evolved. From this period on, one-party rule was established and has continued, along with rapid economic growth based on the financial, export and manufacturing sectors, which ensured that Singapore assumed its natural role as the financial and commercial centre of Southeast Asia – a position bolstered by its extensive port facilities. In 1963 Singapore joined the Federation of Malaysia but was forced to leave two years later in 1965 because of political differences.

The government of Singapore is controlled by the People's Action Party (PAP). The party started as a coalition between an elite of mainly western-educated professionals and a broad-based Communist Party which used the name of Socialist Front (Barisan Socialis) to disguise its ulterior motivations. In the ensuing struggle for power within the coalition, the PAP emerged as the winner and Lee Kuan Yew the new leader. The latter ruled Singapore with the hand of a benevolent dictator from 1965 to 1990 and continues to exert a powerful, behind-the-scenes influence even though he formally handed over the reins of power to the current Prime Minister Goh Chok Tong in 1990. The turbulent 1960s were to be a learning period for the PAP: participatory, democratic politics were to be eschewed; the masses were not suited to a liberal political system and there was a strong feeling that the electorate was too immature to adopt a democratic political culture. With Singapore's ethnic mix and racial divisions, democracy (particularly western-style liberal democracy) would be too dangerous for Singapore's precarious position. Internal racial tensions and ethnic violence in neighbouring countries in the 1960s seemed to confirm this sense of insecurity. And this continues to pervade the elite's political philosophy. In October 1984, Lee Hsien Loong, the elder son of Lee Kuan Yew and a potential future Prime Minister, summed up this 'siege mentality' when he said that 'overnight an oasis can become a desert'.[36] These fears have been mobilized time after time over the last 30 years to justify authoritarian government which has, by and large, been based on the 'politics of survival'. According to one author:

> successive PAP administrations have exercised state power in accordance with a system of restrictive rules and regulation. That system or mode of administering state power which governs the daily lives of all Singaporeans can be referred to as an 'authoritarian regime.' ... the particular form that authoritarianism takes in Singapore is largely shaped by the PAP.[37]

Perhaps the notable aspect of this style of government is that it is based on not having any kind of effective opposition. When the opposition has tried to make changes and gain access to parliament, they have been met with a harsh response from the ruling PAP. In several instances this has resulted in the bankrupting of opposition politicians. The implied social contract the PAP offers Singaporeans is material advancement at the cost of the people tolerating authoritarian and undemocratic policies.

Similarly, the one-party state apparatus in Singapore is coming under increasing pressure as the PAP sees its share of the popular vote declining over time. In October 1990, Lee Kuan Yew stepped down voluntarily after more than 25 years in power and handed over to his hand-picked successor, Goh Chock Tong. He still retains a very powerful and influential position as Senior Minister. In August 1993, the government held elections for an elected presidency which was supposed to have the power to approve budgets, make political appointments and safeguard Singapore's valuable reserves. In a contest in which only two candidates ran, the PAP were the clear winners, but with a less than overwhelming majority (58.7 per cent of the vote). The other candidate who ran against the Deputy Prime Minister, Ong Teong Cheong, staged the most lacklustre campaign in the history of elections, heartily endorsing the PAP candidate for the job before the vote was even cast.

The defensiveness of the government is clearly concerted, with regular propaganda barrages against western decadence, life-styles and the insidious influence of satellite TV (banned in Singapore), which are said to threaten 'traditional' Asian values. As Gary Rodan points out, there is little 'structural economic imperative underlying authoritarian rule' here; rather, the goal of continued political dominance has become the end itself. This continued dominance has been made easier recently with the self-inflicted destruction that the main opposition party, the Social Democratic Party (SDP), appears to be waging against itself. The fact that Singapore is experiencing a rising divorce rate, an increase in drug offenders, more single mothers and increasing alienation as a result of its rapid economic transformation is merely a symptom of most countries, western or eastern, in the process of modernization and rapid industrialization. In another analysis of political change in Southeast Asia, Michael Vatkiosis has argued that 'modern urban existence and the capitalist system has begun to erode the traditional collective values which the ruling elite claim lie at the core of their values'.[38] The most recent election in Singapore (January 1997) saw a slight reversal of this declining vote when the PAP was returned with 63.5 per cent of the vote (up from 61 per cent) and 81 out of the 83 seats in Parliament. This was also a considerable setback for the opposition, who saw their seats halved from four to two.[39] Goh Chock Tong claimed a moral victory, saying that the landslide showed that Singaporeans had 'rejected, Western-style liberal democracy and freedoms'. As Gary Rodan pointed out it was really

> self-interest rather than any clear ideology were probably uppermost in voters minds. They had been given a stark choice: return government candidates and benefit from a range of expensive new public programs, or have these withheld or delayed in retaliation for electing PAP opponents.[40]

Being an opposition politician in Singapore is a high-risk venture. There are only two parties, the Workers Party and the Social Democratic Party, that have won seats from the ruling PAP government since 1996. The government rarely gives more than the minimum required nine days' notice of elections, so preventing campaigning, and there are harsh penalties for those who appear to go against the dominant party.[41] The carrot-and-stick intimidation of the voting populace of Singapore has also been extended to any opposition that dares to speak out or criticize the ruling regime. More recently, Chee Soon Juan, the leader and secretary-general of the opposition party, the Singapore Democratic Party, was arrested and fined for speaking in public without a police permit. He claimed this was a violation of his constitutional right to free speech and as a result of this he was banned from running for political office for five years, and was fined S$1,400 (US$830), although this has since been reduced slightly which will allow Chee back into the political arena. When he refused to pay, he was sent to jail for seven days.[42] The prosecution claimed that the right to free speech was not an 'absolute' right. The personalization of politics has now become a central feature of the political system in Singapore system, much of it encouraged by fears of losing face. It is clear that individual political rights and civil liberties such as freedom of speech and assembly have taken a real battering in the Southeast Asian city-state that lays claim to be a model for other developing and developed economies.

In 1990, the government warned 'their' people about the western vice of individualism and this vice's harmful and 'esoteric' concern with human rights.[43] The notion that the state acts in a managerial capacity to prevent regime threatening change is synonymous with a view of the middle classes as beneficiaries not adversaries of author-itarian forms of governance. In this sense the rule of law means nothing more than preparing citizens for the requirements of a national plan formulated by a wise and virtuous bureaucratic elite than as a mechanism for the protection of individual rights. The notion of law in Singapore is devoid of meaning for the protection of individual rights, and instead is often wielded as the coercive instrument of state power. Asian values and the national plan are attuned to one another in the politics of 'soft' authoritarianism. These values are concerned with asserting the cultural and political 'difference' between East and West and they are typical of the values that Singapore uses in defence of its policies towards its battered opposition. Political change here then is about the management and effective organization of state power and the system of control it exercises over the populace, and, as we will see in the case of Singapore, this is a relentless pursuit.

In 1985 a book entitled *Access to Justice*, Scoble and Wiseberg argued that in Singapore, '[i]n general, the permitted range of political expression and action is quite narrow, the penalties for political deviance quite harsh. In fact, Singapore is an apparently deviant case, when contrasted with the other four ASEAN nations (and with much of the Third World), only to the extent that it has effectively combined political repression with what has generally been regarded as corruption free government.'[44] Fifteen years on, the opposition appears as stifled as ever and the range of expression even narrower given the economic growth and outward sophistica-tion of this state.

Political Economy

Singapore's sense of insecurity and vulnerability may have a lot to do with its size; the island is the smallest geographical member of ASEAN with a land area of only 600 square kilometres. Its population of approximately 3.1 million is made up of 75 per cent Chinese who emigrated there over the last century, 15 per cent Malays and roughly 6–7 per cent Indians, with the remainder Eurasian and expatriate workers. This society is widely regarded as one of the most dynamic economies in ASEAN and a model for many other developing countries. There have been unique accomplishments in urban construction and planning in the city-state, combined with an efficient infrastructure that has raised living standards almost to First World levels. Most Singaporeans have adequate housing, reasonably inexpensive health care and fairly good systems of public education and transportation. Many of the other problems that plague Southeast Asian cities, such as high crime rates, severe traffic congestion, pollution and drug abuse, appear to have been all but eliminated from the city-state. In the twenty-first century, Singapore hopes to achieve the living standards of Switzerland.

In this sense it has done remarkably well for a small, vulnerable island state, assuming an importance in regional affairs out of all proportion to its size. When it was expelled from the Malaysian Federation in 1965, Singapore faced great uncertainty because it had very few natural resources, a tiny agricultural base and a large population for its geographical size. Isolation seemed a recipe for disaster. Singaporean leaders remind us constantly that Singapore's main resource is its people, and certainly the dramatic growth in the years following the separation from Malaysia to a successful NIC would seem to indicate some validity to this claim. To a large extent its growth is based on export-oriented industrialization, a determined emphasis on free trade, massive government intervention in all aspects of life, and the cultivation of large-scale foreign investment, particularly by multinational companies (MNCs). Singapore set out from the beginning to make itself attractive to foreign investment by offering low wages, a largely English-speaking workforce and an uncorrupt government. It also encouraged a mix of local private companies, state enterprises and foreign companies. In the 1970s Singapore felt confident enough to see itself as a global city holding a pivotal position in the global economy. One former foreign minister argued this clearly:

> we are more than a regional city. We draw sustenance not only from the region but also the international economy which as a global city we belong [to] and which will be the final arbiter of whether we prosper or decline.[45]

The analogy was with Venice (strangely enough), but it wasn't to last. One author has noted that in the 1980s this position began to change as Singapore started to see itself as a key regional centre based in an emerging regional economy and not necessarily as a global city in the classical sense.[46]

One cannot deny Singapore's economic success. In 1965, the PAP inherited severe economic problems: poverty, unemployment and homeless. Thirty years later, the change could not have been more dramatic with more than 90 per cent of Singaporeans owning their own homes, GNP growing from $1billion in 1965 to $35 billion in 1992 and one of the highest per capita foreign reserves, not only in the region but at the global level,[47] with an annual per capita income of more than US$18,000 and national reserves of more than S$90 billion.

Even Singapore, however, has not been as immune to the effects of the Asian economic crisis as might have appeared in the initial stages. Despite its huge reserves and low debt, it has also seen unemployment and fiscal deficits as a result of the contagion effect. Naturally there has been a fall in regional demand as a result of the crisis and Singapore has been adversely affected. Unemployment rates were expected to double. One political scientist argued that it was 'estimated that the total number of retrenched workers could go up to 30,000 by the year's end [1998]. As a result, the unemployment rate rose to 3.2 per cent with an estimated 62,800 workers.'[48] Singapore's economy is also affected by other regional activities because nearly a third of its trade is with other ASEAN states (Indonesia, Malaysia, the Philippines and Thailand). In spite of some of these figures, it is clear that Singapore's economy has suffered less than its poorer and weaker regional neighbours. This is probably due to a sound banking system and lack of corruption; in these instances it is clearly the exception to the rule. However, partly because of its comparative economic success and ability to keep its head above the worst of the crisis, relations have become strained in recent years between Singapore and its closest neighbour Malaysia over a whole variety of issues, and this may have implications for future economic cooperation. These disputes belie the typically complex and sensitive nature of bilateral relations in Southeast Asia where 'face' is all-important and relations highly personalized. There is fairly widespread jealousy at Singapore's success. And the economic crisis has brought some of these sensitivities to a head. Singapore, for instance, continues to see itself as a highly competitive economy and its government as one of the most interventionist in the region, regardless of its claims to be totally reliant on the free market. The government argues that everyone in Singapore has to pull their weight; there can be no welfarism along the lines of the European model. Lee Kuan Yew, for instance, argued that people had to get rid of the mentality that: 'You owe me a living. I was born here. According to the Charter of Human Rights, I am entitled to the following things: minimum wage, holidays with pay, education, and so on. It is this attitude we have to set out to dispel. Unless you dispel this belief that the world owes us a living then none of our other problems will even begin to be solved.'[49]

Extensive measures in times of crisis are taken to reduce costs and stimulate the economy. The conditions it imposes may seem difficult at times but the majority of the population still seem to go along with their government's view of things, particularly in terms of running the economy.

Human Rights in Singapore: Measures of Internal Repression

Like Malaysia, Singapore maintains an Internal Security Act inherited from British colonial times. Previously it was justified on the grounds of communist agitation and the threat these types of group posed to colonial society; however, after independence and rapid economic growth, this rationale has become increasingly tendentious. As in Malaysia, the Internal Security Department, Singapore's secret police, has the power to arrest anyone deemed to be 'acting in a manner prejudicial to the security of Singapore' and detain them indefinitely without trial. Defenders of these draconian powers argue that they are necessary to secure law and order and stabilize a fragile society. Detention or exile are also permissible under the Criminal Law (Temporary Provisions Act), the Misuse of Drugs Act and the Undesirable Publications Act; the Criminal Law is used mainly for drug offences, but also has been used for detention of secret society members. Activities of NGOs are also subject to very strict controls, leaving little room for the development of a real civil society. The Societies Act, which came into law in 1967, has made a strong distinction between political and non-political activities. Public policy is seen as something for government not the public. Wong Kan Seng, the Communications and Information Minister in 1985, pointed this out when he argued that 'public policy is the domain of government. It isn't the playground of those who have no responsibility to the people, and who aren't answerable for the livelihood or survival of Singaporeans.'[50]

In more recent times these powers have not been used against radical revolutionaries, but aimed (ironically) at middle-class lawyers, college graduates and accountants, among others. In 1987 and 1988, 22 Singaporeans were arrested by Internal Security on the grounds that they were involved in a Marxist plot to overthrow the government. Their rights were denied them, forced confessions were extracted and they were subjected to physical mistreatment.[51] Under the Act people can be detained indefinitely; Chia Thye Poh, for example, a former member of the Singaporean Parliament and member of the Barisan Socialis Party, was detained in October 1966 without charge or trial, giving him the distinction of being the longest serving political prisoner in modern times. It was not until 1998 that the government finally felt confident enough to remove all the restrictions on him. Tang Fong Har, detained in 1987 for her part in the alleged 'conspiracy', was detained for 85 days, 75 of which were spent in solitary confinement; after their release some of the detainees signed a statement that they had been mistreated in prison and that they denied being part of any plot; the following day those who had signed the statement were rearrested and rein-carcerated. Ms Tang describes another detainee's experience:

The interrogation room was 16 ft. by 12 ft. It was soundproof and two teams of interrogators worked in twelve-hour shifts, round the clock for the first three days. The worst treatment was during the first three days. While I was being questioned and shouted at, I was made to stand continuously for 32 hours in the cold air-conditioned room. My first non-stop interrogation lasted 64 hours. I received my first slap across the face three minutes into the interrogation. It was during the first 36 hours that I received all the slaps and hits. I would have received about 50 hand slaps across my face, chest, stomach and back. According to others, they slapped man or woman alike if they did not get a satisfactory account. The slaps brought on uncontrollable coughing and my head spun. I kept telling myself all the time that I was not a communist. They threatened to slap me more if I did not stop lying. I persisted and was slapped some more. It was incredible. My head was groggy and they threatened to pour cold water on me. But I gave the same answers to the same unreasonable questions. Water was thrown on me and I shivered uncontrollably. My jaws were chattering and I collapsed to the floor.[52]

Lawyers in Singapore commonly admit to the use of the 'aircon room' to extract confessions. Francis Seow, a former Solicitor General of Singapore and one of its most prominent dissidents, was held repeatedly in this room during a 72-day detention in 1988, sometimes for periods as long as 16 hours which left him with cold rashes on his body. He stated that it 'is so cold that even the interrogators cannot stand it, and they often have to leave the room, leaving you inside'.[50] Seow recalls losing all sense of time in this period:

> I then realized that I had been standing in the interrogation room for about sixteen hours warding off questions thrown unremittingly at me. It seemed improbable to me that I could have stood at one spot, almost motionless, for that length of time. I recalled with shame that, when my detainee-clients had previously complained to me that they had been forced to stand for as long as 72 hours at a stretch, without sleep, I had great difficulty believing them.[53]

According to the Home Affairs Minister in 1992, S. Jayakumar, Singapore was also detaining 1,000 'hard-core' gangsters in 1992.[54]

No one has been jailed under formal ISA detention since 1990. However, detainees who have been released, such as Chia Thye Poh (who has now moved back to Singapore from his offshore exile on the Sentosa theme park), cannot be employed, travel abroad or issue public statements without approval of the internal security apparatus. Vincent Cheng, detained under the so-called Marxist conspiracy of 1987 and released in 1990, is under similar restrictions.

Political Legitimacy, Freedom of Speech and Human Rights

The Singapore constitution has placed certain restrictions on the right to freedom of expression. If a publication is deemed to incite violence or threaten national interests or security in any way, it will be prohibited. The PAP government over the years has been fairly liberal in applying this law in the broadest sense to stifle criticism and dissenting views. The Television Corporation of Singapore (TCS, formerly SBC) is controlled by the party and helps the government to develop standards of censorship. It has a monopoly on broadcasting, running all three of Singapore's TV networks and most of the radio stations, with the exception of services such as the BBC World Service and the Malaysian TV channels (which are already censored); satellite dishes are banned for private use. All the mass daily newspapers are controlled by the private Singapore Press Holdings, which has extremely close ties with the political leadership.

In the early 1970s the government closed three local newspapers, the *Nanyang Siang Pau,* the *Eastern Sun* and the *Singapore Herald,* for allegedly promoting Chinese chauvinism, receiving communist support and addressing negative issues, such as national service. At various times the regime has restricted circulation of current affairs journals and newspapers that reported on Singapore, typically on the pretext that their articles have interfered in the internal affairs of Singapore. These include *Time*, the *Asian Wall Street Journal*, *Asiaweek* and the *Far Eastern Economic Review*. In August 1993 it restricted the circulation of the British journal *The Economist* after it published an article on Singapore's prosecution of five people under the Official Secrets Act. In addition, Singapore revoked the newspapers' exemption from various bureaucratic procedures. It is now required, for example, to make a S$200,000 (US$125,000) deposit to the government. The elements in the restriction seem petty in scale, but the control over information and alternative views is highly systematic and staggeringly insidious. As *The Economist* noted in 1990, in response to a new press law that would require journals to obtain a government permit if they published news on Southeast Asia, 'The walls may be tumbling in failed Eastern Europe, but they are rising in successful Singapore.'[55] The regime is particularly sensitive to reports on ethnicity and political stability, again reflecting their vulnerability to anything that might spark political change.

In 1996, the regime announced new laws governing the internet.

The government has a different perspective on the role of the media; its view is that the media exist to reinforce the regime and not attack or criticize their policies or make controversial statements regarding sensitive issues. The case might be made for a harder line against human rights and democratization being taken because the ruling elites are losing legitimacy and some of their credibility. Despite phenomenal economic growth in the Southeast Asian region, many one-party dominant regimes are losing their previous support. In Singapore the government still engages in large-scale social control to stem the tide of democratization. In 1987, Lee Kuan Yew stated: 'Who your neighbour is, how you live, the noise you make, how you spit, or what language you use. We decide what is right. Never mind what the people think.'[56] But, clearly, what the people think and how the vote has declined in contemporary Singapore has become a worrying preoccupation of the one-party regime over the last decade. In 1980, the PAP managed a very respectable 75.5 per cent of the popular vote; in 1984 this had decreased to 62.9 per cent and in 1988 and 1991, 61.8 per cent and 61 per cent respectively. One local commentator noted a sizeable 7.7 per cent swing away from the PAP in terms of votes at the end of the 1980s and beginning of the 1990s.[57] After the election in 1991, the new Prime Minister, Goh Chock Tong, voiced his unhappiness and discontent with the result: 'Life cannot go on as it did before. Certain things have to change now.'[58] The most recent election in Singapore (January 1997) saw a slight reversal of this declining vote when the PAP was returned with 63.5 per cent of the votes cast and 81 out of the 83 seats in Parliament. This was also a considerable setback for the opposition, who saw their seats halved from four to two.[59]

In Singapore the dominance of the People's Action Party (PAP) is criticized by opposition leaders, who seek alternative and more democratic rule. An enormous effort is made to maintain political stability and, some would argue, the authoritarian one-party system, through various methods. In 1988, the regime accused an American diplomat, E. Mason Hendrickson, of backing local lawyers to stand for office against PAP candidates. Goh said that such activity threatened to 'break up the cohesion of our society ... [and that] thirty years of bonding and nation building would come to naught.' In the end the result would be chaos and poverty.[60] Another commentator noted the 'exemplary punishment' the regime reserves for those who question its authority and pose a political challenge: Mr J. B. Jeyeratnam, a leading opponent of the PAP, has been bankrupted for criticizing Lee's autocratic style; and the former Attorney General, Francis Seow, was forced into exile after running as an opposition candidate in 1988.

Academics at institutions such as the National University of Singapore (NUS) and other tertiary institutions are government employees who are loath to criticize government politics and in general eschew any political comments. When they do comment they tend to side with the government and avoid anything that may attract retaliation from the regime. In 1993, Dr Chee Soon Juan, a Singaporean lecturer and the Deputy General of the opposition Singapore Democratic Party, was informed that his contract would not be renewed because of an alleged irregularity involving the use of research funds to post his wife's thesis to the United States. Chee claimed this was necessary for his own research; the sum was fairly small, less than US$150 (S$250). And he appeared to have received sanction for this act from his Head of Department (who was, incidentally, a PAP MP) for the use of funds in this way. After this reprimand the lecturer went on hunger strike and claimed the punishment was politically motivated. In response, NUS fired him with immediate effect. Several university officials, moreover, brought defamation suits against him after he questioned the motivations of his superiors who ordered his dismissal. These resulted in heavy fines, a tactic that has been used repeatedly to intimidate political opponents. Under Singapore law, a history of bankruptcy disqualifies one from political office.[61]

Recently, Chee, now secretary-general of the weak opposition party, the Singapore Democratic Party, has argued that 'The younger generation knows something is amiss. I think a lot of them really want to know more ... They've been in a straitjacket all these years.'[62] In 1999, Chee tried unsuccessfully to speak in public without a permit – which, as far as he is concerned, is his constitutional right, something denied by the ruling government.

Freedom of expression is not high on the agenda. In October 1994, the police interrogated Dr Christopher Lingle, an American teaching at NUS, over an article he wrote for an international newspaper.[63] Lingle's 'crime' apparently was to call into question the 'independence' of the Singapore judiciary, although he did not name Singapore in the article. However, he did the voice the opinion that:

> intolerant regimes in the region reveal considerable ingenuity in their methods of suppressing dissent. Some techniques lack finesse; crushing unarmed students with tanks, or imprisoning dissidents. Others are more subtle: relying upon a compliant judiciary to bankrupt opposition politicians.[64]

In the event, Lingle left Singapore in a hurry after the interrogation for his native America. He was tried *in absentia* for 'contempt of court', a law that forbids 'undermining public confidence in [i.e., criticizing] the judiciary'. The Singapore court found him and his publisher guilty of contempt of court and imposed a S$10,000 fine. In a bizarre, Kafkaesque, but apparently unknowing twist of irony, the prosecutor, Attorney General Chan Sek Kong, claimed unashamedly that Lingle could not have been describing any other country in the region as having a compliant judiciary 'because there is no other such country'. Lingle, in other words, was correct in implying that the PAP elites had a longstanding tradition of suing and bankrupting opposition politicians. Chan noted that 'between 1971 and 1993 ... there had been 11 cases of opposition politicians who had been made bankrupt after being sued'.[65] In addition to this, even after the newspaper had 'unreservedly apologised', Lee Kuan Yew, now officially known as Senior Minister, decided to take both the newspaper and Lingle to court himself.

Despite the judgement in the local press that the Lingle case was about protecting the integrity of the judiciary and 'had nothing to do with freedom of the press', it is clear that it was about freedom of expression, which is severely restricted in Singapore. Criticism of the West and its social, economic and political problems, which fill the pages of the leading English-language daily newspaper the *Straits Times*, flourishes, but this is clearly a one-sided debate; alternative and dissenting views are heavily discouraged, as the Lingle case has dramatically shown.

Singapore has also come under criticism for its human rights record; the city-state has only signed three human rights conventions out of a possible 25 such documents.[66] Asia Watch, an international human rights NGO similar to Amnesty International, has compiled a list of alleged human rights violations in Singapore which include aspects like 'preventive detention', imprisonment without trial, various restrictions on freedom of movement, speech and association, various limits placed on judicial review, and the intimidation and harassment of opposition or potential opposition politicians, to name a few.[67]

Cruel Punishment?

On 6 October 1993, Michael Fay, an 18-year-old American teenager living in Singapore, was arrested along with four other youths for vandalizing cars with spray paint. These cars did not belong to ordinary Singaporeans; they were the property of the elites, including a judicial commissioner of the Singapore Supreme Court. When he appeared in court on the 1 March 1994, Fay pleaded guilty to two counts of vandalism under the Punishment of Vandalism Act, two charges of mischief and one of receiving stolen property. He was sentenced to four months in prison, a fine of US$2,215, and six strokes of the cane, which was later reduced to four after the US President appealed for clemency, on the basis that it seemed disproportionately severe. The argument was made over and over again that the punishment did not fit the crime.

On top of this there appeared to be doubt as to whether Fay's confession was a voluntary one. In a later statement Fay declared that he signed it only 'after he was slapped and punched by police officers who held him in detention for nine days with little sleep and almost no access to his parents or the US embassy'.[68]

In the Covenant of Civil and Political Rights the message is that 'no one shall be subjected to cruel, inhuman or degrading punishment'; this definition fits the caning sentence. Both Fay's father and his lawyer stated that 'blood ran down Fay's legs during his caning ... [and] he was in continual pain, had his flesh ripped and his buttocks covered with bloody slashes and was unable to sit'.[69] Between 1989 and 1993, 14 people (twelve Singaporeans and two foreigners) were charged and sentenced to jail and caning for vandalism offences.

Singaporean authorities often point out in their defence that the British introduced caning, but this argument holds little water. Blaming the hangovers of colonialism is a fairly typical ruse employed by authoritarian governments in Southeast Asia to justify torture and abuse. One author has pointed out that the British had eliminated whipping for most offences by the beginning of the 1950s and had replaced it with caning for violent crimes and rape alone (that is, crimes against the person). The Government of Singapore under Lee, however, reintroduced caning in 1966 for acts of vandalism (that is, a crime against property); it was the by-product of a plan to punish left-wing political graffiti and suppress the political opposition:

> Thereafter, Lee extended caning to many more offences, such as overstaying one's visa, and right now, is contemplating it for recalcitrant drug addicts. It was *not* therefore a British colonial heritage.[70]

The 1966 Punishment for Vandalism Act has made it a crime to paint or mark public or private property, as well as to post flags, bunting or banners without permission, and carries a mandatory caning of between three and eight strokes, fines of up to S$2,000 and imprisonment of up to three years.

Anyone who has an unlicensed gun, carries a knife, extorts, robs, molests or rapes with violence will be caned. Some non-violent offenders, such as vandals, and foreigners who overstay in Singapore beyond 90 days, are also subject to mandatory caning. To inflict torture for overstaying one's visa seems extreme. Lee says he believes such punishment has kept the streets of Singapore safe. In response to the Michael Fay case he said, unapologetically, 'If anyone thinks it is barbaric, well then, please don't bring your 18 year old to Singapore. And if you do bring him, please warn him about the consequences.'[71]

Fay's punishment seems relatively mild when compared to that of Qwek Kee Chong, a 22-year-old at the time, who in 1987 was found guilty on four charges of armed robbery after pleading guilty at a trial where he was not represented by a lawyer. Qwek was sentenced to ten years in prison and twelve strokes of the cane on each of the four charges. On 8 April 1988, he received all 48 strokes of the cane in one session, after which he had to be hospitalized in the Changi Prison hospital.[72] In 1988, the account of a 40-year-old businessman described the fear and pain he had felt when he received twelve strokes of the cane as a 17-year-old, after he had tried to escape from a reform centre where he had been sent for housebreaking:

Then I heard the cane. It sounded like a plank hitting the wall. A split second later I felt it was tearing across my buttocks. I screamed and struggled like a mad animal. All I thought was that I want to run away. If I'm not tied up, one stroke could keep me running for a mile. And I just could not control my screams. It went on and on, one stroke, one minute. Some lashes fall on the same spot, splitting open the skin even more. Some prisoners urinate and even faint because of the pain. I felt giddy and went limp on the trestle at the last stroke. My bleeding buttocks throbbed with pain and felt like they were on fire.[73]

In 1993 caning was used in 3,244 cases judged under the law.

As well as caning, regarded as torture by human rights NGOs, Singapore retains the death penalty by hanging and uses it for a variety of offences, including murder, treason, using a gun in kidnapping, rioting or robbery; but in recent years its most commonly cited use has been for possession of narcotics. A 1975 amendment to the Misuse of Drugs Act made the death penalty mandatory for possession of over 15 grams of heroin or fixed amounts of other drugs (for example, more than 30 grams of morphine).[74]

Singapore's Response to the West

Singapore is a leading exponent of claims that a special set of 'Asian values' separates East Asia from the West and therefore allows Asians the luxury of different human rights standards. Singaporean leaders concentrate on the harmful aspects of western culture which include abuse of drugs, excessive individualism and placing personal over family interests, sexual promiscuity and laziness, among other so-called 'western' characteristics. Asian habits of industriousness, selflessness, filial piety and community before self are continually trotted out to make political points.[75] The most prominent spokesman for these 'Asian values' is Lee Kuan Yew, who consistently champions community over individual rights.

> Whether in periods of golden prosperity or in the depths of disorder, Asia has never valued the individual over society ... The society has always been more important than the individual. I think that is what has saved Asia from greater misery ... I believe that human-rights standards, as distinct from democracy as a form of government, will become universal. It will not be western standards, because the West is but a minority in this world.[76]

In many cases the language of development, human rights and democracy and their implications have become inseparable for East Asian leaders, but this has been primarily achieved in the area of propaganda. Lee Kuan Yew argued such a position in Manila, where he linked these questions with the issue of democracy: 'I don't think democracy leads to development ... But I do think a country needs more discipline than democracy.' This was a clear pointer implying that the problems in the Philippines might be solved by a dose of Singapore-style discipline.[77] Such an argument implies elitism, for the elites are seen to be doing the masses a favour by granting them democracy; the notion that 'good government' and discipline are more important than the right of individuals to participate within their society's politics is clearly a prominent campaign for a 'subject' political culture. Quite clearly, however, we could make a strong case the other way in arguing that an authoritarian, undemocratic regime under Ferdinand Marcos severely retarded economic development in the Philippines.

Similarly, a Deputy Secretary in the Singapore Ministry of Foreign Affairs argued against universal human rights, which he regards as a western invention: 'There is no unified Asian view on human rights and the freedom of the press. These are western concepts. Asians are obliged to react to them. Predictably, there is a whole range of reactions ranging from those who subscribe to these concepts in toto to those who reject them completely.'[78]

It is not the individualistic tendency, however, of western human rights that undermines traditional, family oriented societies in Southeast Asia, but the processes of industrialization and urbaniza- tion, which in turn produce an increasing individualization of society.[79] One-party regimes have even acknowledged the trends towards individual behaviour; in a Government White Paper released in 1991, the People's Action Party stated that 'Traditional Asian ideas of morality, duty and society, which have sustained and guided us in the past, are giving way to a more Westernised, indi- vidualistic and self-centred outlook on life.'[80] Again the Southeast Asian argument is used as a political stick with which to beat opponents. Consequently, when Lee, Mahathir and Suharto cite the moral disintegration and decay in western societies as a result of too many individual rights and democracy, they ignore the argument that individualism is the consequence not of democracy and human rights, but of industrialization, increasing literacy rates and other changes at the societal level that transcend culture.

In 1994, Singapore received a great deal of criticism and attacks from the western media for its draconian policies, particularly over the Michael Fay case. Some critics went as far as to argue that Singapore should be punished by stopping trade or investments and even preventing Americans from travelling to Singapore; dictator- ship was one word used in the *International Herald Tribune* to describe the PAP regime.[81]

Conclusion

The Singapore state is often seen as a model for developing nations because of its extraordinary economic success, its near eradication of poverty and its high-quality social services. Indeed, it has concentrated on the economic and social rights of its citizens to an enormous degree. In this sense it has managed to provide one of the highest living standards for its citizens not only in Asia but also the world. People who visit the island state are always impressed by its cleanliness and efficiency. However, these impressive achievements have been at some cost to individual political rights and civil liberties. Singapore does have a good record in that political or extra-judicial killings are completely absent, and disappearances, common in some other ASEAN states, are non-existent. The social rights of women, children and ethnic minorities have generally been advanced and Singapore certainly has a much better standing in these areas than its ASEAN neighbours. But clearly Singapore falls short in political rights and civil liberties. When he was Prime Minister, Lee stated: 'Nobody has the right to subvert me.'[82] This appears to be a club to batter opposition and anyone who dares to question PAP policy in Singapore.

For dissidents and opposition politicians, the oasis that Singapore has been compared to must seem like the desert. Draconian laws such as the Internal Security Act have been used against political opponents and those who dare to criticize the regime. The continued bankrupting of opposition politicians continues to the present. In 1998, as Lee Lai To points out:

> In fact, in the case of the Worker's Party, Tang Liang Hong, who had been a candidate in the January 1997 election and eventually fled to Australia, was bankrupted as a result of defamation suits brought against him by the PAP leaders. Goh Chok Tong also petitioned to ask the court to bankrupt J.B. Jeyaretnam, the Worker's party chief, for failing to pay the defamation charges owed to him. Earlier, Goh had offered to waive the damages if Jeyaretnam agreed to apologise in the manner sought by him ... The Worker's Party, Jeyaretnum, and veteran member A. Balakrishnam were also asked by the court in another defamation case about an article published in the Worker's party newsletter, *The Hammer*.[83]

The press is not free; it is controlled by the government and any dissent carries severe consequences. Francis Seow, Chee Soon Juan and Christopher Lingle among others have all felt in varying degrees the harshness of a regime bent on stifling opposing viewpoints.

The softer, more liberal and open approach that Goh Chock Tong promised when he took over the reins of government appears to have been abandoned; in fact, some see the regime as even more heavy-handed in its treatment of dissidents and critics. And there are elements that its 'politics of survival' are continuing even though it enjoys a safe and secure economic environment. It is also clear that Singapore is concerned with maintaining a balance between threats to national security (defined as regime security) and any opening up the political system per se to the opposition and democratic forces. The heavier emphasis in the balance is clearly on the former over the latter. Singapore may aspire to be the Switzerland of Southeast Asia and rhetorically promote the arts and high culture, but in reality, it severely limits artistic expression and the development of a creative community. The Singapore press is not free and unabashedly presents itself as a propaganda sheet for the government. In comparing different presses in ASEAN, Vergel Santos has argued, 'the Philippine press is free, the Thai press is free enough, the Malaysian press could use more freedom, Indonesia is losing what little freedom it had and Singapore and Brunei are not free at all'.[84] When unsanctioned political commentary appears it is swiftly and harshly rebutted, as the in the case of Catherine Lim, a local novelist who made some fairly innocuous remarks about the government's heavy-handedness. The PAP's response was to chastise and denigrate the comments and warn against future occurrences.[85]

Moreover, because of the size of Singapore, the general level of fear is magnified. At the university, where one would expect an open and critical intellectual climate among teachers and students, such fear is pervasive. When Dr Chee was fired, no one, neither staff nor student, was willing to speak out or campaign on his behalf; he had become *persona non grata*. When the police visited Lingle to question him, the same thing happened; in fact, the head of his department brought the 'thought' police to his office in a measure of acquiescence against the violation of freedom of speech. Intimidation is a device the state uses frequently to ensure that people learn to remain quiet. The personalization of politics has now become a central feature of the political system in Singapore system, much of it encouraged by fears of losing face. It is clear that individual political rights and civil liberties such as freedom of speech and assembly have taken a real battering in Singapore which lays claim to be a model for other developing and developed economies. In a society where one risks losing one's career and livelihood for saying something politically incorrect, can one really make a case for prioritizing economic, collectivist rights over political ones and civil liberties, and acquiescing in the repressive atmosphere? Societies that rely on fear and coercion to induce respect and legitimacy are outdated and shallow in their long-term thinking. A climate of fear belies Singapore's aspirations to recognition as a model country, a modern blend of East and West and a centre for artistic expression in Southeast Asia.

ASEAN AND HUMAN RIGHTS

> Democracies are not just a moral imperative. They are a practical necessity. Democracies do not threaten their neighbours. They do not practise terrorism. They do not spawn refugees. Some have argued that democracy is somehow unsuited for Asia and that our emphasis on human rights is a mask for Western cultural imperialism. They could not be more wrong. The yearnings for more freedom are not a Western export; they are a human instinct.[86]

The end of the Cold War following the collapse of authoritarian communist regimes marked a watershed in international relations. In the West many were quick to claim that liberal and free market principles were superior to other forms of political and economic systems. Some went as far as to suggest that western liberal democracy constituted an end-point in historical evolution; it was the 'end of history', according to Francis Fukuyama.[87] Others argued that democracy and human rights should be promoted as an intrinsic good and were central to US foreign policy. While geopolitical considerations forced the West to support unsavoury authoritarian governments in the Cold War period, such rationales were redundant in the 1990s and allowed for selective human rights ideals to be promoted in active foreign policy agendas.

As we have seen, this attempted imposition by the West of its value system on East Asian authoritarian governments was unwelcome for a variety of reasons. Several Southeast Asian societies reacted strongly to these attempts to force such views on them. Many of these states had been subject to colonial control by the West in their not too distant histories. Naturally they resented what some saw as a new form of hegemony. They argued that this was contrary to principles of national sovereignty and non-interference in domestic affairs, and that the West was seeking to undermine their rapid economic growth perhaps because it feared the competition the NICs might represent to their own declining economies. Whether these claims could be substantiated is not the point. Rather, it illustrates that these states felt particularly aggrieved and in many ways justifiably so. They pointed out that liberal democracy (which was the project the West was attempting to foist on them) is inappropriate for the political and social culture of East Asia, a culture that promotes 'order', consensus and harmony over confrontation and adversarial forms of politics. Moreover, given their remarkable economic success, many felt they were in a position to resist what some of them regard as a new form of western cultural hegemony. It is in this light that ASEAN's position on human rights issues can be assessed.

A Singaporean official has stated strongly that 'there is no unified view on human rights ... these are Western concepts [and] Asians are obliged to react to them'.[88] If there is no unified view or perspective on human rights in Asia, this has not prevented regional groups such as ASEAN from pursuing a collective policy: acquiescence. Time after time they have refused to condemn violators of human rights in the region and declined to take assertive steps to improve regional versions of rights. The latest in this form of acquiescence was the entry of Myanmar (formerly Burma), one of the region's and the world's worst violators of rights, into the ASEAN club. In the past ASEAN has maintained a fairly ambivalent attitude towards human rights questions; in terms of external foreign policy for instance, while ASEAN did not mind 'references to the principles of human rights, such as self determination, to mobilise the international community against an external foe in Kampuchea, it was reticent to address the human rights situation at home'.[89]

The ASEAN club maintains a policy of 'constructive engagement' towards Myanmar in a similar manner to the previous policies pursued by the West towards South Africa and the People's Republic of China. The hope is that by having a dialogue, maintaining contact and avoiding the isolation of the Myanmar junta, it will eventually come round to appreciating the folly and short-sightedness of its repressive policies and suppression of democracy. Double standards are apparent; while calling for recognition of rights at the international level, the ASEAN governments ultimately consider human rights an internal affair, both regionally and domestically, and carefully avoid discussions of human rights in specific countries even among their close neighbours and erstwhile allies. News is distorted in countries like Singapore and Malaysia in an effort to avoid the discussion of human rights violations within ASEAN states. News about such topics is either given very limited coverage or discussed in such neutral terms that it would be hard for the average reader to determine whether human rights violations had taken place.

Constructive engagement means ASEAN countries continue to trade with Myanmar while others, such as the European Union, maintain economic sanctions. Some have questioned, however, whether ASEAN actually believes trade will improve human rights, or simply lacks any kind of interest in promoting human rights because of the implications this might have for the democratization of their own societies. As one author notes, 'In this connection, the long-term view is admitted: trade in the end will be good for human rights. But in the meantime, the interruption of trade is unlikely to bear any human rights fruit for the usual reasons that make sanctions prone to failure.'[90] Moreover, trade sanctions appear to have had no effect on Myanmar because it is receiving so much help from its ASEAN 'friends'. Thailand, for instance, constantly plays the 'constructive engagement' card in relation to its neighbour. In order to sustain their policies of 'constructive engagement, ASEAN has developed a 'Principle of Situational Uniqueness':

> In pursuing human rights in their comprehensive entirety, the ASEAN countries – as indeed all countries of the world – will be guided by the consideration of the unique blend of factors that condition and constitute each country's total environment, namely its history, demography, culture, economic condition, social situation and political environment. Being in almost all cases young nation states, nation building, that is, the forging of viable, cohesive, integrated and prosperous societies within each state, will be a foremost concern of the ASEAN countries. The ASEAN member nations will promote human rights without sacrificing domestic stability and harmony, which themselves impinge directly and crucially on human rights.[91]

The idea that cultural distinctions make the members of ASEAN different is widespread in this part of the world, providing them with the blanket of 'situational uniqueness'.

Despite rhetorical claims and principled statements, ASEAN countries often use the excuse of constructive engagement to promote their own economic and pragmatic interests. If the Thai policy of constructive engagement towards the military regime in

Rangoon and its close relationship with the Khmer Rouge in Cambodia do little to support human rights, they clearly support Thailand's vested interests in the gem and logging industries.

ASEAN members, moreover, are quick to invoke the national sovereignty principle when it does not involve themselves, such as Indonesia's criticisms of the Vietnamese in their period of occupation of Cambodia, while Jakarta was itself trampling on the right of self-determination in East Timor and Irian Jaya. Selective citations of human rights violations by ASEAN members serve simply to reinforce their own interests and in the process undermine their claims to credibility.

ASEAN's policy is well noted even within ASEAN boundaries. In June 1994, just as an Asia-Pacific Conference on East Timor (APCET) was about to take place in Manila, the Philippine government issued a ban on all foreign participants, including Nobel Peace Prize winners and Danielle Mitterrand, the wife of the then French President. President Ramos, under heavy pressure form neighbouring Indonesia to take action, called the conference 'inimical' to the national interest. Vitit Muntarbhorn has described this policy as more akin to 'instructive derangement'. He argues that it is 'instructive because of the double standards at play and the fact that we – those of us who do believe in democracy and human rights – are willing to live maddening lies that cause innumerable sufferings for the lives of others'.[92]

Christopher Lingle puts this perspective in a historical context:

> During the cold war, the ASEAN states used the image of a Communist menace to great effect. They developed a coherent front that provided legitimacy to their often-repressive methods. It served an end that was applauded by the west. As a reward, developed economies provided the Asian regimes with national security guarantees and generally open markets while turning a blind eye to the boot kept at the throat of their political opponents.[93]

And a Filipino sociologist, Walden Bello, noted in the post-Cold War period that 'part of the authoritarian countries strategy is to build an ASEAN "Berlin Wall" between the democratic movements in Thailand and the Philippines and the pro-democratic forces in their own countries'.[94]

In general, most observers agree, progress in building an Asian human rights organization has been slow. Attempts to replicate the African experience of developing regional seminars on the issue have met with little success. The problem is that economic development is the priority in ASEAN, and therefore prosperity matters more than political liberties. This is reflected in the views of individual leaders in the region, who reiterate the links between certain 'Asian' cultural values and the need for political stability on the one hand, and on the other a view of human rights that upholds the political status quo.

ASEAN and other large groups and trading entities have significantly clashed over versions of human rights and environmental protection. Third-generation ASEAN–EU agreements were delayed, for instance, by Portuguese disapproval of Indonesian troops massacring thousands of protesters in East Timor in 1991. This has large-scale economic implications; after the US and Japan, the EU is ASEAN's third largest trading partner. Additionally, the EU is irritated by ASEAN's negligible role in persuading Myanmar to reform.

In the 1970s and the 1980s many NGOs formed in Southeast Asia around concerns for human rights and were particularly interested in their use as a channel for social change. It has been argued that despite these developments human rights do not enjoy the same legitimacy in the region as in the western liberal democracies. As one author argues:

> It is often said by governments in power that human rights is [*sic*] a Western conflictual notion and that Asian societies are harmony oriented. This is often said to justify widespread violations.[95]

Once again after the coup by Hun Sen in 1997 in Cambodia, the ASEAN powers appeared powerless to do anything apart from delaying the entry of Cambodia to ASEAN. The weak response showed how weak and divided ASEAN were in terms of taking action against any of its members for the blatant disregard of democratic procedures. The position of societies in Southeast Asia has certainly moved to a much more defensive stance, as seen in their media pronouncements and government rhetoric. ASEAN states, from pariah states like Myanmar all the way to Malaysia, Indonesia and even in Singapore (where officials claim they simply react to statements made by the West), have clearly been rattled by western demands that they address human concerns.

The defenders of their domestic rights standards in this region also argue for their own cultural way of life to be taken into consideration; they have a communitarian basis to its society, distinct from the western individualistic ethos. This communitarian tradition seeks consensus, in contrast to the western adversarial tradition. Southeast Asian societies, moreover, are keen to assert the rights of the group over the individual; the group, not the individual, is the starting point in any analysis. This view maintains that obligations to the community are more important than rights procured from it. While individual citizens historically wrested freedoms and rights from reluctant states in the West, the 'Asian' view is that these rights are a 'gift' from the government, not something people are entitled to by virtue of humanity.

Furthermore, the comparisons that regimes in Southeast Asia such as Singapore like to draw between the 'West' and 'Asia' in terms of individualism and collectivism are problematic and often spurious from a sociological point of view. Some governments have even used the broader conception of human rights as a basis for counterattack, saying the West may permit a wide range of individual liberties, but fails to protect its people's socioeconomic rights. One regional critic argues that ASEAN human rights standards 'verge upon an ethnocentric approach which has the impact of reducing universal standards to fragmentation and subordination at the national and local levels'. This 'cultural relativism' is unacceptable when it lowers international human rights standards.[96]

Moreover there are differences within ASEAN states on the question of human rights, which has come about (as Carolina Hernandez points out) because their political systems:

> follow different paths (1) in the way they interpret human rights and democracy, (2) in their assumption of international legal obligations as indicated by their acceptance of international human rights norms embodied in various international human rights documents, (3) in the manner in which they have organized their domestic, constitutional, legal and judicial systems as they relate to human rights concerns, and (4) in the degree of political openness in their societies.[97]

More recently, we have seen that there are clear divergences between some ASEAN members on the policies that should be pursued. Thailand, for instance, with the support of the Philippines, suggested a 'flexible engagement' approach to the question of Myanmar after it was clear that dialogue had achieved little. Of course, most of the other ASEAN states dismissed this, but the very fact that one or two countries from their ranks have different ideas about the delicate balance in handling intra-ASEAN affairs is a signal that conformity is not the norm. Some ASEAN states are all too willing to bend over backwards to support their friend in Asia, often without recognizing the detrimental effects this can have on their populations. Singapore sending arms to Myanmar, for instance, will not help to end civil strife.

3
Myanmar and Vietnam

Myanmar and Vietnam represent two states in Southeast Asia that have seen continuous internecine conflict of one kind or another over the last 50 years. There are several good reasons for placing these countries in the same chapter. War and foreign intervention, civil war, ethnic rebellion, military dictatorship and one-party rule have intermittently characterized their troubled history in the twentieth century. Both have been subjected to international embargoes against their weak economies; both have suffered from the disastrous mismanagement of their political economies. However, both appear to be attempting to make changes within their different systems. Vietnam is gradually experiencing market reforms through the process of *doi moi* (economic reform); Myanmar is making progress much more slowly and is still treated as a pariah state at the international level because of its brutal dictatorship, which has led the country into economic ruin. Here there is still the potential for massive internal disruption. It remains to be seen whether prior ASEAN policies of 'constructive engagement' or western policies of isolation will have the more impact on producing political and social change which may result in the increased respect for human rights. These societies, along with Laos, represent the weakest, most peripheral members of the ASEAN countries, which they have both recently joined. In general, these latecomers have some of the most problematic records on human rights, precisely because of their severely disruptive political and economic histories. Myanmar (formerly named Burma) has one of the worst human rights records in the world and exhibits a severe contrast in terms of poverty compared to its neighbour Thailand, which, at least up until 1997, was riding the boom of the East Asian 'miracle'. Vietnam, although making some promising internal reforms, still has a long way to go in terms of individual rights. Both countries have among the worst records of all the Southeast Asian countries for the protection of individual rights and civil liberties, although Myanmar appears the more reluctant to change in terms of policies and attitudes. More than a decade after pro-democracy demonstrations were brutally put down by the military, the regime continues to exist as a pariah state, calling itself a 'disciplined democracy', a title that bears a striking resemblance to some of the authoritarian justifications used by other leaders in East Asia to prevent human rights taking root in their societies.

MYANMAR

> Truth is true only within a certain period of time ... What was truth once may no longer be truth after many months or years.[1]

Myanmar is cited as one of the worst violators of human rights on a global scale.[2] Its society is ruled by a harsh authoritarian, military regime with a track record for repression and crushing dissent. It is a society that has never experienced democracy and it is ruled by a regime that has never observed civil liberties and political rights of any kind. For more than 35 years, Myanmar has been under the control of a military dictatorship once known as the Orwellian-sounding State Law and Order Restoration Council (SLORC). The present dictatorship assumed power in September 1988 after crushing large-scale pro-democracy demonstrations, which demanded free elections, multiple parties and the development of political and civil liberties.[3] At the start of the new millennium, this regime has shown itself to be equally determined to maintain its military-authoritarian stranglehold on state and society. The junta did, however, in November 1997, change its name, in a cynical public relations exercise, to the gentler sounding State Peace and Development Council (SPDC). This has not, however, prevented the covering up of its continued policies of repression and anti-human rights behaviour, which have become the hallmarks of their rule.

Myanmar enjoys fairly good relations with its Southeast Asian neighbours, which granted it entry to ASEAN in July 1997 and practise 'constructive engagement' or peaceful dialogue, although this has failed to make any inroads in procuring democratic change. Myanmar's *Pyithu Hluttaw* (People's Assembly) with 489 members was elected in May 1990, but was prevented from constituting itself. The party, which dominates politics, is the Taingyintha Silonenyinyutye (National Unity Party). No other parties are allowed in Myanmar.

Like many countries in the region, Myanmar is multi-ethnic. Many of the ethnic groups occupy zones around the periphery of the state, and some have fought hard to retain their independence. Cease-fire accords have been signed with various rebel groups bringing them in line, although the Karen rebels, representing the longest-standing ethnic insurgency, have been decimated.

The junta still appears to enjoy substantial profits from the lucrative heroin trade in the Golden Triangle, despite claims to have cleaned up the drug trade.

Historical Overview/Background

Myanmar is the largest state in mainland Southeast Asia with about 45 million people, and borders several important Asian states including China, India, Thailand, Bangladesh and Laos. It used to be one of the richest countries in Southeast Asia in terms of its natural resources.[4] Now it is one of the poorest in terms of economic and social development. Regime after regime has laid waste to these resources or else exploited them for their own gain, usually at the expense of different ethnic groups.[5]

One of the first groups to inhabit the country we now know as Myanmar were the Mons who retreated to the jungle and into Thailand when the invading Burmese armies arrived from the north. Throughout its history Myanmar has always been an ethnically diverse society despite the fact that the Burmese now account for two-thirds of the population. The throne of Pagan, occupied by King Anurudha in 1044, marked the beginning of the 'golden age' of Burmese history. Pagan developed into a famous city which enjoyed enormous prosperity. In this period, Buddhism was introduced as the state religion and there have been different Buddhist kingdoms reflecting the ethnic make-up throughout its history. Now Theravada Buddhism is the religion of more than three-quarters of the Burmese. Despite the modernizing efforts of the monarchy, by the thirteenth century the country was already in decline. Pagan was sacked in 1287 by Tartar invaders and for nearly 300 years remained in chaotic upheaval constantly clashing with its Thai neighbours. In 1767, Burmese invaded the kingdom of Siam and sacked the capital of Ayuthaya, forcing the Thais to move their capital to Bangkok. Constant border skirmishes and Burmese infighting spreading to neighbouring British India caused the British to intervene. In 1824, 1852 and 1883 the British assumed control of Burmese territory. The usual imperial infrastructure was put in place – railways were built and the rice industry was developed. The country became the world's largest exporter of rice and developed global teak markets. Chinese and Indian immigrants came with the British, adding to the racial mix. The country had a limited form of self-government in the 1930s because of various nationalist challenges to the colonial adminis- tration. In 1937, it was separated from its 'mother' section in India and self-rule appeared likely. Between 1937 and 1941 the country had a fleeting experience with parliamentary government until the Second World War engulfed Asia. Japanese forces occupied the country and dictatorship ensued. After suffering Japanese rule during the Second World War, the Burmese formed a government led by a group called the 'Thirty comrades' who appointed Aung San (the father of Aung San Suu Kyi) as their leader. The campaign for inde- pendence by the Anti-Fascist People's Freedom League (the name of their group) was to bear fruit, but in 1947, Aung San was assassinated along with six members of his cabinet in a plot orchestrated by political rivals. The following year Burma gained independence like many British colonies. The variety of ethnic groups (including the Arakanese, Chin, Kachin, Shan and Karen), the peculiar geography of lowland and upland Myanmar, and the rugged terrain made it difficult to integrate the country. Conflict between various tribal groups and communist rebels was widespread. From this period on, internal conflict has remained a central concern of the government. In 1948, U Nu became Prime Minister, holding office until 1958 and then again between 1960 and 1962. He spent most of this time dealing with internal ethnic minority conflict, which has an immense impact on modern politics. By the mid-1950s, much of the fighting had been contained and U Nu invited General Ne Win to form a caretaker government and hold fresh elections. They reinstated civilian government in 1960, again with U Nu as head of government. However, various crises of a political and social nature plagued U Nu in office. Coping with communist insurgency, various attempts by hill tribes to secede, the disastrous economy and corruption led to the downfall of the government. By 1962, the military had waited long enough and parliamentary democracy gave way to military dictatorship in a violent coup.

Under the dictatorship of General Ne Win the country became an international pariah, with widespread economic and social problems. Ne Win converted an elected civilian government into a one-party state under the control of the military dominated Burmese Socialist Programme Party (BSPP). In 1990, they changed this to the National Unity Party (NUP) in preparation for the elections. Ne Win resigned after the crackdown on democracy but was widely believed to continue to exercise enormous power.

Under Ne Win, the Burmese Way to Socialism, as it was called, created an economic and political isolation that prevented modernization and elevated social, economic and political control to new heights.[6] The government took control of the export of all commodities and goods produced by the Burmese; they nationalized the private sector and discriminated against ethnic entrepreneurs including Indians and Pakistanis, businesspeople and small merchants who were key figures in stimulating the economy; and they prevented foreigners from owning or running businesses, which were appropriated by the state. The paranoia and xenophobic tendencies of the previous regime towards foreigners and ethnic members of its community are still widespread and reflected in government policy to Aung San Suu Kyi, for instance, who was married to a British professor, Michael Aris. They constantly vilified Suu Kyi in SPDC propaganda press, while her husband was alive, for having married a foreigner. The results of Ne Win's programmes were disastrous and Myanmar underwent an economic depression that has lasted to the present day. They sealed the country from the rest of the world; allowed seven-day visas only and then confined visitors to Rangoon. The contrast between the country's backwardness and the progress of neighbouring Southeast Asian economies could not have been more striking. The worse the economy became the more despotic the regime acted. Political parties except the BSPP were outlawed. They strictly censored the media, corruption at all levels was rife, parliamentary democracy of the British kind was declared anathema and incompatible with Burmese culture, foreshadowing the Asian value debate of the 1990s.

Ne Win ran the country with an iron fist, but he was not an efficient or intelligent strongman like Lee Kuan Yew. The government was riven with factions, corrupt and completely inefficient. The policy of autarky (taking Myanmar out of the global economy) turned it from a rich country into one of the world's economic basket cases.

The last straw in this economic and political mismanagement started over a bizarre issue; a disagreement over the music played in a Rangoon tea shop, but once the police ignited the spark with brutal intervention, it escalated into hundreds of thousands protesting for democracy even if no one could define or organize a coherent programme of action around these events. Most people were involved because they had become frustrated with the government's mismanagement of the economy that had seen the currency, the kyat, become worthless. A coup on 18 September 1988 effectively sealed the fate of Ne Win's rule by the chief of the armed forces, General Saw Maung, who declared martial law. The new regime also ended the Burmese Way to Socialism programme, permitting a greater opening of the economy. There was complete suppression of demonstrations and the military killed more than 3,000 students and abolished all state institutions.

SLORC quickly declared themselves as functioning to preserve Burmese culture from alien western ideas, such as democracy and human rights. Despite this, the show of 'people power' did frighten the new junta into some initial concessions. In May 1990, the junta permitted the first free election and that served to conform their worst fears: more than 200 opposition groups registered, most comprising the bodies that had taken part in the events of 1988. They overwhelmingly rejected military rule in favour of the pro-democracy groups headed by the Nobel laureate and daughter of Aung San, Aung San Suu Kyi, who happened to be in Myanmar on family business. By July 1990, the military had still failed to relinquish political power and thousands of people were in detention. For her efforts to bring democracy to Myanmar, Suu Kyi was placed under house arrest, increasing world attention on the violation of human rights.

In its present form the junta is headed by General Than Shwe and Major General Khin Nyunt, the head of military intelligence, also known as Secretary 1. Government policy is based on the elimination of opposition, including widescale extra-judicial killings and disappearances. Under the guise of martial law, they can detain political dissidents indefinitely. The military in Myanmar, known as the *tatmadaw*, has placed large red signs throughout the country bearing Orwellian-type slogans: 'Only when the *tatmadaw* is strong can the nation be strong', while state-controlled newspapers state 'The *tatmadaw* has been sacrificing much of its blood and sweat to prevent disintegration of the union.'[7] Even today the *tatmadaw* claim to be the only historical entity capable of maintaining the country's independence and preventing disintegration.

The military has grown substantially. In 1988, the junta had a force of 180,000 under arms; by late 1993, this had risen to 340,000, or almost double in less than six years, which enabled it to move into nearly every small town and village in formerly rebel-held areas. In other areas, they have moved entire villages into army-controlled areas and new towns, which offer little or nothing in the way of basic services, according to a report by Human Rights Watch Asia.[8] Moreover, the junta has attempted to increase the membership of its political wing, the Union Solidarity Development Association (USDA) which, according to the official figures, numbers some 11 million or 40 per cent of the adult population.

There have been some modest steps to introduce a less harsh form of rule in Myanmar, including reopening the universities and releasing more than 2,000 political prisoners. In January 1993, SLORC initiated a national convention to draw up a new constitution, but this event was stage-managed, the act of a brutal regime seeking to alleviate the effects of isolation from the West. Such façades are typical of a regime desperate to present a moderate appearance to the West in the face of economic hardship. Superficial, cosmetic changes to the image of the regime may invite some sympathy, but the realities of its brutality are not so easily hidden. The widespread use of nationalism in an effort to legitimate the regime, claiming subversion by foreign forces, is simply one more weapon in the arsenal of oppressive techniques against its citizens.[9]

Political Economy

Myanmar is the second largest country in the Southeast Asian region and one of the most resource-rich countries in Southeast Asia, with large reserves of timber, minerals and fish. However, it remains one of the world's poorest countries, a tragic victim of corrupt military regimes, which have successively dragged the economy into the Dark Ages. In the post-Cold War period it has earned the unwelcome distinction of being a UN-designated 'least developed' country. It is one of the few countries (North Korea is another) that have attempted complete isolation (autarky) from the global economy. It has been unable to achieve any substantial export advantage or earnings from its resources, because the price of such commodities has been falling on world markets. The rice market has diminished significantly in global terms. This is problematic; agriculture generates 40 per cent of GDP and provides roughly 65 per cent of the employment within the country.

From independence in 1948, civilian and military leaders alike have been consistent in developing a socialist economy and have opposed capitalism. As one writer argued: 'Under British rule they were leftists and because capitalism had worked to their disadvantage, they mistrusted capital. Because they derive capital from profit, they mistrusted profit as an incentive to industry. They associated capitalism with foreign rule.'[10] In fact, foreign rule and imperialism at the hands of the British left psychological scars on the people, who experienced humiliation and despair at their status as a colony. Between 1948 and 1962 under the civilian government of U Nu, western democratic socialism was tried as an alternative to communism; subsequently, the now defunct Burmese Socialist Party Programme (BSPP) opted for Marxist socialism, denying any role for private enterprise and ruling with an iron fist.

After SLORC assumed power, they tried to change these policies and allow private sector expansion, attract investment and bring in foreign exchange in an attempt to boost their dismal economic position. There are still many restrictions on private sector commerce, however; an enormous bureaucracy and red tape hinder economic decision-making. In addition, the currency is overvalued, there is little infrastructure, and military spending is out of proportion to domestic spending. The World Bank's *Social Indicators of Development Report 1993* showed that the average annual GNP per capita growth for Myanmar between 1965 and 1990 was 1.8 per cent.

In the wake of international protest and condemnation, various US companies, such as Amoco, Levi Strauss and Co. and others have pulled out; those remaining, including UNOCAL, Texaco and Pepsi-Cola, have also come under pressure from human rights groups. However, foreign investment has increased in recent years and signs of a rapprochement by the US have increased hopes for more investment, at least up to the beginning of the Asian economic crisis. The oil company UNOCAL of Los Angeles, Total of France and a Thai energy company have initiated a $1 billion rail project. The railway will run near a pipeline designed to provide gas from an offshore field to energy-needy Thailand, although they do not expect that profits will materialise until well past the year 2000. Companies from China, Japan, Malaysia, Singapore, Britain and Germany have expressed keen interest in Myanmar in recent years, looking to benefit from its timber, minerals, gems, rice and people. The end of the 'Burmese Way to Socialism' in 1988 meant that Myanmar was able to sustain a mini-boom in the 1990s with the development of new roads and bridges, timber exports and rising property prices.

The economic reforms the government initiated in 1988 have had mixed results. In the initial stages the economy experienced a sharp downturn in GDP and massive increases in inflation. The recovery it was to experience only began in 1992 when rice production started to rise as a result of extending the irrigation system and other measures taken to make more use of its natural resources. By the mid-1990s this had fallen back again. The government decided to open the economy and bring in some market liberalization to boost production levels and eliminate corruption. But the people who benefited from the new distribution remained those connected with the military and a small commercial elite.

Following the Asian economic crisis of 1997, the country again sank into the backwater with foreign investment severely down and growth halted. Economic growth was less than 2 per cent in 1998. Inflation became worse because of the weak rice harvest and the introduction of import restrictions on certain goods to prevent the outflow of hard currency. Prices have risen by at least 45 per cent, with rice gaining 25 per cent in one year since the crisis began. Tourism, a key source of foreign currency exchange, also suffered badly as many Asian consumers affected by their own economic crisis at home were travelling less. Construction projects from countries like Singapore have experienced a lack of funding and external investment has again decreased significantly. Many large-scale projects, including projects with UNOCAL and Total, were abandoned. It is a country where economic stagnation has become the accepted way of life. The government simply has not addressed the basics of economic reform that many observers agree must be initiated if economic growth is to take place. This would include a devaluation of the currency, which is now worth at most one-thirtieth its official value, some control over the money supply to prevent inflation, and an overhaul of the major public sector industries taking corruption to the task. Unfortunately, none of these may be on the cards. It is hard though to imagine economic reform without political reform as the ruling powers benefit from the mismanagement of the economy.

Political Rights and Civil Liberties

It is important to note that freedom of speech and other universal human rights have never existed in Myanmar. There are severe limitations on freedom of speech and the press and these have increased not decreased steadily over time. The Burmese military dictatorship is a true believer in the development-democracy dictum of other authoritarians, that development must come first. In Myanmar, however, it appears that democracy is so low on the regime's list of priorities it may never see the light of day. It may well be that the regime wants the sort of electoral politics that helped to legitimate the governments in Kuala Lumpur and Jakarta. Indonesia (at least the Indonesia of Suharto) was often cited as a development model for Myanmar. However, it is clear to most observers that elections are a long way off. The junta tolerates little dissent or alternative views. It controls all the television and radio stations and uses these to pursue its political policies; the two national dailies (one in Burmese, the other English) and papers published by the Rangoon city government and the central (Mandalay area) military command are all under the control of SLORC. All forms of media, including books, plays and films, among others, are heavily censored and people in these areas often engage in self-censorship. Academics in higher education are restricted in the same way as other government employees and discouraged from criticizing the government, engaging in politics or even discussing politics and meeting with foreign officials.

In 1990, Amnesty International reported on a clampdown on cultural activists. A 29-year-old dentistry student, Zar Gana, who became popular during the 1988 democracy demonstrations for his use of satire and humour to depict the authorities, was arrested, released in 1989 and rearrested in May 1990 and is still being held. Other examples of detainees include musicians and artists who staged plays and wrote songs about the authoritarian regime in the hope that there would be a change of attitude. They arrested and incarcerated most of them in Insein Prison.[11]

There are various laws the state can use to enforce their opposition to human rights, including the State Protection Law of 1975 under which suspects can be held for up to three years without being charged or tried for actions that 'endanger the peace of most citizens or the security and sovereignty of the state'.[12] In addition, the Emergency Provision Act of 1950, which was initially put into force during the civil war, continues to be enforced. Under this Act, they can prosecute people for 'spreading a false news item or a rumour to excite dissatisfaction' or for 'causing disintegration of the moral character of the people using methods that cause harm to security, the law and order and rehabilitation of the state'.[13]

The case of Nay Min is one example. He was a lawyer detained under these provisions and facing a 14-year jail sentence with hard labour in October 1988, after they accused him of 'sending false news and rumours' to the British Broadcasting Corporation. Sentenced by military tribunal, Amnesty International has reported that he has developed an acute heart condition in prison.[14]

Amnesty International reports that 1,500 opponents of Myanmar's military rule are held in detention. Two of the 26 democratically elected National League for Democracy (NLD) parliamentarians are held for no other reason than their peaceful opposition to the junta: they are U Kyi Maung, arrested in December 1990, and Dr Aung Khin Sint. The former dissident is in his seventies and reputed to be in poor health. Amnesty has also noted that the military junta had made some improvements by releasing 2,000 political prisoners since April 1992.[15] After briefly raising some hopes in late 1997 in the human rights NGO community that change might be on the cards, the junta, newly named the SPDC, began another crackdown. Between December 1997 and February 1998, there were widespread new arrests of student activists and dissidents, some of them accused of bomb plots against the regime. As one report notes, 'thirty-three others were given harsh sentences, including Aung Tun, sentenced to 15 years under the 1962 Printers and Publishers Registration Act and the 1950 Emergency Provisions Act for publishing a book describing the history of the student movement in Myanmar. In connection with Aung Tun's research, the veteran politician and independence hero Thakin Ohn Myint, aged 80, was sentenced on 5 May to seven years' imprisonment with hard labour.'[16]

Freedom of assembly is not on the agenda either; following the demonstrations in 1988, just about everyone that participated was a target for arrest by SLORC. People like Nan Zing La, a prominent Kachin lawyer, arrested because he gave two speeches during the demonstrations in the late 1980s; and Ko Hong, a former policeman arrested in November 1988 because he had advocated democracy and peaceful political activities to a mass rally.[17] There are enormous tensions when it comes to holding any kind of rallies around anniversaries. The date of the 27 May 1990 election is crucial. When the SPDC allowed the NLD to hold a party meeting in 1999 on this anniversary at Aung San Suu Kyi's home, they cynically detained over 200 NLD members for either trying to or actually being at the meeting. In their refusal to obey travel restrictions imposed upon them (forcing them to report their daily whereabouts by signing in with local authorities), many parliamentarians were also detained. It is clear that the regime uses many of these meetings (at first allowing them and appearing 'liberal') simply as a pretext to clamp down on the opposition. Students also bore the brunt of the regime, which cracked down heavily on demonstrations in Rangoon.

Prison conditions for most of those detained are deplorable with several detainees dying in custody, their deaths exacerbated by ill health and maltreatment. Foreigners were (in line with the xenophobia of the junta) treated with little more grace, and arrests were made of people who had flouted immigration laws, including a dual Australian/British passport holder, James Mawdsley, who had entered illegally via Thailand in April 1999 and was sentenced to five years' imprisonment. (He was released later as a humanitarian gesture.) Most international reporting and attempts by the foreign press to gain access is generally denied.

Aung San Suu Kyi

The best-known dissident is the opposition leader and democratic activist Aung San Suu Kyi, who won the Nobel Peace Prize in 1991 for her non-violent struggle for democracy and human rights. In addition, Norway awarded the activist the Rafto human rights prize in 1990. She is the daughter of Aung San, the Burmese independence leader assassinated in July 1947. After the bloodshed of the street confrontations in 1988, she formed the National League for Democracy, mobilizing tens of thousands of Burmese to campaign for elections and the restoration of democracy. Clearly, the junta was terrified of this prospect; after more demonstrations and more bloodshed, which Aung San Suu Kyi did everything possible to avoid, they arrested her along with thousands of supporters and placed her under house arrest. After this she embarked on a hunger strike, which again led to heightened tensions, but called this off after elections were scheduled for May 1990. The National League for Democracy won these overwhelmingly, but SLORC would not accept the results and refused to release Aung San Suu Kyi, unless she abandoned her political views and left the country, which she refused to do. They have allowed her limited visits but she remains under house arrest at the whim of the military dictatorship. Various international organizations, such as the UN, the Red Cross and Amnesty International, have tried unsuccessfully to put pressure on the junta to release her.

In recent years, the junta has vacillated between taking hard and soft lines on its most famous dissident. On 20 September 1994, the Chairman of SLORC, General Than Shwe, and his military intelligence chief, General Khin Nyunt, met her in a public relations move to increase the confidence of investors in the Burmese economy. In July, Khin Nyunt had declared that 'Daw Aung San Suu Kyi is not an enemy.'[18] In February of the same year the junta allowed an American congressman, Bill Richardson, to visit Suu Kyi. Again the softening of the hard-line position taken by the junta reflects the intensity with which it hopes to win over reluctant friends in ASEAN, who believe 'they require … constructive engagement' as the way to produce change in the regime. Despite the apparent softening of the regime towards its most famous prisoner of conscience, it seems unlikely that it will release her before the new constitution has come into effect.

Suu Kyi has tried all means possible in her efforts to talk to the junta, but in vain. In 1998, on the tenth anniversary of the Rangoon demonstrations, she attempted to hold meetings with various members of her party outside the main capital. The first two of these trips were allowed to take place even if under modified circumstances, but they stopped the third when they blockaded her car. She remained for six days in a village outside the capital, subsequently being driven home by the junta who claimed they were doing this for her health and safety.

The final stand-off of that summer took place on 12–24 August. Secretary 1, Khin Nyunt, had invited the Chairman of the NLD, Aung Shwe, to a meeting on 18 August, a meeting that they did not inform Suu Kyi about until the following day. This was seen as a typical and cynical ploy by the junta to divide the opposition leadership. After 13 days on the road her doctor managed to persuade her to return to Rangoon, such was the poor state of her health by this time.[19]

The opposition leader has argued that between 1,000 and 2,000 dissidents languish in jail and more than 78 of the parliamentarians who were elected in 1990 under the auspices of her movement have spent time in jail. One of the more bizarre incidents was the case of one who was jailed for three years after a search of his house found his young child playing with two Singaporean coins. He was charged with illegal possession of foreign currency.[20] At least 20 more elected NLD members are in exile and more than 112 resigned or are disqualified from holding any position.

Development, Forced Labour and Human Rights

One major issue facing Myanmar is the alarming increase in the numbers of refugees and the implications for human rights and their violation. In fact there is widespread abuse of human rights in relation to its policies on refugees.

By the end of April 1990, more than 40,000 refugees had flooded into Thailand, including some 28,000 of the ethnic Karen group in more than twelve camps north and south of Mae Sot, Tak Province in Thailand, and various other ethnic groups. One of the reasons Thailand continues to support the regime is that it fears that the political violence and instability in Myanmar will trigger a mass exodus of refugees across the border. A development aid expert in Bangkok in May 1994 argued that 'the Thais are quite open about putting their money in Myanmar as an alternative to what they see as chaos'. They have managed to separate the ethnic issue and the civil war from the question of democracy.[21] The Thai regime is very concerned with the flood of people across their borders; surveys in 1994 have shown up to 72,000 ethnic Burmese in Thailand with 8,550 belonging to the Mon ethnic group.

The reasons for refugee flight are increasingly clear. Many members of the various ethnic groups are being used as forced labour. Documents produced in Bangkok highlight the abuses of ethnic groups at the hands of the military, including forced labour, rape and murder during the building of the 176-kilometre rail link from Ye to the southern town of Tavoy. On Myanmar's eastern border with Thailand, one source noted that they enslaved nearly 13,493 people in one area of construction alone as of early February. The source noted that a report by the New Mon State Party (NMSP) stated that up to 500,000 people in Mon state were facing the 'appalling consequences' of forced labour in the construction of the railway line:

The usual procedure is to force every family in each village to provide one family member for labour for rotating shifts of fifteen days, though this can vary ... People who do not work to the satisfaction of the soldiers are often beaten, and many people have died from beatings, sickness and lack of food.[22]

Forced labour is a common measure inflicted on ethnic minorities and prisoners by SLORC. The *Bangkok Post* carried a report in May 1994 on forced labour on the SLORC railway. This was based on reports by two ethnic groups involved in the forced building of a railway line from Ye to Tavoy districts in Mon State, southern Myanmar that began in 1993. The report noted that in April 1994 there were approximately 50,000 workers, but since the project started between 120,000 and 150,000 local civilians had been forced to work on the railway. Again, conditions were poor, the labour unpaid for and the workers had to provide their own food. The report cited the appalling working conditions: 'intense heat, endemic malaria, contaminated water, and malnutrition – many of the workers have become ill and hundreds may have died'.[23] In July 1994, Amnesty International charged that 'SLORC troops routinely beat and kick porters who have become weak and unable to carry heavy loads of ammunition. They rarely tell the porters how long they will be forced to serve, are typically given little or nothing to eat and are sometimes tortured or killed.'[24]

The refugee/migrant issue has a clear international dimension; the policy of appeasing and engaging the regime has allowed refugees to become pawns in the game of constructive engagement. Refugees such as the Mons have been placed in temporary shelters along the Thai–Burmese border as Thai authorities are reluctant to offend and damage relationships between the Myanmar authorities and themselves. Rebel leaders of ethnic groups argue that the Thai authorities use the threat of repatriation of refugees as a bargaining chip to convince ethnic rebel groups to enter cease-fire negotiations with the junta.[25]

In the late 1990s, Burmese troops and the Democratic Karen Buddhist Army, which was a pro-regime militia of defectors from the Karen National Unity, launched widespread attacks against Karen refugee camps in Thailand, killing many and destroying homes.

The relatively liberal view taken by Thailand towards refugees from Myanmar changed in the 1980s. Some argue that the authorities have in turn pursued policies to return students to their unwelcoming home in Myanmar. Thai authorities in exchange have sacrificed students from Myanmar for certain lucrative enticements.[26] The Thai military benefited from many forest franchises along the Thai–Myanmar border in the 1980s and 1990s. Moreover, the opening of new checkpoints for Thai logging companies to accept timber from Myanmar, it was argued:

> will only help strengthen the repressive military junta in Rangoon. For the money paid by Thai logging firms to the State Law and Restoration Council (SLORC) will be used to purchase arms and ammunition to bolster their capability to crush pro-democracy elements and keep down the Burmese people.[27]

Violations against Ethnic Minorities

There is some overlap between refugees and ethnic minorities here. Human rights violations have been so severe that in the 1990s more than 100,000 Karen, Karenni, Shan and Mon refugees flooded into Thailand. In the main, they have excluded Myanmar's ethnic minorities from government and the military leadership.[28] There is a wide gap between the living conditions of these people and the ethnic Burmese. Since 1989, the regime has managed to co-opt 15 ethnic rebel armies in cease-fire negotiations which allowed them to maintain their arms. There is a thin line between some of these ethnic warlords and drug trafficking which has become a major source of income for the regime. Moreover, discrimination against ethnic groups is widespread, not surprisingly from a state that is imbued with so much nationalist paranoia.

In Arakan state, for instance, the Rohingyas have largely been discriminated against; they are denied national identity cards and they restrict the Muslims' travel and freedom of movement. In 1982 a Citizenship Act had effectively removed citizenship from this group making them ineligible for basic social services, health and education. In early 1992 as many as 250,000 of these Burmese Muslims fled into neighbouring Bangladesh, claiming that the army had been engaging in plunder, rape and massacres against them, aimed at expelling them from the country. Although the majority have returned, they still claim that they face discrimination and unequal rights; between 1996 and 1997, many of them tried to establish their case for asylum in Bangladesh citing the potentially fatal threat that awaited then if they returned.

Forced porterage is one of the most commonly reported human rights abuse. The army forces thousands of civilians to carry their supplies, food and ammunition. They kidnap these porters in the middle of the night or even during the day. They can be forced to work for a few days or even a few months at a time, usually without pay and typically under difficult conditions of disease, malnutrition and highly dangerous terrain. Sometimes porters are forced to walk in front of soldiers in areas that are known to be mined. Similarly, some porters have been forced to wear army uniforms in areas where they could serve as targets for enemy guerrillas.

> Maung Htway (an ethnic Karen) told of being forced to carry two 120mm mortar shells – weighing a total of 56 pounds – on his back as he walked barefoot through the mountainous jungles of the Karen state with Burmese troops. He said he and other porters were given little food and water, routinely were beaten and often tied together with nylon ropes around their necks to prevent escape ... One day when he could barely walk, he said, a soldier struck him in the back and chest with a rifle butt, knocking him down. 'Even now I cannot breathe very freely,' he said, more than three weeks after his escape.[29]

In 1993, SLORC issued orders making it compulsory for every village and district in Myanmar to provide at least one soldier. According to the *Bangkok Post*, this was causing tremendous hardship among the rural people, who were already supplying porters for the army and contributing a great deal of labour and material to civil works and road improvement projects.[30] In the ancient city of Mandalay, there has been widespread use of forced labour to renovate the site of the nineteenth-century Gold Palace. One report noted that every day 'thousands of men, women and children are forced to work without pay under the blistering tropical sun, dredging silt and filth from the bottom of the palace's 8.3 km moat and hammering rocks into its banks'. Each family in Mandalay had to send one person a week to help this project, without any form of compensation.[31] In late 1993, one irate Burmese exile wrote a stinging letter to the conservative business magazine, *Asia Inc.* arguing vehemently that:

The rape of Burma's natural resources by SLORC, fuelled by the multinational traders in Thailand, Singapore and China, is turning Burma into an environmental disaster. SLORC generals are the only beneficiaries of this tragedy. Whatever spill over from their pockets goes into arms-buying binges to use against ethnic minorities. Lt. Gen. Tun Kyi is perhaps the most prominent looter, but the rank and file soldiers also exact their toll. In fact, the whole population is now enslaved to the military – if not as forced porters and chain gang road builders then in the more subtle but equally debilitating form of economic slavery of having to buy basic necessities at exorbitant prices from the soldiers. There is a system to this SLORC madness.[32]

The regime continues to commit widespread atrocities and human rights abuses against minorities along its borders. The most recent attacks on the Karens and other minority groups show that this policy will continue for some time to come. The dictatorship has maintained its crude yet effective carrot and stick approach, managing to divide the Karens. The pro-junta Karen Democratic Buddhist Army (DKBA) managed to burn down the Karen National Union's (KNU) refugee camp at Huay kaloke (Thailand) in March 1998. Thousands of people were forced back into the jungle. In April 1998, Amnesty International produced a report that stated that there had been a profound deterioration in the human rights situation between 1996 and 1998 'throughout the central Shan state in Myanmar' with the junta going after people suspected of aiding the Shan State Army. As many as 300,000 people were forcibly moved inside the central Shan state while 80,000 decided to take their chances in Thailand.[33]

Rape has also been used against ethnic refugees; at least two-thirds of several hundred refugees examined by Danish doctors in Thailand in 1999 were found to have been raped and suffered physical abuse. In short, the systematic policies of oppression and abuse against ethnic members of the community have not ceased despite Myanmar's entry into a multi-cultural ASEAN community.

The West and Myanmar

The West views Myanmar as one of the worst violators of human rights in Asia, and has tried diplomatically and economically to isolate the country, arguing that it is 'a serious violator of human rights norms'.[34] This contrasts sharply with the ASEAN approach of 'constructive engagement'. The US responded to the 1988 crackdown on the democracy protesters by suspending $12 million worth of assistance; this comprised $8 million in anti-drug funding and $4 million in AID development assistance. The US has banned arms sales and opposed further international aid to the country. However, the US administration stopped short of calling for a UN economic embargo. Germany and Japan suspended their respective contributions of $100 million and $300 million, which resulted in the effective suspension of 90 per cent of the country's foreign currency exchange.[35]

In 1990, an amendment to a mini-trade bill called for the US President to impose a boycott of Burmese goods if certain steps towards democratic rule were not certified. Annual trade between the two countries amounted to roughly US$22 million at the time.

ASEAN states have pursued a very different policy. Shortly after the crushing of the pro-democracy movement in 1988, Singapore sent an arms shipment to Myanmar. In fact, Singapore is the largest supplier of small arms to Myanmar in the ASEAN region. In November of the same year, Thailand sent a major trade delegation to improve economic ties. In 1994, Singapore Prime Minister, Goh Chock Tong, ended ASEAN's diplomatic isolation of Myanmar by visiting Rangoon with a delegation of businesspeople. The Rangoon regime has sold logging concessions to companies in Hong Kong, Japan, Singapore and Taiwan, managing to generate more than $112 million a year. At least ten oil companies, including Amoco, UNOCAL and Royal Dutch Shell, have invested several hundred million dollars in oil exploration, and major Southeast Asian corporations are opening department stores and hotel chains. Pepsi-Cola has opened a new bottling plant.[36]

The West has changed its policy over the years. It started with a hard-line policy of attempting to isolate and punish Rangoon in the hope that the regime would change. This has been a failure, partly because ASEAN would not participate in the economic sanctions and boycotts, preferring constructive engagement. In recent years the West has come round more in favour a policy of reconciliation and dialogue, similar to the ASEAN approach. The European Union has shifted its policy to one called 'critical dialogue'. This was openly expressed at the ASEAN–EU meeting in Bangkok in July 1994.[37] Australia also has adopted this approach, arguing that the policy of pressure had not worked. Gareth Evans, the Australian Foreign Minister, stated at the ASEAN meeting in Bangkok in July 1994 that 'it would be better to focus on encouraging the ASEAN countries, which are closer to Myanmar, to see what progress can be made.'[38] This is clearly an implicit endorsement of ASEAN's policy of appeasement. Australia and Japan have also argued that an open Myanmar will be more conducive to change than a closed one; in other words, neo-liberal policies should be encouraged. Asian countries, such as India, previously critical of the human rights situation, have also come round to accepting the situation and are increasing their investment in Myanmar. Critics of these policies and 'constructive engagement' argue that the 'single most important factor sustaining the junta's rule against the will of the Burmese people has been the willingness of nations around the world to invest, trade and establish economic ties with Myanmar'.[39] More recently, Australia and the United States have proposed setting up a human rights commission as an independent body within Myanmar, but many of these ideas have failed to materialize and there appears no reason why we should think they will.

Burmese Reaction to Western Demands

In November 1992, Lieutenant General Khin Nyunt argued that 'traditionally in Myanmar there has never been any torture of those who have violated the laws'.[40] In fact, the SLORC has admitted to detaining political prisoners only once, in April 1992. They have consistently refused Amnesty International access to Myanmar to investigate these allegations. They regard these and other efforts as western interference. In June 1993, Than Shwe said in a speech carried by the *Voice of Myanmar*:

> The external forces that bear malice towards us are inciting the people by using human rights and democracy as an excuse. The Western countries' human rights and standards of democracy cannot be the same as our Asian standards. We must choose the human rights standard and the democratic path compatible with the tradition of our country and people.[41]

In June 1993, Foreign Minister U Ohn Gyaw addressed the United Nations conference on human rights. Challenging western ideas about the international policing of human rights, he said that 'there is no unique model of human rights implementation that can be superimposed on a given country'.[42] Despite this rhetoric, however, the junta has been keen to improve its image. The regime hired a New York Congressman, Lester Wolff, as its registered lobbyist in Washington, paying him roughly $10,000 a month, and had dealings with Van Kloberg Associates, a Washington public relations firm that specializes in advising and promoting Third World dictators to clean up their image. In order to show the regime in a more favourable light the junta twists even visits by US congressmen and other politicians. As one exiled activist has put it: 'Visits to Burma, even so-called "private" tours, send mixed signals to a delighted Burmese junta in need of legitimacy and recognition at home and abroad.'[43] The junta is also using the most recent investment and foreign currency reserves not to improve the conditions of the people but to expand its army and militarize the economy even further.

Human rights groups have criticized US policy on Myanmar, arguing that curbs have been placed on refugees fleeing its military rule; President Clinton is carrying over the Bush administration's policy that favoured restrictive policies towards Burmese refugees. They asked that relief agencies stop distributing aid to refugees on the Burmese side of the border.[44]

At the Bangkok conference on human rights, the Burmese delegation with enormous cynicism reflected the prevalent mood of many ASEAN countries when it replied to western criticism: 'Asian countries with their own norms and standards of human rights, should not be dictated [to] by a group of other countries who are far distant geographically, politically, economically and socially.'[45]

The rhetoric continues to this day, using a mix of internal propaganda against foreign influences (one of these being Aung San Suu Kyi). In January 1998, for instance, the government propaganda broadsheet, *New Light of Myanmar,* argued:

> Western countries are using the Internet to spread disinformation with intent to destabilise some developing countries. The Internet creates cultural problems –and it is essential for Myanmar people to preserve and adhere to Buddhist ethics and try not to lose their culture.

> (Khin Nyunt, in *New Light of Myanmar,* 9 January 1998)[46]

The justification for military rule, the threat of the external, negative influences, has often been cited, that is the threat from the 'alien dark force' (*meit sa deitti*) of westernization and globalization, despite the fact that the ruling junta enjoy substantial benefits for themselves and their children from these very forces. Yet it is clear that they act in a paternalistic and authoritarian way to prevent citizens from receiving the same.[47] Therein lies the irony and paradox of many of their policies. Myanmar will only develop if it opens up, and yet if it does open up like so many dictatorships they fear the democratizing influences that will inevitably undermine their power base and ultimately their rule.

Conclusion

Summer 1988 saw a climax in the Burmese people's struggle to secure human rights. Thousands of Burmese took to the streets to call a halt to 30 years of economic devastation and political repression under a brutal military regime. At least 10,000 civilians died as a result as the junta presided over a bloody massacre. Since then, the regime has been at the forefront of a systematic campaign of terror and the denial of human rights and democracy. We will never know how many thousands of political opponents have been tortured, jailed or disappeared. Several million of its population has been displaced during their rule, as exiles or forcibly removed from towns into the countryside. Ethnic and religious minorities have been accorded particular attention under the restrictions of martial law, to their detriment. Documented evidence has shown that the regime forced villagers to walk into mine fields to clear them. Nearly half a million refugees, such as the Arakanese Muslims and the Karens, have been forced into the neighbouring countries of Thailand, Bangladesh and southern China. More than 1 million people are believed to be internally displaced. To fund these forms of internal repression and military excursions against minorities, the SPDC has sold enormous logging and fishing concessions which have resulted in the systematic destruction of the country's environment and major problems for the region's ecological system. Moreover, the regime has become actively involved in drug production; Myanmar now supplies half the world's heroin. There may be stagnation over the Burmese issue as well, as its government appears secure. Fifteen rebellions have been stopped by cease-fires that have freed the military for other functions of deployment and control. The fact that Myanmar has gained entry to ASEAN seems to reinforce its position.[48] In fact, the main motivating factor in Burmese society now may be fear as one defector from the regime has stated:

> People are terrified. The problem is that the Defence Services have become the instruments of just one man. It was the same with Marcos in the Philippines and Ceaucescu in Romania. Everything that happens is down to Ne Win and no more than 100 officers, Get rid of them and our problems will be solved. But if they try to hang on forever, then the army will begin to split and that will be the biggest disaster for our country.[49]

One student in her mid-twenties summed much of this up when she said:

> The people want to control their own lives, but there is almost no hope for us ... the Tatmadaw has all the power. Our true leaders are still in prison. My country is not important enough so that other big nations will come to help save us.[50]

The junta's policies have clearly not softened since they joined ASEAN in 1997; the policy of constructive engagement has been a complete failure. The regime continues to control the judicial system and has severely and ruthlessly clamped down on any individualistic or even collectivist notions of human rights. Forced labour, arbitrary beatings and executions and rape are among some of the more common techniques to drive the population into submission. The press is completely controlled by the regime, several thousand dissidents remain in jails, and Aung San Suu Kyi herself has argued that the country remains under a 'blanket of fear'. In April 1999, the UN Special Rapporteur for Myanmar argued that, based on extensive documentation, 'extra-judicial, summary or arbitrary executions, the practice of torture, portering, and forced labour continue to occur in Myanmar, particularly in the context of development programs and of counterinsurgency operations in military-regions'.[51] Now more integrated in the region, there has been no spillover effect as ASEAN continued with its much vaunted principle of non-interference into neighbours' internal affairs. Michael Aris, the Oxford professor and husband of Aung San Suu Kyi, who died in 1999, was refused a last request to visit his wife as he was dying, in what must rank as one of the most cynical and inhumane gestures of a government that we can only describe as evil and cruel. With the abandonment of its disastrous economic policies and an opening up of its economy and closer relations with its nearby neighbours in ASEAN, it remains to be seen how long the junta can continue to inflict such high levels of human rights abuses, authoritarian policies and cruelty upon its population.

VIETNAM

Vietnam has had one of the most turbulent and strife-ridden histories of modern times. Its society was subject to colonization and large-scale intervention from first French and then American military forces. It has been the subject of countless books, films (about the US war) and has inspired a great deal of reflective thought on the nature of conflict. If one issue has caused difficult memories for the American public, it has been the Vietnam war and how to remember it. Since the end of the war, however, Vietnam is transforming itself from an economic backwater in Southeast Asia to a country that appears to have a dynamic future. For a population of 76 million people, the dynamic changes it has undergone since the end of the war must seem sweet relief in comparison to the historical background. It has been a socialist republic under the control of the Communist Party since the mid-1970s, but recent reforms and economic changes suggest that there have been major political compromises in the way society is to be organized. In 1997, Vietnam took another step into the mainstream of Southeast Asian politics with admission to ASEAN. As one of the weaker economies of the region, Vietnam has not escaped the burden of the implications of the Asian economic crisis from this period onwards, However, given its international isolation for so long and its unconvertible currency, it has weathered the crisis far more successfully than many of its counterparts.

Historical Background/Overview

Like Myanmar, Vietnam has had a history of foreign intervention. However, their experience of such intervention has been far longer and deeper. The shape of that intervention and the responses of the Vietnamese to it have played a major role in forging their national identity and current perspectives. The French, the United States and the Chinese, three formidable opponents, have all made their mark in the political history of the Vietnamese over the last century, much of which caused significant damage engendering a strong sense of political nationalism. The Chinese played a significant role in determining the Vietnamese geopolitical outlook. Ignoring such a powerful neighbour is difficult and their histories have often been intertwined in various forms. Vietnam, however, has emerged with a far more positive outlook, despite its hardships, than Myanmar.

In AD 939, almost 1,000 years of Chinese rule ended in what we now know as Vietnam, the basis of which was situated around the Red River delta. Two historical processes have encapsulated Vietnamese history ever since: defining their identity through resistance to Chinese control and expanding their borders southwards at the expense of the Khmer empire and weaker kingdoms. By 1428 the Chinese had withdrawn after failing to establish any significant control over Vietnam and ceded Saigon at the end of the sixteenth century. Until the beginning of the twentieth century, Vietnam's economy was mainly feudalistic and agricultural. The French arrived in 1858 and four years later had established control over most of the Mekong delta; the following year they had taken over Cambodia as a protectorate. By 1885 they had extended their control over the entire country, forming French Indochina, which included, after 1893, Vietnam, Cambodia and Laos. This had the unintended consequence of helping Vietnamese expansionist plans. The French were never secure in their possessions and faced constant rebellion and resistance from the Vietnamese. In 1930, the Indochinese Communist Party was formed under the control of Nguyen Ai Quoc (Ho Chi Minh) and, by the outbreak of the Second World War, it had a powerful army. Ho Chi Minh declared independence at the beginning of September 1945. The Japanese surrendered and the Viet Minh seized power under 'Uncle' Ho in the principal northern city of Hanoi, while the French regained control of the south in 1946. The French, unlike the British, were not willing to give up their colonial possessions.

That same year, the first Indochina war began. Eight years later the Viet Minh emerged victorious with the final capture of the French fortification of Dien Bien Phu in 1954. An international conference subsequently obliged the French to leave Vietnam and divided the country into the Democratic Republic of Vietnam (the north), controlled by Ho Chi Minh and the Republic of Vietnam (the south), controlled and backed by the United States who were concerned at the possibility of communist expansion in Southeast Asia. Both Saigon and Hanoi aspired to control a united Vietnam and this led to increasing tensions. Gradually US support for the south and the anti-communist regime of Ngo Dinh Die deepened under Presidents Kennedy and Johnson. US involvement was not the result of a dramatic intervention, however; it built up gradually. Johnson used the 1964 Gulf of Tonkin incident, when US warships were allegedly attacked by the North Vietnamese navy, to obtain congressional approval for an open-ended military commitment to defending the south.

The Vietnam war was a nightmare and disaster for all parties concerned, but most of all the Vietnamese. In 1965 the second Indochina war (the Vietnam war) began in earnest with the introduction of American ground forces allied with the south; increasing military intervention by US forces, large-scale bombing of the north and the southern countryside and widespread economic and environmental destruction through the use of toxic agents such as Agent Orange. Michael Parenti has indicated the extent of the destruction:

> The total firepower used by the United States in Vietnam 'probably exceeded the amount used in all previous wars combined.' In Vietnam, the US dropped eight million tons of bombs (leaving 21 million bomb craters), and nearly 400,000 tons of napalm. With a minor assist from troops from other Western nations, the US military killed about 2.2 million Vietnamese, Cambodians and Laotians, maimed and wounded 3.2 million more, and left over 14 million IndoChinese homeless or displaced, with over 300,000 missing in Vietnam alone. The US war effort also left Vietnam with an estimated 83,000 amputees, 40,000 blind or deaf, and hundred of thousands of orphans, prostitutes, disabled, mentally ill and drug addicts.[52]

The United States' failure to defeat the Vietnamese militarily and the growth of opposition at home led to the abandonment of the war. The breaking point came with the communists' Tet offensive in 1968, in which the north suffered tactical defeat and fearsome casualties, but succeeded in turning US public opinion irreversibly against the war. Even today the scars of the war have left Americans embittered and angry. Many are unable to deal with the memory of a war that they never understood and which was ultimately lost. The conflict tore US society apart. A Third World nation had defeated the world's greatest superpower. It had worn down the US just as it had the French before them.

US forces began withdrawing in 1969, and in January 1973 the Paris Peace Agreements were signed, followed by the withdrawal of the last US forces. In March 1975, communist forces launched their final military offensive against the south and, at the end of April 1975, made their triumphal entry into Saigon.

Vietnam is now a socialist republic ruled by a one-party system under the control of the Communist Party. It is run by a 13-member politburo and a central committee who are nominally elected every five years. Internationally, Vietnam has experienced some success in the post-Cold War years. In 1989, it pleased the international community by withdrawing its forces from Cambodia. Vietnam signed ASEAN's Treaty of Amity and Cooperation in July 1992 and was accorded observer status at ASEAN's regular meetings of foreign ministers and a member of various security forums in the region thereafter. In this it has achieved a far greater degree of integration and status than Myanmar, which for many is still a pariah state.

In 1992 they adopted a new constitution that allowed for the 'rule of law' and a measure of respect for human rights, but in reality the government continues to use this selectively and aims at restricting individual rights, ostensibly on grounds of national security.

The Vietnamese parliament, the *Quoc Hoi* (National Assembly), has 450 members who are elected for a five-year term. In the last elections in July 1997, a party called the Vietnamese Fatherland Front, a front organization for the Dang Cong San Vietnam (DCSV: Communist Party of Vietnam) was the only party allowed to participate. This party obtained 447 seats with 384 of these belonging to the DCSV. In practice, the communists control the entire structure of Vietnamese society in a Leninist-style polity.

Political Economy

There is no doubt that the series of wars that Vietnam fought in the name of nationalism devastated the agricultural basis of the economy. Nevertheless, the Vietnamese rebounded in a way that might be expected of a society that has fought three major wars on their own territory in the twentieth century and emerged as the victor every time. Vietnam lies in the mainland of Southeast Asia and has a sizeable population of 76 million, mostly homogeneous in ethnic origin. Hill tribes make up smaller minorities than in Thailand or Myanmar.

When Vietnam was reunified in 1976, the Communist Party decided to create a socialist state but was severely hindered, politically and economically, by its involvement in the Cambodian conflict. Military and foreign intervention had destroyed much of the infrastructure in the previous 21 years. They sent northern technicians and planners to the south to supervise the construction of the economy along socialist lines. Following Soviet models, they emphasized the construction of heavy industry and a command-type economy in which the centre would be directed from Hanoi. They abandoned the free market; agricultural surpluses were appropriated by the state and equal pay to all workers no matter their skills became the norm. Like many socialist-type economies there were constant food shortages, rationing and hyperinflation. The ethnic Chinese in Vietnam, who were the traditional entrepreneurs, now became the subject of government crackdowns. They were forced to leave after their businesses, savings and goods were confiscated, forcing hundreds of thousands to escape by boat for more welcoming shores. In the event the Vietnamese boat people, as they became known, were subject to harassment and intimidation and many lives were lost to piracy.

Vietnam was also to suffer in turn from a vindictive US economic embargo, causing a lack of foreign capital and investment in their economy. Moreover, not content with seeing the economy in ruins the Vietnamese decided to initiate a disastrous invasion of Cambodia in late 1978, where they found that the Khmer Rouge had allied with the Chinese. Although the Vietnamese prevailed to a large extent, their economy was beginning to resemble a shambles. In the mid-1980s the Communist Party decided to reform their economic policy. At the Party's sixth national congress, the policy of *doi moi* (economic renovation) was adopted and market-driven economics stressed the reconstruction of the economy with the emphasis shifted from agriculture to industry and increasing reliance on market forces. As Melanie Beresford has argued, economic reform was encouraged for two reasons:

> First, the attempt to extract resources from a largely agricultural economy to promote industrialisation ran into physical limita-

tions as farm productivity stagnated. Conflicts between peasants and the bureaucracy sharpened as the former increasingly avoided the official collective and state-run economy. Meanwhile the difficulty in obtaining agricultural surpluses led to shortages of food in the cities so that urban workers also became disaffected and productivity in industry fell. Second, the industrialisation programme, the very *raison d'être* of the Communist regime, itself was in danger. Reform, or the shift towards a market economy, was thus a process that began from below and, when it was seen to produce results, was encouraged from above as well.[53]

The inefficiency of the centrally planned economy was castigated and a new programme of restructuring introduced. A government report acknowledged that controlled industries had displayed embarrassing inefficiency since losing subsidies and monopoly rights. In the words of one writer, 'the industries have failed to produce a more service and customer-oriented economy. Consequently, managers have been instructed to operate their factories profitably, to find out for the first time what their customers want and to get rid of surplus labour.'[54] *Doi moi* was the product of earlier attempts at renovating the economy; price controls were gradually removed and they established commercial banks. Moreover, the government initiated a legal framework for conducting business in Vietnam. In August 1994, one German expert in economic development stated that Vietnam was set to become the fifth 'tiger' economy in Southeast Asia. He argued that 'two years of *doi moi* had transformed Vietnam from a net importer to the world's third largest exporter of rice'.[55] The high economic growth rate of 8 per cent in 1994 is largely the result of the reforms initiated by Bguyen Xuan Oanh, who holds a doctorate in economics from Harvard University and was South Vietnam's Prime Minister for a brief period in the 1960s. Vietnam's economic surge is also due to a rise in the exports of oil, marine products, garments and rice, which rose 27 per cent in 1994 compared with 15.2 per cent in 1993. In 1995, rice exports were expected to exceed 2 million tons, placing the country among the top three rice exporters (the other two are the United States and Thailand).[56] Reducing the inflation rate to 4.9 per cent and registering an 8–10 per cent growth rate meant that Vietnam's 'efforts to transform the communist state economy into a market economy have been surprisingly successful – they have triggered a hectic bout of economic activity'.[57]

The flirtation with capitalism has had its negative side, however. While the private sector grew quickly, Vietnamese farmers and people in rural areas were still suffering. There were only modest political changes to accompany the economic *perestroika*. The party still follows the Leninist line of playing the 'leading role', but there have been some efforts to change some structures.

After the thaw in US–Vietnamese relations and the lifting of the economic embargo in 1994, many American companies and their finance capital started to invest in the country. France, Japan, South Korea, Taiwan, Singapore and Hong Kong were already investing heavily. By the beginning of 1993, Taiwan was Vietnam's largest investor with US$1.5 billion committed, followed by Hong Kong (US$1.2 billion) and Australia (US$536 million). Singapore is the country's biggest trading partner (US$1.3 billion in annual bilateral trade). Several countries were actively interested in the search for Vietnam's high-quality, low-sulphur oil.

The lifting of the economic embargo has helped Hanoi, as loans from international institutions previously disallowed are now permitted. At a conference in Paris in 1993, 23 donor nations committed a package of $1 billion in new loans and in June 1994, the International Monetary Fund (IMF) provided an additional systemic transformation facility (STF) credit of $17 million following a positive review of Vietnam's economy. This was in addition to major loans provided by the World Bank for a dam project, an education scheme and highway improvement.[58] In 1994 there was massive investment in the Vietnamese economy. The Vietnamese State Committee for Cooperation and Investment (SCCI) approved more than 300 projects with a combined value of $3.1 billion. In the same year foreign donors also committed more than $1.86 billion in grants and concessional loans, and pledged another $2 billion for 1995. International banks like Bank of America and CitiBank have been opening offices as inflation has been cut from the 60 per cent of 1990 and 1991 to under 4 per cent. Commitments from the World Bank and other international financial institutions have gone some way to engendering more openness in the Vietnamese economy. Vietnam in some senses has never really made any contribution to the Asian values debate. Its government has always pursued the line of economic development, reform and change before any political liberalization.

There are, of course, still many problems as Vietnam tries to balance a market economy with a socialist ideology and political system. Throughout 1994, inflation increased to more than 14 per cent from a previous low of 5.2 per cent in the previous year, at a time when the average yearly income remained roughly $220. There are an increasing number of strikes and many commentators have noticed a growing disillusionment over *doi moi*. A Hanoi University professor, Tran Quoc Vong, has stated: 'we must limit the widening gap between the rich and poor. The people demand social justice.'[59] Nevertheless, it is clear that overall economic growth after the Cold War has increased dramatically, with 8–9 per cent growth every year since 1990. However, again we must be cautious in asserting that more economic growth in authoritarian states means better conditions or improved human rights records. In fact, we have often seen the opposite: improved economic performance leads to increasing abuse of human rights, perhaps because authoritarian governments feel they have so much more to lose.

With the death of the older communist hard-liners, such as Party General Secretary Truong Chinh and his colleague Le Duc Tho in the late 1980s, the way appeared open in the post-Cold War period for economic liberals such as Nguyen Vanlinh and Vo Van Kiet. It was in effect a political swing to the pragmatists. Without its old-style patrons the command economy appears to have given way to market forces and this will probably force the Communist Party to liberalize. One analyst has argued succinctly that despite the efforts of the Communist Party to integrate a socialist view to a market strategy, this has in effect only succeeded in optimizing the worst aspects of each, a worst of both worlds. The government in that sense lost control after 1986 and was in danger of winning the war, but losing the peace in terms of the socialist programme they would like to impose.[60]

The Effect of the Asian Economic Crisis

Vietnam has not been immune to the Asian economic crisis; its economic growth has definitely been curtailed compared with the early 1990s. There have been problems within the banking sector, the role of state-owned enterprise and the labour sectors among others. There was a substantial decrease in foreign direct investment, for instance, which previously had accounted for nearly 30 per cent of total investment in Vietnam as well as jobs for several hundred thousand people. Asian investment in particular decreased significantly as the shrinking of their new export markets also took a toll. Unemployment has increased, first in urban then rural areas, especially where there were many foreign and joint venture enterprises. Poverty continues to be a major issue in rural and urban areas, and corruption, a hallmark of many of the regimes in Southeast Asia, has not diminished despite the official party rhetoric. Rural areas were one of the hardest hit by the crisis. The country's agricultural sector continued to show anger through 1998 and 1999 at the levels of corruption, high taxation, unfair prices and the land confiscation issue, among others. Since 1997, there had been various outbreaks of rural unrest, which the regime noted publicly in an effort to make the public understand that it was attempting to solve the issues.[61]

Developments in Human Rights after the Cold War

In 1990, there appeared to be a sharp curtailment of the limited reforms in human rights that had accompanied changes in Vietnam's economic policy. Disturbed by various changes in Eastern Europe and the Soviet Union, the Communist Party, like its counterpart in Beijing, attempted to tighten its control over society. For most communists there was a strong belief that the economic system should take precedence over the politics surrounding it. Therefore, it should come as no surprise that Vietnamese leaders are not very interested in the political, individual rights and liberties espoused by the West. After 21 years of engagement with the United States, which committed what amounts to human rights atrocities against large sections of the Vietnamese population, they certainly felt they were justified in pushing their own perspective. Democracy for them is a western façade controlled by capitalists who have vested economic interests at stake. It is not a reflection of reality.

To increase their control over society the party decided to initiate a series of anti-human rights laws. One of these was Directive 135, issued by the Council of Ministers in late 1989 and promulgated by the National Assembly in April 1990, which established a paramilitary police force and a series of campaigns directed against crime, corruption and opposition to official party policies. It was against any form of political pluralism for good measure. Thousands were arrested, many citizens (in particular former 're-education prisoners') were forced to attend study sessions on Directive 135, and the interrogation and harassment of small-time businesspeople was stepped up.

In April 1992, The National Assembly adopted a new constitution that apparently allows for such basic human rights as free expression, association and movement. Article 50 specifically says that in Vietnam 'all human rights in the political, civil, economic, cultural and social fields are respected and manifested as citizen rights stipulated in the Constitution and Law'. Amnesty International was pleased with the new constitution, the release of more than 100 ex-officials of the former regime in 1992 from re-education camps and the release of some prisoners of conscience in early 1993. These included the Catholic priest Dominic Tran Dinh Thu, the Protestant pastor Tran Mai and the economist Do Ngoc Long.[62] Amnesty remained quite concerned, however, with the practice of detention without trial and prolonged house arrest without trial, unfair trials, the arbitrary application of national security legislation and the use of the death penalty.

In 1998 almost 8,000 prisoners, many of whom were criminals, were released under the terms of two general amnesties. Also released were a number of religious and political dissidents, including the writer and teacher Doan Viet Hoat who was arrested in 1990 for publishing the pro-democracy bulletin 'Freedom Forum'; the physician Nguyen dan Que and Thich Quang Do, secretary-general of the Unified Buddhist Church of Vietnam (UBCV). However, the authorities confined some of the released to homes or pagodas and denied them permission to leave Vietnam or meet foreign officials.[63]

Despite official government pronouncements, there are still quite a number of people advocating human rights and democratization who are in prison – or under administrative detainment, as the euphemism goes – and various other forms of pressure from the authorities.

Freedom of the Press and Expression

In 1990, the government imposed new restrictions on the press. They issued procedures for the banning of publications and the punishment of 'politically reactionary' authors, and called for various 'councils of arts' nation-wide to censor literary and artistic publications and to review the existing works which they published in the north before 1945 and the south before April 1975. They also compelled newspaper editors and publishers to be registered party members. In addition, the government banned *Tap Chi Phap Luat,* a legal journal in the Quang Nam-Danang province, and had the deputy director of the provincial judicial service removed from his position for allowing its publication.[64]

One of the best-known prisoners in 1991 was Duong Thu Huong, a novelist from Hanoi and an active feminist who resigned from the Communist Party and was openly critical of the government. Vietnamese émigrés in the West argued that they arrested her because she sent a new novel outside Vietnam for publication. The official line at the time as stated by Lt. Gen. Tran Cong Man was that 'this case does not concern freedom ... it concerns criminal activity, acts that are forbidden by law'.[65] Following the 1992 constitution, article 69 proclaimed to offer Vietnamese citizens freedom of speech, expression and assembly in legal form, however as we have seen under directive 135, this is not something that they can work out in practice. A Law of Publishing passed in July 1993 allows the prohibition of various publications that advocated opposing the government, disseminating reactionary thinking and decadent lifestyles, the distortion of history and the repudiation of revolutionary endeavour.[66]

In 1993, the activist Dr Doan Vet Hoat, already jailed for two years, was sentenced to 20 years in prison for allegedly plotting to overthrow the Vietnamese government after he published a typewritten newsletter entitled *Freedom Forum.* The director of Asia Watch, Sidney Jones, stated: 'we believe Dr. Hoat was arrested, detained and convicted solely for exercising his rights to freedom of expression and association as proclaimed in articles nineteen and twenty of the Universal Declaration of Human Rights'.[67] (As noted earlier, Hoat was released in 1998.)

In 1993 the government tightened its control of the media under a new law that forced the press and publishing houses to 'fight against all thoughts and acts which compromise national interests, the dignity and the way of life of Vietnamese people'. Under these new criteria all publications were to reinforce the policy of *doi moi.* Among the works that were banned or forbidden are those 'hostile to the socialist homeland, divulging state or party secrets, falsifying history or denying the gains of the revolution'. In part this is in response to the flood of such materials originating from Hong Kong, Thailand and elsewhere in the region, which despite being seized by customs officials still cause enormous headaches for the authorities. The widespread pirating and copying of 'culturally unhealthy products', such as videos and foreign books have increased dramatically in recent years, as in many peripheral states, such as Cambodia and Laos.[68]

Although many western officials agree that Vietnam is not in the same league as Myanmar's military junta, they argue that repression is practised. Hanoi displays no real tolerance of democratic discussion and has imposed severe restrictions on freedom of speech, religion and political opposition. Political reform has clearly failed to maintain pace with economic reforms. In Vietnam, as one report notes, 'it is illegal ... even to endorse a multi-party political system and criticism of party decisions and government policies are met with arrests and lengthy prison sentences'.[69] Throughout 1998 and 1999, the government maintained tight control of the press. Little criticism of the government is published in the media and in a reminder to journalists to 'toe the line', Nguyen Hoang Linh, the editor of *Doanh Nghiep* (*Enterprise*) newspaper was brought to trial in October 1998 and found guilty of 'taking advantage of democracy to harm the state' for which he was sentenced to one year and 13 days' imprisonment. In 1997, the same editor had reported on high-level corruption.[70]

Freedom of Religion: Persecution of Religious Minorities

Under the Vietnamese constitution, the rights to freedom of worship and religious practice are guaranteed, but the same document also argues that no one should misuse religion to violate state law and policies. Various incidents have emerged in the post-Cold War period that suggests that the government is violating the right to freedom of religion. Nearly 75 per cent of the population are Buddhists despite widespread official claims that only 6 million practise it.

The Unified Buddhist Church of Vietnam (UBCV) was established in 1951 and played a prominent role in the anti-war movement in the 1960s, the most famous incident being the self-immolation by the monk Thich Quang Duc on 11 June 1963, which caused worldwide protest against the Diem government. The church was outlawed in 1981 when the government created the official Vietnam Buddhist Church as an umbrella organization for all followers of the faith. In 1986, the initiation of *doi moi* appeared to go hand in hand with a relaxation of control on religious institutions. In 1991, however, the government appeared to reverse this position in a series of new regulations. These included Resolution 297, which stated that 'any act which, posing as religion, attempts to sabotage national independence and goes against the state will be punished according to the law'. By the end of 1993, the government had issued new criteria for the approval of priests and other religious officials on the basis of 'their good performance of their civic duties'.[71]

In 1992 the Unified Buddhists (An Quang sect) began protesting against increasing governmental control, particularly after the death of Thich Don Hau, the Buddhist patriarch. In early 1993, some of the middle- and low-level leaders of this group were arrested in central Vietnam and Vung Tau in south Vietnam.[72] In August 1993, the military newspaper *Quan Noi Nhan Dan* argued that Buddhist conspirators were attempting to overthrow the Communist Party. They claimed that this was inspired by exiles abroad who wanted to undermine the economic success of the Vietnamese, and the government claimed that Unified Buddhist Church of Vietnam members were engaged in anti-government activities at home and abroad. Several monks arrested between 1978 and 1993 are still in prison or under house arrest, according to Amnesty International, for alleged 'disruptions of the public order'. These include Thich Quang Do and Thich Huyen Quang, who have been under house arrest since 1982 for criticizing the authorities over alleged persecution, violations of human rights and attempts at state control over Buddhist institutions.[73] Thich Quang Do was released in 1998 but with restrictions on his movements. In August 1993, the officially recognized Church of Buddhism denounced leading dissidents, saying they were using religion to sabotage national solidarity. This was aimed at Thich Huyen Quang, the leader of the Unified Buddhist Church of Vietnam, who has argued strongly for the separation of church and state. The state placed surveillance on him after this incident. These kinds of conflicts are reminiscent in some ways of the confrontations between the Buddhists and the authorities running South Vietnam more than 30 years ago. In November 1993, they jailed four dissident monks for instigating anti-government unrest in the Vietnamese city of Hue in May of that year.[74]

Towards the end of the 1990s, there seems to have been an improvement in the authorities' relationship with the religious groups. In 1998, the authorities allowed the appointment of an

Archbishop in Ho Chi Minh City and provided support for 'non-sanctioned religious observances' at La Vang during the summer of 1998, but there were also some problems with allowing access to dissident religious figures from the United Nations Rapporteur on religious intolerance.[75] The Papal visit to La vang to celebrate its 200th anniversary was abandoned after the Vietnamese refused permission.

Despite the superficial claims of religious freedom in the republic's constitution, both national government and local agencies exercise tight control over this area. Even in the late 1990s the government continued to make certain that all religious activity had to be approved by the state and applied various travel restrictions on religious figures. The approval of candidates for enrolment and ordination in seminaries is under government supervision. Similarly, ministers and clergymen are unable to practise legally without sanction from the government. A directive issued in July 1998 prevented the distribution of bibles and banned 'excessive mobilization' of the population, with general threats couched in legal terms against those that sought to abuse religion to create social unrest.

Economic and Social Rights

One argument that socialist societies (among others) have used against the West in response to criticism of their human rights policies is that they are more interested in securing economic and social rights for their people than individual, political forms of rights. This emphasis has long been suspected by Western NGOs and human rights organizations as a cover for various forms of abuses by their authorities. It is important, then, to look at the records of some of these states and see just how far they have been protecting the rights they are most keen to emphasize. To some extent we have seen that in all newly developing countries, and in particular where there appears to be sharp rates of growth, disparities between rich and poor actually increase in the short term. This has been the case in Indonesia, Vietnam, Myanmar and Thailand among the states we have looked at here. It may in fact be a by-product of the introduction of free market and capitalist ideas into their economy in such a short space of time. Despite high growth rates, this does not necessarily mean that wealth is evenly distributed. Moreover, despite attempts by many governments who preach socialism to portray themselves as meeting the needs of the people, more often than not they succumb to the difficult choices that dictate such fast growth strategies in Southeast Asia. In 1997, for instance, many groups – mainly women and children – were on the losing end of the new market reforms that Vietnam initiated. One report published by UNICEF noted that 40 per cent of children under the age of five and 60 per cent of ethnic minority children were suffering from malnutrition and nearly 200,000 babies were born underweight every year. The burden on women in the countryside, many of them faced with multiple tasks, had reached alarming proportions. The report also detailed how market forces had led to the increasing exploitation of children in the organized sex industry with more than 20,000 children under the age of 18 involved; an increase of more than 33 per cent in the number of those involved only six years previously. There were also reports of a great deal of child labour in the mines. In response the government decided to initiate a national Committee on Food Security in July 1997. Like many other states in Asia, Vietnam is no exception to being exploited by American multinational corporations. Nike, Walt Disney and McDonald's have all come under attack from various NGOs for allowing harsh and difficult working conditions.[76]

With the opening of their economy and moves towards a free market, Vietnamese authorities are now facing growing labour problems and militancy on a number of issues ranging from minimum wages to improved working conditions. Official estimates have put the number of strikes and walkouts in Ho Chi Minh City (formerly known as Saigon) at more than 50 in recent years. In 1993, 600 workers at a South Korean-run firm in Ho Chi Minh City went on strike to protest against long working hours and the regular beating of employees for being slow at their jobs. There are serious problems with strikes and walkouts by workers earning low wages. In fact, workers received the 'right' to strike only recently after the Vietnamese Assembly passed a new bill. The term 'strike' was seen as an alien concept in a socialist state. Currently, trade unions are demanding a minimum wage of US$50 a month while government legislation requires employers to pay a minimum of US$30.

Unemployment is also a problem. In 1994 several estimates showed that 6 per cent of the Vietnam's 34 million workers were unemployed. The Asian Development Bank in Manila, however, has argued that the figure was closer to 20 per cent.

Although the specific economic rights in the standard universal documents are few and far between which mention freedom from hunger, the right to medical care and the right to an adequate standard of living, there is clearly no right implied that says come and do business in our country at everyone else's expense.[77] The Vietnamese position on economic rights reflects some of the international intent but attempts to balance it within its political system. For instance article 15 of the 1992 constitution argues that it has a 'multi-component economy functioning in accordance with market mechanisms under the management of the State and following a socialist orientation', while the constitution generally is reflective of the debate about incorporating private property and production within a framework of Marxist-Leninism.[78] Another part of the constitution allows for the private and individual sectors to adopt their own ways of organizing production, hardly things one would consider compatible with a Marxist state, but all fitting the process of *doi moi*. While conservatives in Vietnam are unlikely to give the private sector much credence in the development of the economy, it appears that they have opened a Pandora's box which will be difficult to close. The more conservative state officials would deny the notion of individual rights in society, and stress collective rights vis-à-vis mobilization campaigns which litter the history of socialist and indeed nationalist regimes (family planning campaigns are a case in point). However, it appears to be fighting a losing battle if it believes such propaganda and policies have much effect on people and the economy. The people involved in the private sector would clearly like a more level playing field and therefore emphasize individual rights in their discourse. This would mean the institutionalization of rights to protect them from arbitrary action by the state. It is clear that the notion of socialist authoritarianism is still concerned with the illiberal doctrine of rule by law rather than the liberal democratic perspective of the rule of law.[79] This is typical of what states that promulgated the Asian values thesis attempted. Individuals must first and foremost show their loyalty to the state; individual companies are expected to show adherence to the rights and obligations that the state lays down; it is still the state which has to be seen as the driving force behind the economy and its likely that most Vietnamese believe that it is their duty to pursue national development.

Other Violations of Human Rights

Vietnam retains the death penalty, but since the reunification of the country statistics on this are fairly vague. In 1985, Justice Minister

Phan Hien was reported as saying, 'several dozen executions are carried out every year'; these are mainly for violent crimes but sometimes also for economic offences, which are considered to constitute crimes against state security. Amnesty International noted eight new death sentences and three executions as reported by the official media between 1985 and 1988, but they believed that the actual figure was far higher. A revised Code of Criminal Law which came into force in January 1986 stipulates that crimes that are punishable by death include 'counter-revolutionary' acts such as high treason; espionage against the independence and territorial integrity of the Republic; acts of terrorism, sabotage, banditry and hijacking among others. Apart from offences against 'national security', there are many other provisions for the imposition of the death penalty.[80]

Examples of these include the following.

On the 28 May 1993, Wong Shi Shing, a Hong Kong resident, was sentenced to death for trying to smuggle 5 kilograms of heroin into Vietnam. Tran Ngoc Minh, a former Vietnamese refugee in Hong Kong who was deported to Vietnam, was sentenced to death in June 1993 for committing two murders earlier in the year. The only recourse available in case of such judgments is to seek commutation from the president.[81]

More recently, the government has gone some way to releasing political prisoners. Doan Viet Hoat, a prominent detainee, was released in 1998, but there has been sharp criticism within their own camp. Sidel points out that members of the National Assembly have criticized abuses by police and prosecution: 'the call had been made in response to a report that nearly 29 per cent of arrests made by the end of October were of innocent individuals'.[82] And a senior official, Hu Tho, the chair of the party's commission for ideology and culture, accused the police, the court system and other institutions of 'violations of democracy', arbitrary arrests and corruption.[83]

Vietnam and the West

Much of Vietnam's relationship with the West, and particularly the United States, has of course been influenced by the war. It was only in February 1993 that the United States decided to lift a full-scale economic embargo, which had been in force since the war ended. In July 1993 the Clinton administration announced there was no more objection to IMF lending to Vietnam and opened the door for hundreds of millions of dollars worth of aid projects to flood into the country.

In this sense human rights abuses within Vietnam played less of a role in the normalization of relations with the US than other external factors. Perhaps the two key issues for the normalization of these rights were some progress on the Cambodian issue and (and perhaps more importantly in light of the Cambodian settlement) progress in finding the missing American prisoners of war in Vietnam – the so-called MIAs.[84]

However, human rights as an issue continued to hinder ties between the United States and Vietnam. In a position typical of the Southeast Asian states, Vietnam regards any proposals by the United States for improvement as violating its sovereignty or denying the principle of non-interference in the domestic affairs of a nation. With the lifting of the economic embargo, it seemed natural to proceed to normalization of relations. This was not as smooth as hoped. Even after the embargo, Winston Lord, the US Assistant Secretary of State for East Asian Affairs, informed the US Congress that 'in Vietnam, freedom of expression, the press and assembly are limited and so are labour rights and the people's right to participate in politics'.[85]

Conclusion

Since the end of communism in the former Soviet Union and Eastern Europe, Vietnamese officials have been concerned about economic and social change and the threat that political liberalization might accompany this. One problem is how to maintain their political control in the face of change, which may undermine the regime through a process of 'peaceful evolution'. Like the Chinese Communist Party, Hanoi fears democracy, multi-partyism, human rights and freedom of expression, or any other concepts that challenge the ruling regime. Moreover, the attempts to balance a market economy with a socialist ideology have put a significant strain on the system. Their economic policies of *doi moi* or economic renovation after 1986 have, to some extent, seen an opening of the system in line with liberal ideology. This, however, leaves the party vulnerable, a situation it has always tried to avoid. Gabriel Kolko, an expert on the Vietnamese system has argued that:

Democracy and human rights are inextricably linked to the party's inability to define viable socialist economic policies, for they are the pre-condition for its long-term survival. The party's factions have responded to these topics in a manner that has muddled the relationship between such crucial issues almost beyond comprehension ... as late as March 1989, its formal position was to 'encourage freedom of speech [and] promote straightforward discussion and debate,' although it warned against these rights leading to what it called 'sabotage.' From the inception, the compromises that the senior leaders struck on these issues were full of obvious and irreconcilable tensions between freedom and control. What emerged was a plethora of contradictions and banal rhetoric. Democracy, they stated, was to be implemented through much greater economic freedom, and by the party, state, and political system operating in a self- renewing manner, a goal which they have consistently admitted has not been attained.[86]

Freedom of religion within Vietnam, for instance, may be a serious problem for a Communist Party that is increasingly becoming anachronistic in modern Vietnam. It appears contradictory to have an open market system side by side with a dictatorial communist elite that has sought to defuse challenges by means of repressive control over Christian and Buddhist organizations. This section has noted the fairly violent methods of preventing religious organizations from expressing their views in a peaceful manner. Despite the adoption of a new constitution in April 1992, which appeared to guarantee fundamental rights, violations are still taking place. Several Buddhist monks were arrested, for instance, on grounds of national security in October 1992. Dubious allegations of 'undermining the policy of unity' and 'circulating anti-socialist propaganda' appear difficult to prove against people simply trying to practise their religion. On the positive side, the refugee crisis combined with overseas migration involving the nearly 1.5 million refugees who fled after the fall of Saigon in 1975 has finally wound down. The exodus has stopped and many are returning to take part in Vietnam's economic boom. The release of more than 100 ex-officials of the former Republic of Vietnam who had been detained in 're-education' camps since 1975 and various prisoners of conscience represents an increasingly deliberative effort to come to terms with their past.

While the regime emphasizes economic and social rights in their defence of violating individual liberties (and their records on the protection of women and children's rights are highly regarded), we can see that abuses such as the practice of detention without trial, unfair trials and the abuse of national security legislation remain causes for concern. Despite rhetorical commitment to human rights, violations in areas such as freedom of the press, assembly and association and labour rights and the right of people to change their own government are widespread. The processes of globalization and the financial crises may hit countries like Vietnam with more devastating effects than, say, Myanmar (because of the latter's long isolation), but they also seem better equipped and able to weather these storms than the Myanmar junta. Their pragmatic attitude towards life and their politics will clearly prove useful. After all, they have fended off the French, the Americans and the Chinese in the last 100 years and this will stand them in good stead as they try to deflect external pressures that are the result of global processes. What is clear is that their attitude and stance towards human rights are much more refined and workable than the Myanmar version; Vietnam is striving hard to work within the system while Myanmar is steadfastly remaining outside global trends. It remains to be seen whether the economic liberalization that Vietnam is undergoing will have similar repercussions for their political system and human rights agenda. On the face of it, it seems that the legitimacy of the regime, like many in Southeast Asia, will be determined by its progress towards democratization and increasing respect for human rights.

4
Indonesia

Indonesia is one of the most important states in Southeast Asia and one of the most volatile in terms of its consequences for the region and the global community. It has never had a good human rights record and some of the worst atrocities in Southeast Asia have been committed on the archipelago's territory. Moreover, there are few precedents in Indonesian history that offer the basis for the establishment of democracy and a human rights culture. Nevertheless, in recent years, progress towards democracy has been made. Civil society, social movements and NGOs have emerged to make demands and resistance to authoritarianism has been expressed in various forms. The former strongman, President Suharto, one of the longest serving dictators in Southeast Asia, stepped down in 1998, opening the door to the creation of more political space and opportunity for the development of an alternative political framework in Indonesia, one more receptive to the rule of law and democratic values.

Indonesia is also important because of its sheer size and diversity. Territorially, it is the largest state in Southeast Asia, stretching for almost 5,000 kilometres from the mainland of Asia to the Pacific Ocean. It is also the most heavily populated, with 198 million people. In addition, Indonesia is one of the most diverse societies in Asia inhabited by 300 ethnic groups speaking as many languages and dialects. One report captured this diversity:

> To go from Aceh, the Muslim-minded province on the northwest end of Sumatra, to the country's eastern border with Papua New Guinea is like going from Los Angeles to New York. The difference is that in between there are 13,667 islands, with people living on about 6,000 of them. And for all the 'melting-pot' nature of America, it has nothing on Indonesia. There are Javanese, Sundanese, Balinese, Bataks, Sasaks and so on. They are just the Malay stock; in addition, there are Melanesians, Micronesians, Chinese, Arabs and Indians. Together, the Indonesians speak perhaps 300 distinct languages and dialects; cultures range from

the deferential court-system of Java to the stone age animism of Irian Jaya.[1]

As the report also argued: 'for a visiting journalist trying to understand the place, it has the intangibility of a mirage. If Indonesia did not exist, surely nobody would invent it.'[2]

One of the mottoes of the country is unity in diversity, a rhetorical effort which pays lip service to different cultures and seeks to hide the fact that the central government in Java has been trying (without much success) to enforce Indonesianization, especially in the outer islands. Given the diversity of society here, unity is an ill-conceived notion and it appears only recently that the changes wrought in the Indonesian political system are beginning to take these real differences into consideration.

The development of an Indonesian empire extending outwards from central Java has by and large been ignored by international actors who have often had vested interests in the area. Indonesia's stability appears to have survived the trauma of the Asian economic crash of 1997, but there have been simmering tensions for years over economic distribution, difficulties between Muslims and Christians, the growth of various independence movements in Aceh and Irian Jaya and, of course, the thorn in Indonesia's side, East Timor, which still witnesses daily bloodshed by various paramilitary groups, even after an historic referendum which saw a decisive vote in favour of independence in 1999. On 7 June 1999 Indonesia held democratic elections for the first time in over 30 years, in what will be represented as a watershed for future prospects of democratization and, hopefully, improved human rights throughout the region.

Historical Overview

Indonesia has a long and complex cultural and social history, which has been intermittently interrupted by bouts of severe repression and violations of basic rights. In some ways it is a country that still has to deal with its traumatic past, from massacres in 1965 to the problematic issue of East Timor, which some scholars have argued is equivalent to genocide.

Evidence of early Hindu and Buddhist temple kingdoms dates back to as early as the fifth and sixth centuries. Beginning in the seventh century, the Malay kingdom of Srivjaya-Palembang developed as an entrepot for trade with China and in the following century Chinese traders were active in Java and Sumatra. Between the twelfth and fifteenth centuries, predominant political control was in the hands of the Javanese Majapahit kingdom. In the thirteenth century Islam started to make inroads along with influxes of Indian traders; as a result coastal areas became more important and attempted to influence the central stronghold of the inland aristocracy. As seen in the case of Malaysia, a strong Muslim empire had emerged by the fifteenth century, centred in Malacca on the Malay Peninsula. After it fell to the Portuguese, Malacca remained the centre, but internal resistance was always imminent. By the end of the sixteenth century the struggle had been dissipated by the Dutch, who became the colonial masters, based in Batavia (Jakarta); they formed the Dutch East India Company and controlled the spice trade and Java. Their imperial acquisition lasted from then until the middle of the twentieth century and was to have lasting implications for Indonesia, but it was an empire in relative decline by the beginning of the nineteenth century. During the Japanese occupation in the 1940s, many atrocities were committed against the local population.   Following the Second World War, Sukarno and his Indonesian Nationalist Party declared independence. Following a four-year, vicious struggle against the Dutch, they gained independence in 1949 but continued a superficial link with the former colonial power. In 1954, this nominal union was completely severed because of continued Dutch possession of Irian Barat (now known as Irian Jaya). Thereafter, the country enjoyed a short-lived period of liberal democracy between 1950 and 1957, which ended when President Sukarno declared martial law, overthrew parliament and installed 'guided democracy', his personal brand of authoritarianism. It was not a happy period. Indonesia suffered from ethnic, religious and class conflicts; inflation spiralled out of control and corruption was rampant. Human rights were largely ignored. The last free election with multi-party competition was held in 1955; 44 years later, they would try to repeat this.

Sukarno was a nationalist who disliked constitutional and liberal democracy; his aim was to try to unify the thousands of islands within one Indonesian territory. It was a major task and the ramifications of this kind of policy remain today. Western liberalism and the ideas of equality and democracy were dismissed by the new strongman of Southeast Asia, who had the full support of his army. Democracy in this view was a western import, a source of division and contention. Javanese society, on the other hand, was one in which hierarchy ruled through a rigid system of patron–client relations. In Sukarno's version of democracy the state was responsible for guiding the people, not the other way round. Despite the fact that Indonesia is made up of many different ethnic, religious and tribal groups, a common state ideology was imposed to try to achieve this unity.

The ideology of 'Pancasila' entails belief in five basic principles: monotheism (belief in one supreme god), national unity (nationalism), humanitarianism, social justice and democracy. However, in Indonesia's case we can argue that these are really rhetorical principles rather than having any practical value.[3] As an ideology, Pancasila appears supportive of the idea of human rights. Its 'open' and vague character however, has left it open to interpretation and subsequent widespread misuse. It has been employed to justify limiting press freedom, reducing the number of political parties and decoupling parties from their constituents. Labour and trade union rights appear almost non-existent under these directions of the Pancasila. As one writer argues, 'the right to *organize* appears, in reality, to be the right *to be organized'*.[4]

Moreover the government has traditionally interpreted Pancasila in relation to the *integralistic staatsidee* which sees the state as the embodiment of the entire people. The idea that individuals owe certain duties to the family and the state is clearly emphasized. In so far as the state exists to protect the rights of the people, human rights do not require a guarantee for individuals because they themselves form the state. Duties towards the state are stressed as more important than rights against the state. Again, this is a view reflective of rights as privileges not entitlements. The notion of democracy in Indonesia relies on its interpretation, defined as *musyawarah* and *mufakat,* which means consultation and consensus, words widely used in ASEAN circles. Deferential values are more important than directness, and open criticism is strictly off limits. Voting is regarded as divisive and few Indonesians take issue with the preference for reaching consensus; in this system parliament fulfils a merely ceremonial role.

The position one occupied in Javanese society was also important, of course. The Javanese had a tradition of mutual aid (*gotong rojong*) which Sukarno believed to be one of the bases of his guided democracy. It was an expression of fusing unity and community together, a way in which to ensure that traditional patron–client relationships were honoured by deferential respect for one's superiors. In this case it prevented dissent from authority, allowed the regime to claim indigenous principles of government (which appealed to nationalism) and made certain that people knew their place within the system. As one author has argued: 'in practice *gotong rojong* was merely an excuse for Suharto to insist that everyone agree with his personal decisions.[5] The army was keen to maintain an important role in power because of the various influences that could upset the structure of Indonesia politics, including the Communist Party and the conservative Muslims among others.

In 1963 Indonesia declared its opposition to the new Malaysian Federation so beginning a period of relations between Indonesia and Malaysia known as the *Konfrontasi* (confrontation). This proved to be a disaster for Indonesia. It had been an attempt to divert attention, like many attempts by authoritarian regimes, from a failing economy, rampant inflation and increasingly uncontrolled corruption. Indonesia was rapidly descending into chaos and political anarchy. Intense competition between the president, the army and the communists followed and led to massive internal strife which saw a political and violent climax between 1965 and 1966, including an attempted uprising by dissident army officers. Over a period of two years, hundreds of thousands of people were massacred in a combination of ethnic cleansing against the Chinese population and people associated with the Communist Party (PKI), as well as people who had nothing to do with the communists. The abortive coup of 1965, blamed on the Communist Party, was swiftly put down. Sukarno was discredited in the event and forced to transfer executive authority (*supersemar*) to Suharto, who ruled as a quasi-monarchical president until 1997 when he fell from power in a series of events which have created political instability in Indonesia but which appear as the direct result of the exposure of the weakness of Indonesia's economy following the East Asian economic crisis.

The new leader rapidly installed the 'New Order' regime ruled by the dominant Golongon Karya (Golkar) Party. Golkar is heavily supported by the Armed Forces of the Republic of Indonesia (ABRI) who provide it with an effective coercive arm, which since the mid-1960s has played a pre-eminent role in the national polity. Hopes for real democracy and an improvement in the human rights situation were quickly dashed when Suharto came to power. He reinstituted the political ideology of the Pancasila and added various elements which again boded ill for democracy and the establishment of a human rights culture. These included anti-communism, a doctrine of *dwi fungsi* (dual function) which allowed for military involvement in civilian politics, the notion of the floating mass which excluded people from any organized politics except during elections and emphasized economic nationalism (aimed at achieving a kind of autarkic self-reliance).

The New Order based its legitimacy in prioritizing development. Central to this overall programme were growth, equality and stability, both for internal and external consumption. Of all the states we have examined in Southeast Asia, the Indonesian emphasis on linking economic development and legitimacy seems the most striking given the precarious balance of ethnic and social forces which make it up. In part this helps to explain why the Asian crisis of 1997 had such a devastating effect on the legitimacy of the ruling elite. Politically, the New Order regime continued in the footsteps of the former system, clamping down on opposition and ignoring human rights and civil liberties. As the chairman of the Indonesian Legal Aid Foundation argues, the regime has been characterized by 'institutional paternalism, press censorship and other forms of social and political repression'.[6] Suharto did attempt to address some of Indonesia's economic problems and prevent the worst excesses which characterized the Sukarno years, but his record was blighted by the invasion of East Timor in 1975 and the Dili massacre in 1991 which showed that his regime could be as just as excessive when it feared losing control.

Since independence, concepts of western democracy have been reduced in scope; the number of political parties was reduced to roughly three; and the elected parliament has been replaced by an appointed one. Candidates for political office are vetted by government officials and barred from making critical comments about government policy during election campaigns. The military has *dwi fungsi* to justify their role in political and social issues such as human rights among others. This has been established as a permanent right of the Indonesian military. It has also led to the development of the 'security approach', a role which involves the full use of repression to prevent any perceived threats to the security of the Indonesian state. This has been widely criticized by human rights organizations for violating rights in East Timor, Aceh and Irian Jaya among other regions.

In March 1993, the People's Consultative Assembly, made up of MPs and political appointments, along with members of the armed forces, re-elected President Suharto for a sixth consecutive five-year term, but things started to go wrong in July 1996 when the regime cracked down on supporters of the opposition leader, Megawati Sukarnoputri, the daughter of Sukarno. This was the first sign that there was serious discontent with Suharto's brand of authoritarianism, the widening economic disparities and the level of corruption, most notably and visibly among Suharto's own family. The rioting was among the worst experienced by Indonesia since the mid-1970s. Troops were responsible for at least five deaths and they arrested 249 demonstrators. Various party members, leaders and trade unionists were imprisoned. The Asian economic crisis from mid-1997 onwards affected the Indonesian currency, the rupiah, in a devastating fashion. The currency was very weak, prices rose and the economy was severely affected. By January 1998, the rupiah had been declared the world's worst performing currency; 2.5 million people had lost their employment and the IMF moved in to impose austerity measures as conditions in the provision of loans to the government. The country's stock market further deteriorated in a dramatic fashion and there was widespread panic buying.

In addition, Indonesia, along with its neighbours, suffered from environmental disasters in the years leading up to Suharto's fall. In Indonesian political culture these can be seen as portents that the leader has lost his power to rule. Massive forest fires caused terrible smog and haze over entire regions, affecting people's respiratory system. Satellite photos taken in 1997 showed that in Kalimantan, a 1 million hectare rice plantation project, mandated by the president and set in a peat bog, was smouldering uncontrollably.[7] For many weeks the archipelago was enveloped in smoke, causing airports to close and ships to collide at sea, so thick was the haze enveloping Indonesia.

In March 1998, Suharto declared he would have another five years in office. Food shortages, price increases and the start of more anti-government demonstrations followed. For the first time in 30 years there was terrible economic discontent. The coffee crop had been destroyed and the prospects for the next rice crop looked appalling. Moreover, bilateral dialogue between some of the ASEAN members was becoming acrimonious. Indonesia's neighbours, including Singapore and Malaysia, appeared annoyed and disgruntled at the effects of the haze and the problems it was causing in their urban settings, an unusual sign given the typical non-interference of

ASEAN members in other members' domestic affairs and the policy of constructive engagement.

By May, 1998 the streets were in flames again as Indonesian troops shot dead six students; in the riots which followed more than 500 people died in Jakarta and there was widespread fears among the Chinese community that the massacres of 1965 would be repeated. Thousands of ethnic Chinese fled to Singapore and Malaysia. Suharto was forced to leave office to be replaced by his vice-president, Jusuf Habibie, a successor who struggled to maintain order and political legitimacy. The economic crisis had important reper-cussions for a dictator who based legitimacy on economic growth; mass demonstrations against his rule and loss of support from the military forced him to step down. The new president promised some economic reforms, some autonomy for East Timor and tried to make some concessions, but they were limited and did little in the way of real social change. In June 1998, Habibie called for an action plan for human rights which sought to ratify key human rights treaties. By the end of 1998, they had ratified the Convention Against Torture and other Cruel, Inhuman or Degrading Treatment or Punishment and the International Labour Organization's Convention 87 Concerning Freedom of Association and Protection of the Right to Organize. Controls on the formation of political parties were also lifted and the print and broadcast media were allowed more or less full freedom in the aftermath of Suharto's fall.

Indonesia is clearly in a time of transition. In August of the same year, the National Commission on Human Rights declared its interest in setting up a Truth Commission in Indonesia to look into previous abuses. General Wiranto (who was so heavily involved with the East Timor problem) apologized to the people of Aceh for some of the abuses they had suffered.

By November 1998, tensions had again risen as ethnic violence erupted (especially on the islands of Ambon and Kalimantan) with Muslims and Christians engaged in fierce conflict among others. On East Timor, problems erupted as well with pro-independence forces clashing with their counterparts.

After May 1998, Indonesia's transition consisted of two phases. There was to be, first, a parliamentary election in June 1999 and, second, the election of a president by a special assembly that met in November 1999. The months in between these two elections were to see lawlessness and a great deal of politicking among the competing players. Much of this was conducted against a backdrop of intimidation and political violence.

The first democratic elections for decades, however, held in June 1999, have proved to be a qualified success for the forces of opposition, particularly Megawati. It is clear that they will have a difficult job managing the ethnic amalgam and the sociocultural divisions that pervade Indonesian politics. Suharto managed this with an authoritarian style of leadership until the economic crisis exposed the flaws and revealed massive social injustices in the system. However, he still successfully oversaw the transfer of power to his successor, who came to power in the middle of the political crises that Indonesia then faced. Suharto's legitimacy based on economic performance and political astuteness had faltered. He could no longer control the great game he had played in the previous 30 years. Indonesia had begun to emerge as one of the world's largest democracies.

In the presidential election of 20 October 1999, Abdurraham Wahid, a Muslim cleric, emerged as the outright winner in Indonesia's first ever free and democratic presidential elections in 54 years of independence by a vote of 373 to Megawati's 313. Despite the latter's party being the winner in the June elections, she was unable to gain as much support for the highest position in the country. However, in a conciliatory mood, Wahid made her his vice-president. Wahid, more commonly known as Gus Dur, is the head of an organization which claims 30 million members and appears committed to promoting sectarian and social tolerance across the archipelago. There was some violence during the election; a small bomb injured five people at a Megawati rally in Jakarta; thousands of Habibie supporters protested on his home island of Sulawesi. It clearly remains to be seen, however, whether the new political dispensation which has not fully run the course of its own transition period can engender economic and political stability which will nurture the roots of human rights and democracy as Indonesia moves into the new century.

Political Economy

Suharto not only changed the Indonesian political system, he also sought to change the social and economic make-up of this vast country. In fact the political legitimacy of the New Order, especially since the 1970s, has depended on the economic growth it enjoyed. We can see that despite large-scale corruption and an unequal distribution of developmental goods, there have been sufficient resources to raise the living standards of large sections of the population. The private sector and market mechanisms became much more important during Suharto's regime, and increasing openness in the economy resulted in more foreign investment. There is still, however, significant government intervention. Despite the restrictions on its democracy, Indonesia's economy has witnessed rapid growth in recent years at least until the economic crash of 1997; its authoritarian government has provided a relatively stable environment in which to exploit the vast natural resources of the archipelago, particularly oil and gas reserves.

Deregulation ensured that the country was not left out in this growth period for all ASEAN countries. Agriculture, oil and gas powered this states dynamism, but a diverse and expanding manufacturing sector also helped to produce an increase in exports. Twenty-five years ago, Indonesia had a per capita annual income of $75; in 1994 this had risen to $750. GDP has shown a 17-fold increase, rising from $8 billion in 1969 to $142 billion in 1994. The Asian Development Bank (ADB) has forecast 6.7 per cent GDP growth for 1994 and 7 per cent for 1995.[8] Despite this, large sections of the population live in poverty and poor social conditions.

Indonesia had high growth in the 1980s. *The Social Indicators of Development 1993* report, which is published by the World Bank, indicated that the average annual GNP per capita growth for Indonesia between 1965 and 1990 was 4.3 per cent, for 1991 for instance the per capita GNP was US$610 – the lowest of all members of ASEAN in that year. This growth has been helped by somewhat successful attempts to reduce population growth. GDP growth was expected to be 6.5 per cent for 1993 and inflation seemed to have been brought under control.

The disparities in income distribution in Indonesia are quite striking. In 1993, the top 20 per cent of households received 41 per cent of the national income while the poorest 20 per cent received 21 per cent.[9] Economic growth has also meant that fewer Indonesians live in what the World Bank call 'absolute poverty' – that is, consuming fewer than 2,150 calories a day. In 1970 three-fifths of the people lived below this poverty line; by 1980 this had decreased to 29 per cent and by 1990, even further to 15 per cent.[10]

In education and health, Indonesia also improved. By 1990, it had achieved universal primary school enrolment; this has to be qualified by the fact that 23 per cent of the people aged 15 and over remained illiterate (the highest percentage of illiteracy in ASEAN). Infant mortality fell dramatically in Indonesia after the start of the 1990s. Average life expectancy has increased from 45.7 years in 1967 to 62.7 years in 1994. At the same time the family planning programme has managed to bring down the population growth rate from 2.32 per cent in the 1970s to about 1.8 per cent in the 1980s.[11] What kinds of factors helped to explain this growth? One explanation lies in state intervention within a capitalist framework. The state in Indonesia has been described as being a *dirigiste* entity with two facets: mercantilism and patrimonial rent-seeking. As Richard Robison argues:

> On the one hand the state intervenes in mercantilist fashion to protect national enterprise and national economic agendas, including the development of such upstream manufacturing industries as steel and petrochemicals, through tariffs, monopolies and state funded industrial projects. In another dimension, its officials appropriate state resources and authority on behalf of specific political and corporate interests. Under this *dirigiste* regime the growth of a capitalist class has proceeded with great rapidity. Between 1977 and 1990 approved domestic investment increased from Rp.574 billion to 59,878 billion with the private sector share now clearly outstripping that of the state sector both in terms of capital formation and share of value added.[12]

Foreign investment increased dramatically in recent years. By the mid-1990s there were at least six major projects, including four oil refineries, one steel mill and the country's first private power station – all indicators of the interest in mega-projects in the region. In the first few months of 1994, $15.4 billion was pledged in investment, with an estimate of a record $18 billion for the whole year.[13] Foreign aid was dispensed at an accelerated rate; in 1993, Indonesia received aid worth a record $5.1 billion. Debt, however, has also grown; the current debt stands at $83 billion and roughly 32 per cent of Indonesia's export earnings service debt payments; by 1999 this debt was expected to increase to $95 billion, but with the hope that the economy would grow quickly enough to offset additional payments. The World Bank argued that if this level of development was sustained, Indonesia could become a solid, middle-income country with a per capita income of $1,000 by the end of the twentieth century.[14]

The crisis that affected Indonesia from 1997 onwards along with many of the other Southeast Asian states appeared to outsiders in the first instance as economic. Indonesia's economy, however, was prone to widespread corruption and influence peddling. In 1987 an article in the *Wall Street Journal* argued that Indonesia's limited freedoms had at the same time hindered development. Such an atmosphere had produced many monopoly import concessions which had typically gone to companies controlled by Suharto's relatives, which in turn serve to 'strangle' an economy already suf-focating under complex regulations, high tariff barriers and mismanaged state enterprises.[15] The collapse of their currency and the failure of their banking system in 1997 to take preventative measures was, however, part and parcel of a larger picture of decay and simply helped to highlight the political problems, including leadership succession, widespread corruption and the prevalent dis-satisfaction with issues of social justice. By the beginning of August 1997, the economic crisis had forced the government to float the rupiah. The result of bad borrowing and incompetent investment decisions left Indonesian business with nearly US$80 million in debt. When capital flight began, these companies started selling the Indonesian currency to cover their debts in dollars. The result was catastrophic as the fall of the rupiah served to exacerbate the bankruptcy of most of these businesses. By late October the government had agreed a bail-out package from the IMF to the tune of US$43 billion, along with a package designed to reduce the corruption of family influence. In addition, the dramatic fall of the rupiah – almost 70 per cent of its value between July 1997 and January 1998 – meant that food prices increased dramatically. The resulting ethnic tensions were plain.

Many Indonesians believed the Chinese had made their wealth through connections with Suharto and were very quick to use the Chinese as scapegoats for their poor economic fortunes. On Java, for instance, from 1997 there were sporadic outbreaks of rioting, much of it targeted against ethnic Chinese and Christian minorities, but which can also be explained by the pent-up frustration of those who have not been the recipients of the New Order's substantial economic growth rate. These marginalized people are the losers in economic growth and globalization; left out by development, they have helped to contribute to it and at the same time in financial crisis they suffer most from the negative social and economic effects. The threat was seen to Indonesian's national security:

> Over the last 18 months, Indonesia has seen dozens of riots across the country, protesting everything from land seizures to police abuse. Several small riots have broken out in recent days over increases in food prices and perceptions of price gouging. The disturbances were first seen in eastern Java, and by late Tuesday they had spread to within 350 miles of Jakarta. Small protests and strikes have also been staged at factories over wages and working conditions.[16]

In April 1999, the Taman Siswa, an Indonesian educational institution, issued a press release which recommended various measures to prevent national disintegration, so great was its belief that Indonesia was on the verge of collapse.[17]

Habibie's leadership in 1998 did initially provide some hope for the economy. A technocrat, he agreed to the measures suggested by the IMF to restructure the Indonesian economy; however, his abilities in economic matters were severely questioned by his critics. By the end of 1998, the Indonesian economy had stumbled though some of the worst of the Asian economic crisis. Although private sector debt remained a major problem, GDP growth appeared to be moving back in a positive direction and the rupiah was showing signs of recovery. Things were beginning to look more like normal. However, one might add that even at conservative estimates it might be several decades before the real roots of economic recovery and reform of Indonesia's financial institutions are felt.

Human Rights and Development

The form of rule of Suharto imposed for over 30 years was what most political scientists would call a dictatorship. There was little opposition and, if any emerged, it tended to be crushed ruthlessly through the broad powers he accrued to himself and the regime. He established political stability where there was anarchy at least up until 1997 and was regarded as having produced successful economic development. Along with Lee Kuan Yew of Singapore and Mohammed Mahathir of Malaysia he made up the triumvirate of leaders who proclaimed Asian values, Asian democracy and antipathy towards notions of liberal, democratic-based human rights cultures. As long as development goals were reached he was tolerated within the framework of Indonesian society. Suharto reinforced notions of communitarianism, consensus and status over individual versions of rights. It is the classic case of justifying political legitimacy by appealing to the fact that political stability and economic development had been achieved. Increasingly it was an argument that would prove difficult to sustain in the light of economic turmoil and the collapse of Asian currencies.

The disparity between rich and poor in Indonesia has led to labour disputes and industrial unrest, in a much more conflictual and open fashion than in Indonesia's closest neighbours, Singapore and Malaysia. In August 1994, the International Confederation of Free Trade Unions (ICFTU) argued for the release of detained independent trade unionists in Indonesia. The Confederation was protesting at the fact that on 13 August, the leader (Muchtar Pakpahan) of Indonesia's independent trade union group, Sejahtera Buruh Serikat Indonesia (SBSI) was arrested. The SBSI, which has 125,000 members, had been campaigning for months to double the minimum wage to 7,000 rupiahs ($3.3 dollars) a day and to improve working conditions. They stated that Pakpahan's arrest was a direct violation of the ILO's Convention 87 which guarantees 'freedom of association and protection of the right to organize', and legal aid lawyers in Indonesia have said that Pakpahan and supporters were simply informing workers of their rights. Indonesia did not sign this Convention but is a member of the ILO.[18] Moreover the ICFTU was alarmed at the 'continuing harassment of SBSI activists at factory level and the continuing trials of SBSI leaders in Medan'.[19] Jakarta stated that the labour leader was responsible for whipping up anti-government sentiment in Medan. In June 1994, the government officially banned SBSI. As noted, the argument is generally made in Southeast Asia that economic development should precede political liberalization; 'development before democracy' is the oft-quoted maxim of authoritarian rulers in this part of the world. However, we are entitled to understand at whose expense development is taking place. Are the have-nots really experiencing development themselves, or is this simply economic exploitation to benefit the few elites?

The role of multinational corporations in Southeast Asia is clearly not to the benefit the masses, but in a rather crude fashion procures cheap labour for the West. The economic practices of Nike, the sports and footwear company, is instructive. In the 1980s they closed their US factories and moved to the Far East where minimum wages were unheard of. When the South Korean workers gained the right to form independent unions and strike, Nike simply relocated its Korean factories to other, less developed, countries such as Thailand, Malaysia, China and Indonesia, where they built six factories. In 1991, their net profits reached record levels. What was the human price of this global rearrangement in labour markets? One article illustrated the detrimental effects of these moves on Indonesian workers with reference to a young woman named Sadisah who worked in a Nike factory. On average, Sadisah worked six days a week, ten and a half hours a day for a monthly wage equivalent to US\$37.46 – roughly half the retail price of one pair of the sneakers she produced. The daily wage for seven and a half hours' work at the time was approximately \$1.03 per day, or just under 14 cents an hour, which was less than the Indonesian government's figure 'minimum physical need'. However, the author notes that Sadisah and other workers in the factory are

> compelled to put in extra hours, both by economic necessity and by employer fiat. Each production line of 115 workers is expected to produce about 1,600 pairs of Nikes a day ... Sadisah worked 63 hours during this pay period, for which she received an extra 2 cents per hour. At this factory, which makes mid priced Nikes, each pair of shoes requires .84 man-hours to produce; working on an assembly line, Sadisah assembled the equivalent of 13.9 pairs every day. The profit margin on each pair is enormous. The labour costs to manufacture a pair of Nikes that sells for \$80 in the United States is approximately 12 cents.[20]

The costs to social development are enormous. The author quotes an ILO survey which found that 88 per cent of women working at Sadisah's wage rates are malnourished; and most workers in this factory (over 80 per cent) are women. With seldom more than elementary school education, they are generally in their teens or early twenties, and have come from outlying agricultural areas in search of city jobs and a better life. Sadisah's wages allow her to rent a shanty lacking electricity or running water.[21]

Workers like Sadisah are not only subject to the bare minimum in terms of living conditions and economic rights, they are also murdered if they speak up about such conditions – as in the case of Marsinah, a 24-year-old labour activist who was murdered in East Java in May 1993. This was a short time after she had instigated a protest against the dismissal of some of her colleagues who were detained by the military for trying to organize a strike in the factory where she worked. Her treatment was brutal: 'a postmortem indicated she died as a result of injuries inflicted by torture including severe beating which caused internal bleeding and having had a sharp object inserted into her vagina. Later reports indicated strangulation as well.'[22] Eight civilians and one military officer were arrested and according to reports all of these had various rights violated. However, the striking aspect of the case was not only the violent message of retribution for labour organizers, but also the role of the military forces in applying the 'security approach' to labour disputes and strikes.

The Transmigration Programme

One of the most important attempts at state-controlled development lies in Indonesia's programme of resettling the Javanese population, a policy that has had disastrous consequences for migrants and indigenous locals in the area to which they have migrated. The Transmigration Programme (*transmigrasi*) is probably the grandest historical plan to resettle entire populations. It involves the transferral of peasant farmers and military units from the overcrowded core of Java to the less populated and underdeveloped peripheries of the Indonesian archipelago. This has been conducted with the collusion of the World Bank and other aid donors to the tune of billions of dollars annually. At the end of the 1980s, 6 million had already been removed, with several more million by the end of 1994 and at least another 65 million by 2010, in an effort to expand Java's total control to the hinterlands. Indonesia's 1984–89 five-year plan was to remove 5 million people from Java, Madura and Bali to areas that specifically were resisting the imposition of Javanese sovereignty, areas such as Kalimantan, Sulawesi, the south Moluccas and East Timor and Irian Jaya (formerly West Papua). The resulting human rights abuses, environmental destruction and uneven development have been dramatic.

In addition, transmigration has caused problems between the 'settlers' and the 'natives', creating large numbers of refugees. The general policy is one of 'assimilation' into the mainstream of all Indonesia's tribal groups, which will produce a more homogeneous Indonesia, or, as the Transmigration Minister put it: 'The different ethnic groups of Indonesia will in the long run disappear ... and there will be one kind of man.' This policy has also been called 'the Javanese version of Nazi Germany's *lebensraum*', calling as it does for the removal of over 800,000 indigenous people from their homesteads and villages to resettlement sites.[23]

Cultural Survival, an organization that supports the rights of indigenous peoples', claims that resettlement has had extremely destructive effects on these communities, including the 'destruction of local governments, economies, means of sustainable resource use ... [and] the widespread use of military force to pacify areas and break local resistance by bombing and massacring civilians'.[24]

Indonesia, which likes to cite the notion that economic development should precede the luxury of political and civil rights, has a fairly poor record in terms of labour rights and social conditions for its workers. The transmigration programmes have not only infringed the rights of indigenous populations; they have also forced the dislocation of poor farmers into areas that have poor soil and difficult terrain. In Third World countries with rapidly expanding economies such as in East Asia the costs to the poor of economic development, particularly through enforced migration programmes, can be seen to outweigh starkly the benefits.

Under Suharto the development before democracy maxim reached its peak. To ensure his monopoly on power he relied on a variety of laws, some established, some created for the purposes of legitimating his rule. What kinds of institutional measures did Suharto use against opponents of his regime in this postcolonial period? In 1963 an anti-subversion law came into practice which makes it a capital offence to engage in 'acts that could distort, undermine or deviate from the state ideology or broad outlines of state policy, or which could disseminate feelings of hostility or arouse hostility, disturbances, or anxiety among the people'.[25] This extensive law has been widely used to clamp down on dissent, allowing for the heavy-handed prosecution of state critics. The criminal code, like many legal procedures in Southeast Asia, is a legacy of colonial rule; in this case the Dutch Empire. The regime managed to preserve features of the code that resembled some of the worst elements of the colonial period while reforming it with even more repressive contributions. One of these additions is the death sentence or life imprisonment for anyone found who opposes the Pancasila or 'who expresses hostile feelings, hatred, or contempt for the government, such as might disturb stability in the field of politics or security'.[26]

Even as Indonesia developed rapidly, institutional measures were being taken to provide a tight grip on power. Laws established early 1970s made the judiciary formally independent of the executive branch's Ministry of Justice and provided the chief justice with ministerial status. However, judges and most civil servants are almost always members of the ruling party, Golkar; furthermore, the courts nominal power to review laws is rarely if ever invoked.

In addition to subversion the death penalty is also imposed for drug trafficking by Law 9/1976. This has increased sharply in recent years. As one report states: 'between 1974 and 1984, there were four executions; between 1985 and 1987 there were 19 ... but the true total may be much higher: the government does not make such statistics available'.[27] There were few executions before Suharto came to power, but in the wake of the 1965 coup the numbers increased dramatically as Suharto sought to purge potential threats to his regime. An estimated 500,000 were killed in this period in a wave of anti-communist sentiment and hundred of thousands more were imprisoned. Most of the detainees were released in the 1970s and are now known as ex-Tapols. Most are still subject to severe constraints on their basic civil rights, all imposed without any due process in law. These include various restraints in terms of employment, residence and freedom of speech.[28]

Despite the lull in politically motivated killings since the disruptions of 1965–66, they appeared to have returned by the early 1980s (although not on the same scale). In the period 1980–85, widespread extra-judicial killings occurred; one report cited as many as 4,000 such deaths in 1984.[29] While the killings of criminal suspects appear to have decreased since then, politically motivated executions still continue, notably in East Timor and Irian Jaya. In September 1993, for instance, a force of local army and police opened fire on several hundred villagers who were protesting against the construction of the Nipah Dam on the island of Madura off the coast of East Java; four were killed and three wounded. As a result four army officers were transferred and the military has admitted that there were violations of procedure. But regardless of these admissions and palliatives the intimidation of villagers who protested against the dam's construction continued after the shootings and constitutes a serious violation of freedom of assembly and expression.[30]

The post-Cold War era appeared (at least on the surface) to promote a policy of 'openness', a prescription that Suharto himself endorsed. It seemed to indicate an Indonesian *glasnost* in which press controls were relaxed, demonstrations by students and activists were more common and new NGOs appeared willing to criticize the government. The new mood was a result of a growing middle class and their increased demands for a voice in society; however, some critics argued that this was a top-down imposition and one that could be reversed. In the event 'openness' has proved to be a façade for internal Indonesian politics, freedom of speech and the press were still severely constrained.

Freedom of Speech

The press in Indonesia is subject to an extensive array of controls by the state; the media are constantly under threat of closure and journalists operate in a climate of fear (*budaya takut*), which enforces constant self-censorship. This has changed to some extent after the political downfall of Suharto, but there are still tight controls on the press. The first eight years of the New Order displayed some tolerance, certainly more than was ever shown under the Sukarno regime, but over the past 30 years there has been a marked tendency for the regime to close down publications they find politically unacceptable. Officials in Jakarta have conceded that in this period, nearly 2,000 books have been banned by the Indonesian government.

The most famous political writer in the country is Pramoedya Ananta Toer, whose works were considered to be communist propaganda by the government; he was imprisoned for 14 years in 1965, ten of these years spent on the island of Buru. Since 1979 he has been under state surveillance at his home in Jakarta. He has angered the government so much that three students are now serving jail terms for having distributed his works. As a general rule, authors who have served their sentences are still deprived of their rights to publish and often this punishment extends itself to the next generation.[31]

In June 1994, the government banned three leading journals, *Tempo*, *Editor* and *Detik*. In the case of *Tempo* (which had a weekly circulation of more than 200,000) the authorities argued that it violated laws relating to national stability; recent coverage of divisions between the Indonesian cabinet and the military apparently proved to be the decisive point in closing down the journal, but the government argued that it had been violating these laws for several years. The Information Minister, Harmoko, described the candour of these journals' reporting as akin to 'alcoholic journalism'.[32] In a scathing condemnation of the closures one human rights NGO stated that the ban

> exposed the policy of 'openness' as a political device, promoted as long as it served the central government's interests, cast off when its natural consequences, such as a freer press, began to hit home. It exposed the arbitrariness with which power is exercised in Indonesia, and it prompted a rash of demonstrations that were a telling display of popular disaffection with the petty sensitivities of the leadership. In violating a basic right, the Indonesian government did more damage to itself than it could ever have done to a free-spirited press.[33]

The dubious reasons given for the closure of the other two magazines were of an 'administrative' nature.[34] One author noted that in order to survive in the different type of political climates in Indonesia, the 'press has its own list of do's and don't's – a system that some have hit as self-censorship. Taboo topics included direct criticism of President Suharto and his family.'[35] After the democratic changes of 1997–98, *Tempo* began publishing again.

Human rights activists are also suffering from actions taken against them on grounds of 'defamation' against the national leadership in the form of President Suharto. In January 1994, 21 students were indicted in Jakarta over claims that they had defamed the President during demonstrations and were sentenced to six months in jail. The charges alleged that in one instance they had been guilty of distributing stickers which claimed that Suharto was to blame for many of Indonesia's problems. Nuku Soelaiman, the chairman of the Pijar Foundation, which had distributed many of the stickers was sentenced to four years in prison for defamation.[36]

Indonesia and East Timor

> The luck of the Timorese is to be born in tears, to live in tears and to die in tears.[37]

At the heart of the nexus of human rights developmental issues, the East Timor case seems central. Timor is part of the Lesser Sundas group of the chain of islands that make up Indonesia. The eastern part of the island was colonized by Portugal more than 450 years ago. They took steps to insulate their half of the island from the upheavals and problems which affected the western (Dutch) part of the island. Historically, the East Timorese have little in common with the rest of the archipelago; as a Portuguese colony its inclinations lay in trade as opposed to Dutch colonial settlement. Descendants from the Atoni people of the Highlands and mixed with Malay and Melanesian immigrants, they have few similarities to the Javanese or Indonesian counterparts. Whereas most Indonesians are Muslim or Hindu, the people of East Timor are overwhelmingly Catholic. In 1974, the 'Carnation revolution' which produced radical political and social change in Portugal sealed the fate of this seafaring empire. After the overthrow of the government in Portugal, the Timorese Democratic Union (UDT), led by members of the colonial administrative elite, called for a Federation with Portugal and eventual full independence. However, East Timor was abandoned to a large-scale invasion by the Indonesian military, who subjected the inhabitants of the principal city of Dili to what one historian has described as 'systematic killing, gratuitous violence and primitive plunder'.[38] One interpretation of the background to the East Timor issue argues that the US not only tacitly complied with the invasion and provided material support, but has also maintained a blanket of silence over the human rights violations in the early stages. The United States blocked any UN action on the matter at the time as Indonesia was central to American geopolitical strategy in the postwar period. As Noam Chomsky argues: 'with its wealth of raw materials, Indonesia was to play a central role in the emerging global system, with Japanese and Western European capitalism reconstructed within a broader framework managed by the United States and ultimately subordinated to U.S. interests'.[39]

The thorn in the Indonesian military's side was the *Frente Revolucionaria do Timor Leste Independente* more commonly known as Fretilin, the guerrilla organization fighting for self-rule in East Timor.[40] In May Fretilin demanded complete self-rule for the former colony and by September 1975 they had established control over the administrative capital, Dili, managing to eliminate the competition except for those along the border with West Timor. The threat of a civil war, unrest and the notion that Fretilin would wage a communist insurgency prompted Indonesia to pursue a form of police action to defuse the tensions. This, however, simply exacerbated the situation. Fretilin announced the independence of the Democratic Republic of East Timor on 28 November 1975. The following day, the pro-Indonesian elements backed by the government declared East Timor an integral part of the Indonesian state. Adam Malik, the Foreign Minister, formalized this and ABRI forces invaded the island on 7 December 1975. On 17 July 1976, East Timor was declared the 27th province of the Indonesian Republic.

The invasion was denounced by the West, but little else; the United Nations rhetoric had no effect despite its refusal to endorse the annexation. Armed resistance by Fretilin has been piecemeal and limited in the face of far superior Indonesian technology and numbers. The militaristic 'security approach' was widely used in East Timor under the notion of 'total people's defence', which meant an effort to mobilize the local population against Fretilin, despite the refusal of the UN to recognize East Timor as part of Indonesia.

In November 1991 new evidence of atrocities emerged with film of Indonesian troops shooting unarmed civilians in Dili. The numbers suggested by human rights NGOs are problematic in this case; Asia Watch, for instance, stated that between 75 and 200 unarmed demonstrators were killed.[41] The consequences in this period were fairly devastating. In 1993 the Australian parliament's foreign affairs committee stated that 'at least 200,000 had died under occupation by Indonesia'.[42] In April 1994 *The Economist* reported Abilio Soares, the Governor of East Timor, as saying that it was 'probably true that between 100,000 and 200,000 people had died as a result of the war in east Timor'.[43] Just a few days before, Ali Alatas, the Foreign Minister, had dismissed the figure of 200,000 dead – a little under a third of the pre-1975 population – as a '"canard" without a shred of evidence ... [however] the impact of the killing was underlined by a schoolteacher who said that 70 per cent of the children in his class had lost one or both of their parents to war or famine'.[44]

In August 1994, the Roman Catholic Bishop of East Timor, Carlos Belo, launched a scathing attack on the Indonesian government for alleged killings and torture after troops used tear gas and batons in July to break up a demonstration, which left dozens injured. The same month a delegation of Japanese legislators called for immediate withdrawal of Indonesian troops from East Timor.

The scale of genocide on East Timor has been compared to Cambodia under Pol Pot; James Dunn, the former Australian consul to the island, completed a study of the census statistics after 1975. He argued that:

> before the invasion, East Timor had a population of 688,000 which was growing at 2 per cent per annum. Assuming it didn't grow any faster, the population today ought to be 980,000 or more, almost a million people. If you look at the recent Indonesian census, the Timorese population is probably 650,000. That means it's actually less than it was 18 years ago. I don't think there is any case in post world war 2 history where such a decline of population has occurred in these circumstances. It's incredible; worse than Cambodia or Ethiopia.[45]

Whatever the numbers, it is clear that the death toll is in the hundreds of thousands. The Indonesian Foreign Minister once stated that 'East Timor is a pebble in Indonesia's shoe'[46] and the standard line of the regime has been to disregard any right to self-determination on the part of the East Timorese, to deny in fact that East Timor has any claim to nationhood. In an address to over 400 military and civilian personnel in East Timor, General Benny Moerdiano (sometimes referred to as the 'butcher' of Timor), who led the invasion in the 1970s, summed up the efforts to prevent Timorese self-determination when he said:

> There is no such thing as a Timorese patriot, there is only an Indonesian patriot. There is no such thing as an East Timorese nation, there is only an Indonesian nation ... In the past, there were some small states that wanted to stand on their own and without hesitation, the Indonesian government took steps to stop that. All the forces at our disposal were used to prevent the creation of small states ... If you try to make your own state and the movement is strong, it will be crushed by ABRI (the armed forces). There have been bigger rebellions ... than the small number calling themselves Fretilin or whoever their sympathisers are here. We will crush them all! I repeat we will crush them all.[47]

Ironically, the Indonesians who fought for the right to independence and self-determination from the Dutch deprived the people of East Timor of this universally recognized right which they themselves claimed in the wake of empire.

Recently, there has been immense progress towards a solution to the East Timor problem, and in specific in the aftermath of the economic crisis. In the post-Suharto period, the East Timor question opened up. After Suharto stepped down and Habibie came to power, the latter pushed the autonomy proposal in June 1998, and proposed a gradual devolution of domestic legislative and judicial administrative control to the province with control of foreign policy, external security and the budget remaining under the control of Jakarta. The plan was problematic from the beginning as it failed to accede to Timorese demands for independence and self-rule. In that sense the autonomy solution could be viewed only as one stage in the road to a referendum in the province's future. From this period, however, international interest in the problem of East Timor widened and it became increasingly an international media topic. Meanwhile the fighting continued as Timor began to prepare for elections and in fact it looked on the surface as if political and social change was under way. In reality stalemate existed.

On 30 August 1999, the East Timorese turned out *en masse* to vote 21.5 per cent in favour and 78.5 per cent against the proposed special autonomy. This was a massive vote in favour of independence from Indonesia. This followed weeks of organized harassment from various terrorist militias, many of them supported by the Indonesian army and police. The police and army in fact helped to coordinate and direct the militia violence and following the referendum, continued to carry out this policy of terrorism. Hundreds of people were reported to have been massacred by these groups and 150,000 people were living as refugees in fear of their lives, many of them in West Timor and many subjected to brutal abuse by the Indonesian orchestrated militias.[48] One human rights groups reported that militiamen going from house to house had murdered 77 people. Moreover a UN investigator in the first week of December 1999, argued that her team had found evidence of systematic murder in East Timor, something that points to a great deal of collusion between the military and the militias.[49]

After several weeks of what can only be described as anarchy, during which the United Nations evacuated most of its personnel and abandoned its bases, the Indonesian government agreed to allow a UN-sponsored peace-keeping force on East Timor, mainly composed of Australians. This group, known as Interfet, have been given the mandate of providing stability and order in the transitional period now that the Indonesian troops have left East Timor.

Other Peripheries, Other Human Rights Abuses: Aceh

The other major problem for the Indonesian regime lies in the northern periphery of Sumatra. Aceh, a mainly Muslim province of 3.4 million, is roughly 1,000 miles from Jakarta, and yet has seen more than its fair share of conflict. Its peripheral, provincial status underlies a traditional history of resistance to centralized authority; and like many other peripheries it suffers from uneven economic development and the lack of respect for local traditions by central government bureaucrats. Despite this, Aceh is important to the Indonesian economy because it contains rich supplies of oil and gas. The province, however, has always had the potential for strife and a bitter guerrilla conflict is being fought by Indonesian armed forces against Islamic independence fighters. In fact, this territory serves to illustrate in some ways the precarious unity of the Indonesian archipelago. Military repression in the province by central government troops over the years has only served to fuel resentment against Javanese rule in Jakarta. In 1976, this resistance found middle-class expression in the inception of the Aceh Independence Movement made up of business people and professionals who felt alienated from the Jakarta regime. Hasan di Tiro, a businessman now in exile in Sweden, was instrumental in pushing for separatist aims.

In 1989, Indonesian security forces initiated counter-insurgency measures against the armed resistance movement. In four years it was estimated that roughly 2,000 civilians, including elderly and children, suffered as a result of extra-judicial killings. More than 1,000 people were arbitrarily arrested for supporting the rebel group Aceh Merdeka (Free Aceh). Disappearances are common and at least 50 people in this period were sentenced to lengthy prison sentences.[50] The fact that there is an armed separatist struggle in Aceh coinciding with demands for a fully Islamic government in the province have caused the Indonesian authorities even greater headaches than the case of East Timor in some respects.

Aceh is less well known when it comes to international and regional media publicity of human rights violations, in comparison to East Timor and other regions of the world. As Amnesty noted:

the international community was appalled by the massacre of more than 200 East Timorese at the Santa Cruz cemetery in November 1991, but it has turned a blind eye to the fate of some 2,000 Acehnese killed by Indonesian forces since 1989. Widespread condemnation followed the sentencing of east Timorese resistance leader, Xanana Gusmao, to life imprisonment after a blatantly unfair trial in May 1993, but few voices have been raised in protest at the imprisonment of at least 50 alleged members of Aceh Merdeka since 1991 after equally unfair trials.[51]

In 1993, 73 people accused of being members of Aceh Merdeka were released without trial or charges after periods of detention that sometimes exceeded two years. The confrontations between the Indonesian military and citizens of Aceh have served to highlight the diversity of Indonesia but also has pointed to one of its longest standing problems: the growth of Islam and militant tendencies. The difference between Aceh and East Timor is that the former was part of Indonesia at the time of independence, unlike East Timor and West Papua. This means it will be far more difficult to justify letting it go and it may be that the Indonesian military, who feel already humiliated by the withdrawal from East Timor, will cling to this province far more. Several thousand troops and police are based there; at least 50 members of the security forces were killed there in 1999. Civilians have also been targeted by the military. In July 1999, more than 70 people died in a massacre by these forces (who suspect them of aiding the separatists) in the mountain village of Beutong Ateuh with a further 150,000 civilians fleeing the potential reprisals of the military.[52] In 1999, more than 250 people were killed in the province signalling the increased willingness of the Indonesian military to keep Aceh within the archipelago. Despite this it is clear that pro-independent sentiment has increased over time due to the brutality and human rights violations of the Indonesian armed forces. Now their demands have taken on extra political value with East Timor's positive vote in favour of independence. It seems unlikely, however, that Aceh will receive the same kind of treatment that East Timor did. Aceh has always been regarded as an integral part of the Indonesian state whereas East Timor was always one of its colonies. Shortly after the fall of Suharto in 1998, the head of Indonesia's armed forces, General Wiranto, took the unusual step of apologizing to the people of Aceh for the abuses of the previous ten years. However, this had the contrary effect of prompting Acehnese students to become more aggressive in the push for independence. They appear to think that a referendum along the lines that Jakarta organized for East Timor is at hand. Summing up the problem of this move in the eyes of the Indonesians, Dewi Fortuna Anwar (the president's spokeswoman) said:

> The Acehnese need to understand that Aceh is not East Timor ... Indonesia is an abstract concept, based on the former Netherlands East Indies. If we start allowing different parts to break away, it will be dismembered before we know where we are.[53]

In this sense it will be much more difficult to extricate itself from the new Indonesian dispensation.

In addition to Aceh and East Timor, the other problem for Indonesia and its programme of unifying the archipelago is in Irian Jaya (formerly West Papua) one of the poorest parts of the archipelago where they have a distinct language and cultural tradition. The main benefit for Indonesia and particularly American capital is the vast mineral wealth and natural resources there. Irian Jaya was incorporated under Indonesian control in 1961 just as it was about to gain independence from the Dutch. Alongside Aceh, it has one of the most serious campaigns to seek greater autonomy and control over their resources. Unfortunately, this province has attracted even less media attention than East Timor and the integration of Irian Jaya into Indonesia has been accepted by the UN despite the manipulation of the referendum in 1969 by the Indonesian authorities on the question of independence. Recent events suggest that with the media attention given to East Timor these other peripheries are now seizing the chance to try to break away from the hold of Jakarta. At the beginning of December 1999, Indonesian security forces fired on roughly 2,000 demonstrators who were demanding independence for Irian Jaya, wounding dozens of people according to human rights reports.[54]

The Muslim Trials

In the 1980s many Muslims were arrested and prosecuted on political charges in Indonesia on a variety of charges ranging from attempting to establish an Islamic state by force to undermining Pancasila. Most were convicted, and while some of the accusations may have had some basis, many people were convicted for simply exercising their right to express and practise their religious beliefs. The government appears very frightened of the spectre of Islamic fundamentalism and mistrusts any form of Islamic political agenda. Over 85 per cent of the Indonesian population is Muslim, but the majority are not fundamentalist and they are clearly not interested in establishing an Islamic state. Muslim leaders have charged, however, that the sole reason for government prosecutions is to discredit political Islam by linking it with violent fundamentalist extremism.[55] Beginning in the 1970s Muslim preachers whose lectures contained a political content have been brought to trial.

In 1987, in Jakarta, for instance, a series of trials started to prosecute twelve members of an Islamic prayer group on charges of subversion. Allegations of torture while in custody were prominent in these cases. In January 1988 Bambang Supriyanto, who acted as a courier for one of the leaders of the prayer group, and who later was sentenced to seven years' imprisonment on grounds of subversion, said that after his arrest,

> He was detained in a dark room for three months, and during the first month was interrogated every night 'with a great deal of torture.' According to his lawyers, Supriyanto was given electric shocks on his kneecaps and shoulder blades, and his toes were stamped on with the legs of chairs.[56]

It is clear that the intelligence services in Indonesia are using the judicial process and abusing human rights for political reasons. Efforts to discredit political Islam are part of a larger strategy to discredit potential rivals and all other groups that political involvement and participation will not be tolerated. Independent political expression, whether of a moderate or more animated form is not welcome at any level and clamping down on Islamic groups is one way the government has tried to get this message across.

Indonesian Reaction to Claims of Human Rights Violations

Like Malaysia, Indonesia has been vociferously critical of western demands for democratic reforms and changes in their policies on human rights. Ali Alatas, Indonesia's Foreign Minister, was in the forefront of the indignant responses to western accusations. At a United Nations Conference in Vienna in 1993 he argued:

> In a world where domination of the strong over the weak and interference between states are still a painful reality, no country or group of countries should arrogate unto itself the role of judge, jury, and executioner over other countries on this critical and sensitive issue. Any approach to human rights questions which is not motivated by a sincere desire to protect these rights, but by disguised political purposes or, worse, to serve as a pretext to wage a political campaign against another country cannot be justified.[57]

Alatas also criticized Australia for allowing East Timorese activists and protesters to hold demonstrations outside Indonesian consulates in Australia.[58] And when Amnesty International released a critical report on the human rights situation entitled 'Indonesia and East Timor: Power and Impunity', in September 1994, it was heavily criticized by government officials, diplomats and political analysts based in Jakarta. They argued that it was blowing the situation out of proportion: 'to say that ideological conformity is enforced at gunpoint is clearly an exaggeration', stated one diplomat.[59]

In June 1993, the Indonesian government announced the setting up of the Indonesian Commission on Human Rights. Critics argued, however, that the Commission has no real enforcement powers; it can only propose or offer suggestions to the government. Moreover, there was no consultation of other human rights groups in setting this body; all the 25 members were appointed by Suharto, which hardly lends credibility to its claims of impartiality.[60]

In the case of murdered trade unionist Marsinah, who led a strike at a watch-making factory, the same commission made the surprising move of actually claiming that torture was used to extract confessions from suspects. Despite this the body was strongly criticized by Frans Winarta of the legal aid foundation, who pointed out that the military was heavily involved in the investigation process and that the group was not based on the rule of law, but by presidential decree, and as such can be revoked anytime.[61]

When the US terminated the International Military and Training Programme for Indonesia, Indonesia responded by saying that it could 'live without IMET' and upheld the claim that East Timor was part of Indonesia.[62] Moreover, East Timor was declared off limits to outside visitors, and there were new arrests of suspected dissidents.

After the Dutch government cut off aid to the Suharto regime following the Dili massacre, the regime responded by stopping all transfers of aid from Dutch NGOs to their Indonesian counterparts in 1992. This had a negative effect on the Legal Aid Institute (LBH) which tried to bring attention to human rights abuses as well as providing free legal aid. The LBH was receiving 88 per cent of its $650,000 annual budget from a single Dutch NGO, Novib.[63]

The Jakarta regime also tried and was partly successful in using strong-arm tactics on its ASEAN neighbours to prevent international conferences on East Timor taking place. In 1994 pressure was placed on the Philippines, Malaysia and Thailand to stop these. However, these tactics unwittingly served to generate enormous publicity for the plight of the Timorese against what otherwise would have passed off unnoticed. In an effort to coerce the Philippines in line with 'ASEAN' solidarity, the Indonesian government announced that 250 Filipino fishermen had been caught and detained while they were fishing inside Indonesian waters, and at the same time twelve joint ventures between the two countries worth between $200 million and $300 million were to be cancelled. This tactic paid off because the same day, the President of the Philippines decided to ban East Timorese and other foreigners from attending the Manila conference on East Timor, in an explicit palliative to the Jakarta government.

The West's Response to Human Rights Violations in Indonesia

After Myanmar, the main target of western pressure for changing human rights in Southeast Asia is Indonesia. This, however, is a fairly recent development. Throughout the postwar period the United States paid little attention to human rights abuses in Indonesia; they certainly never assumed any priority under the Reagan administration. More recently, after increasing attention focused on Indonesian violations of rights in East Timor in 1975–76, the status of human rights has assumed a new importance. This significance was heightened by the 1991 Dili massacre, when Indonesian troops stationed in East Timor fired on a funeral procession that had become the focus of a political demonstration. In spite of the fact that central government in Jakarta transferred the blame to local military commanders the incident prompted efforts to persuade Indonesia to withdraw its troops and allow for the self-determination of the East Timorese. The contrast in the lenient punishment meted out to a few soldiers and the harsh sentences given to the Timorese 'instigators' after the Dili incident was seen as further evidence of Indonesia's oppression.

The US embassy in Jakarta sent several teams to Dili between November 1991 and February 1992. Various US State Department officials called upon the Indonesian government to investigate and impose appropriate punishments on those responsible for the murders. In addition the US Congress called for a solution based on self-determination for East Timor and, in 1993, they stopped Jordan from supplying Indonesia with US-made F5E fighter planes.[64]

More recently, the issue of East Timor gained international coverage when Indonesia played host to the Asia Pacific Economic Co-operation (APEC) meetings in the mid-1990s. Bad timing undermined plans for Suharto's attempt to showcase Indonesia as a leader in the Asia-Pacific region; the meetings coincided with the third anniversary of the Dili massacre. Twenty-nine East Timorese scaled the walls of the US Embassy compound in Jakarta and staged a sit-in protest over the continued occupation of the former colony by Indonesia; this coincided with three days of anti-Indonesian rioting in Dili. Human rights groups noted that over 120 people were arrested in East Timor following the unrest in Dili in November 1994 and at least 27 were arrested in conjunction with the protest in Jakarta. Warren Christopher, the US Secretary of State, asserted at the time, 'the relationship between the U.S. and Indonesia can never reach its highest level unless Americans have the confidence that there is effort here to respect human rights'.[65] Unfortunately, the grand ideals of human rights widely touted by the United States in the post-Cold War period appear to have been superseded by more practical and cynical economic goals.

During the APEC meetings Indonesia signed at least 17 business deals with US corporations worth over US$40 billion, including a giant natural gas liquefaction project with Exxon and telecommunication deals with Motorola and AT&T. Disregarding his previously high-brow stance on rights, President Bill Clinton stated at the APEC summit: 'We reject the notion that increasing economic ties and trade undermines the human rights agenda. We believe they advance together.'[66]

The British connection with East Timor has resulted in a major scandal for British foreign policy. Before the massacre in Dili in 1991, the Foreign Secretary, Douglas Hurd, urged the European Community to stop aid to countries that violated human rights, but shortly after the massacre, the British government increased its aid to the Indonesian regime by 250 per cent. Baroness Chalker, the Minister for Overseas Aid, claimed that this was to help the poor of Indonesia, but a large proportion of such aid comes with trade ties and a great deal of this is concerned with the supply of weapons.[67]

The European Union and some of its individual members also tied improvements in human rights to their relationship with Indonesia; Portugal has repeatedly condemned human rights abuses in Indonesia, particularly in relation to its former colony of East Timor, repeatedly calling for it to be given independence. After Catholic students were attacked by the Indonesian army at the University of East Timor (Universitas Timor or UNTIM), the Portuguese Foreign Minister described the incidents as 'grave' and 'serious' and stated that 'Indonesia's attitude does not surprise me [because] what can you expect from a dictatorship like that of Jakarta.'[68]

The US Congress also managed to override the executive branch of government in terminating the US$2.3 million for IMET (the International Military and Training Programme for Indonesia). This was one of the recommendations by Amnesty International and Asia Watch. Under this programme, Indonesian military officers were also brought to the United States for military education and training. The end of the programme, it was argued, would put pressure on the Indonesian government to hold the army to account. The US State Department objected, however, arguing this would undermine the Indonesian government, which had already established a committee of inquiry to investigate the killings. In the end the Congress managed to procure the termination.

Even these modest efforts to promote human rights in Indonesia have been mostly unsuccessful. This is partly due to the tendency of other ASEAN states to support Indonesia and the policy of 'constructive engagement'. Even non-ASEAN nations such as Australia, hoping to promote their own economic interests, have played down the human rights issue.

In May 1994, a conference on East Timor, which was held in the Philippines, was elevated to the status of an international incident. Diplomatic relations were slightly soured when the Indonesians decided to avoid a business gathering in Mindanao in May; this was exacerbated when the Indonesian Industry Minister failed to attend an official meeting with the Philippine President, Fidel Ramos. Ramos decided to ban foreign participants from the Asia-Pacific Conference on East Timor (APCET). Among those banned were

Danielle Mitterrand, the wife of the French President, and several Nobel laureates. The conference chairman, Renato Constantino Jr, argued that this was a clear 'surrender to Indonesian pressure ... the Ramos administration is acting as if the Philippines is Indonesia's 28th Province'.[69] Ramos defended his move as necessary to protect $700 million worth of business deals with Indonesia, including $250 million in investment and $450 million in joint venture schemes.[70]

Conclusion

Indonesia is the strongman of ASEAN, a vast archipelago of different cultures, religions and peoples melded into one by a state-sanctioned ideology, the Pancasila. It is a fast-developing society, accompanied with the usual strains that modernization and industrialization brings: urbanization, dislocation and the inevitable disparities between rich and poor. Given the diversity of Indonesia, it seems a miracle that the whole thing holds together. However, coercion and violations of human rights have played a large part in the glue holding these different entities together. The threat of disintegration in the Indonesian political structure has always been most prevalent when looked at from the perspective of its outlying peripheral areas. East Timor, West Papua and Aceh all require an acceptable democratic solution if Indonesia is to develop a human rights culture and continue down the path of democratization it has appeared to be following since 1997.

The case of East Timor, is the most striking. Unlike Cambodia's Pol Pot regime and other well publicized human rights violators, East Timor was little in the news over the past 30 years; indeed, it seemed like a conspiracy of silence to blot out any hint of the systematic destruction of the East Timorese nation. The invasion itself violated the basic and fundamental right to self-determination. In East Timor, the Indonesian regime has violated every conceivable human rights principle; the level and ferocity of the destruction has been immense. And in proportion to the population, the genocide in East Timor has been on a much larger scale than that under Pol Pot in Cambodia. The recent referendum which has been seen over-whelmingly as a vote in favour of complete independence for East Timor is but a step in the movement towards human rights and self-determination in the province after many years of repression and political violence. It is now necessary for Indonesia to tighten its rein on the army and militia forces to ensure a peaceful transition. This has proved problematic given the collusion between the Indonesian military forces and the pro-Indonesia militia.

While posing as a democratic formula for society, the Pancasila has been used repeatedly to suppress human rights by serving as the ideological basis for government restrictions on political activity. The New Order government still invokes 'the cult of stability' to maintain its legitimacy, constantly presenting images of economic and social instability from the past in order to justify human rights violations in the present and the future. The growing disparity between the haves and the have-nots has caused widespread tension and labour riots, which have been met with the heavy hand of the state. Labour leaders such as Pakpahan have been arrested and had their rights violated on the pretext of maintaining internal order. Other activists have been murdered for their efforts to improve the dire conditions of many Indonesian workers.

Freedom of expression is not high on the agenda either, with the closure of journals and newspapers, which may appear critical of government, and this is despite the rhetoric of 'openness' the Jakarta regime has recently promoted. When reacting to the controversial closure of the three journals in 1994, Suharto argued: 'Openness does not mean unlimited freedom, even worse, freedom to be hostile, pitting one party against another and unconstitutionally imposing one's ideas.'[71] One of Indonesia's most famous writers and a long-term prisoner of conscience, Pramoedya, who has been accused of disparaging national moral values in his literature, has summed up many of these sentiments:

> How happy European children are. They are free to criticize, to declare their disbelief in a policy, and without being punished, let alone exiled. Those who are criticized and those who criticize lose nothing, let alone their freedom. Rather, they advance by correcting each other ... Try to criticize your Kings. You would have been killed by the sword before uttering your final words ...[72]

Pramoedya is one man who has suffered severely for expressing ideas that have seemingly conflicted with the government's views. However, in very recent years and more specifically since the Asian economic crisis, signs have appeared that the Indonesians are softening in their version of authoritarianism. There is an argument that as a result of over 30 years of developmental policy pushed by the New Order, a new middle class has taken root which wants to increase the speed of political liberalization and is demanding greater democratization. Fewer military personnel have been appointed to top roles; widespread protests and dissatisfaction with the Suharto leadership saw its end and replacement with that of President Habibie, who was seen as more amenable and softer than Suharto and who opened up a dialogue on the East Timor issue, for instance. Perhaps this was one reason for his rapid decline. Democratization has also been taking place more rapidly in civil society; there are now hundreds of protest movements led by trade unionists and students as well as the development of quasi-opposition groups within society. The fall of Suharto opened the door to a more democratic civil society and a large number of new political groups have appeared. Since May 1998, the number of political parties has gone from roughly three to about 100, many of them with a weak social base, but all indicative of the burgeoning need in Indonesian politics to engender processes of democratization and end the paternal dictatorship. The establishment of the Independent Committee for Monitoring General Elections (Komite Independen Permantau Pernilu, or KIPP) has indicated a softer line in the regime. Others have argued that this top-down democratization is simply the state stage-managing politics in a cynical bid to maintain power. Despite the removal of Suharto, the upsurge in NGOs and the development of protest at economic conditions, the underlying conditions for authoritarianism still remain. The removal of Suharto and the exposure of the levels of corruption may be simply the first step in creating a more open and transparent Indonesian polity.

Poverty has also been an obstacle to democratization and the development of a human rights policy; as we have seen, many leaders in Southeast Asia have rested their case on delivering the goods and while Suharto's regime has improved many Indonesians lifestyles there is still a great deal of work to be done. Indonesia still retains enormous gaps between the haves and the have-nots.

In June 1999, Indonesia held its first democratic elections since the 1950s, in a bid to stave off the pressure from growing opposition. However, the growth of an independent civil society will not take place overnight; years of authoritarianism have produced an authoritarian political culture which will not simply disappear. The fact that many parts of the archipelago suffer from severe poverty, partly as a result of the economic crisis, partly as the result of economic corruption, will prevent the development of a human rights culture and processes of democratization in the short term. Democratic movements will also need to establish legitimacy on the basis of providing economic growth and development. Indonesia in that sense has a long way to go to dissolve the legacies of authoritarian government and disrespect for human rights.

5
Thailand and the Philippines

This chapter looks at the attitudes and records of Thailand and the Philippines towards human rights. In recent years these two states, of all the ASEAN members, appear to have improved their records in the areas of political and civil rights, appear less prone to coups and authoritarian regimes which characterized their societies previously and have made deliberative efforts in the further democratization of their societies. Both are now (at different levels) faced with managing political and social change in the transition to newly industrializing countries (NICs) status. The fact, however, that they appear to be approaching their 'human rights' situation in an open manner, allowing for freedom of speech and dialogue, suggests they will be in a better position to manage the trends towards democratization in the near future than regimes that appear determined to silence any kind of open, critical dialogue. Both societies have often been compared with one another as being more politically liberal in their views surrounding Asian values and its corollary arguments. Thailand, as far as one of the leading experts on Southeast Asia is concerned, 'has today the nearest approximation to Western style bourgeois democracy'.[1] The Philippines, which explicitly has as its model a western-style form of democracy, has often been seen as the economic basket case of Southeast Asia and has been vilified by authoritarians like Lee Kuan Yew, who use it as an example to vindicate their development before democracy thesis. However, it is a country that has had its legacy of authoritarian rule, and clearly to the detriment of developing a human rights culture. In the post-Marcos period of adjustment and political stability, it has made a brave effort to pursue long-term reforms, including the democratization of society and social change among others.

Both countries have come a long way in their prospects for democracy and human rights in comparison to other Southeast Asian states such as Singapore and Malaysia, which, given their level of economic development, have made little progress in the sphere of political liberalization. Despite this, the fact remains that these countries have major socioeconomic problems, which are seen in the poverty and maldevelopment in their countries.

THAILAND

Thailand is one of the most interesting and dynamic societies in Southeast Asia. It has a long tradition and a rich and diverse cultural heritage. In part this has been maintained because Thailand is the only state in the region which has never been colonized; it has maintained its independence and always managed to manipulate external powers to its benefit. This has enabled it to be free of foreign influence in the shaping of its political institutions in an indigenous fashion. The Thai population of 56 million is made up mainly of ethnic Tai who practise the Theravada form of Buddhism and includes tribal minorities such as the Hmong in the north. Furthermore, Thailand has a sizeable Chinese population of 10 per cent, many of whom have intermarried with the Thais.

Historical Overview

Like many states in Southeast Asia, Thailand has been subject to migration and movements of people. In the tenth century, migrations of ethnic Tai from south-west China started to congregate on the central plain which was under the control of the Cambodian Empire at Angkor. From the thirteenth century, two early states took form in what we now know as Thailand: Sukhotai (1220) and Chiang Mai (1296) both claimed these titles after victory in war. Slowly the basis of centralized authority began to take shape and between the fourteenth and eighteenth centuries (1350–1767), a kingdom named Ayuthaya in the Chao Phraya Basin predominated and managed to absorb Sukothai. In this period, fighting between these core Thai areas and Burma, Chiang Mai and Laos continued. Theravada Buddhists from Sri Lanka also made important inroads into Thai culture in this period, which ended with a Burmese invasion and the transfer of the capital to Thon Buri. In 1792, the Chakri Dynasty founded by King Rama I took over and shifted the seat of power to Bangkok. Just over 40 years later (1826) the British defeated the Burmese and with it, Thai–Burmese rivalry. Between 1836 and 1932, the Thai royal family made extensive efforts to modernize the economy and government and managed to control society and maintain their independence without being colonized. Trading routes were opened to the West and rice cultivation became the staple commercial activity in the economy.

Thailand has a very powerful mixture of military and bureaucratic influence within its political system and to some extent as a result also a fairly long history of violent coups. In this sense it resembles a 'bureaucratic polity', controlled by groups which have influence within the structure; it is not characterized by any form of democratic autonomy. In 1932, a coup brought the absolute monarchy to an end and military government to the forefront of Thai politics. The latter proclaimed a constitutional democracy, but in essence, the term democracy was used, as it has been countless times by military authorities, as a front for centralized authoritarian control. The first election was conducted the following year and regular elections took place thereafter. This should not obscure the fact, however, that most of the regimes that have come to power in Thailand have been undemocratic and typically controlled by the army. Between the 1930s and 1960s, the typical pattern was military government with intermittent civilian rule. Thailand, then, is unusual in that it has seen more than its fair share of cyclical alteration between democratic governments and military regimes, despite the fact that democracy has a record that dates to at least 1932, well ahead of most of the other former colonial states. In the 60 years between 1932 and 1992 there were 17 attempted military coups, many of them conducted at the level of internal faction fighting within the army itself. The more complicated and difficult problem of finding an appropriate formula in which power should be distributed has taken far longer and is still continuing in Thai society. Between 1932 and 1991, for instance, Thailand experienced at least 13 changes to its constitution. There has been stability in the Thai kingdom, however, notwithstanding the present formula, particularly in its most recent history between 1978 and 1998, when there was a power-sharing scheme between the military-bureaucratic elite on the one level and politicians on the other, known as a period of semi-democracy which allowed the middle classes in Thailand to develop in size and political strength.[2] The near bloodless seizure of power by the military in 1992 was a return to the old pattern of coups in Thailand. As one report put it: 'the culmination of a long period of animosity between the military and the aristocracy, whose traditional strength has been eroding in a period of democracy'.[3]

The Kingdom of Thailand is a democracy, governed by a constitutional monarchy under the present King Bhumibol Adulyadej who can theoretically exercise a great deal of influence in the country's political and economic affairs.

The most recent period of political tension resulted in the return of a popularly elected civilian government in 1992. In March 1992, elections to the Assembly saw three pro-military parties win 190 seats between them to capture a slim majority in the House of Representatives, which comprised 360 seats. The coup leader, Suchinda Kraprayoon, who was not a candidate in the elections, was then named Prime Minister much to the dismay of democratic forces. This was followed by the violent suppression of pro-democracy demonstrations in May 1992 which saw monarchical intervention into politics and the resignation of the Kraprayoon government. NGO sources argue that more than 50 protesters were killed during the bloodshed, a period which violated rights of freedom of expression, assembly and association. After free elections were staged in September 1992 in which the constitution was amended to make sure prime ministers could only be chosen from elected MPs, the Democratic Party established a five-party, pro-democracy coalition under the premiership of Chuan Leekpai. This was short-lived, however; the eruption of a scandal in May 1995 over land reform brought down the longest serving elected prime minister in Thai history. Two months later, new elections returned the rural-based Thai Nation Party under the leadership of Barnharn Silpa-Archa, who in April 1996 substantially reduced the role of the military in politics by reducing their representation in the Senate. By September, this government was in difficulties itself after a spate of corruption scandals. A three-day no confidence debate in the government saw the collapse of the Assembly and fresh elections slated for November 1996. In this election the New Aspiration Party (NAP) were returned by a two seat margin and formed a coalition of five political parties, and its leader, the former general Chavalit Yongchaiyudh, became the new prime minister. This coalition was also short-lived and, in late 1997, the veteran Chuan Leekpai resumed control of the Thai government after popular outrage brought down Yongchaiyudh's coalition who were credited with the failure of the Thai baht and the Asian economic crisis. Leekpai's government was the seventh in as many years, a coalition that characterized the state of Thai politics. The proliferation of political parties and the subsequent construction of coalition governments with slim majorities have been

portrayed as a central weakness in Thai politics, causing fragmentation, division and weak, fragile government. On October 11, 1997,
after the Asian economic crisis had started, a new constitution came
into force, which promised radical changes aimed at open and
democratic means involving participation from different sectors. The
result has been called a 'people's constitution', which changes the
rules in elections (previously attuned to vote buying and corrupt
practices). The new arrangements allow voters to elect two entities:
a district representative and a political party. This was specifically
designed to reduce the vote-buying nature of Thai elections and
allow for more democratic and open procedures. In itself this is a
positive step forward for the Thai political system.

The political system headed by Prime Minister Chuan Leekpai
enjoys widespread support for its reinvigorated commitment to
democracy; human rights and the pursuit of civil liberties has been
given a wider prominence under his direction with the new constitution aiming to control corruption and limit money politics. The
Thai democracy of the 1990s promoted the expansion of freedom of
speech and assembly. In comparison with Singapore, for instance,
Thai newspapers have a critical function and have offered alternative
viewpoints after the relaxation on constraints on the media. The
Chuan administration has made an effort to increase the number of
women in government and pursued policies designed to prevent and
control the notorious sex industry in Thailand with measures aimed
at curbing child prostitution and under-age labour. Human rights
NGOs have been given more credibility and respect than in the past.
Of 25 laws stipulated by the 1997 constitution, one of the key bills
is on the development of the National Human Rights Commission.

Political Economy

Since 1997, Thailand has had one of the most difficult economic
times in the region. It was where some people argue the Asian
economic crisis began, and many blame it on financial mismanagement, including the accumulation of bad debts through
over-lending, the weakness of the central banking system and poor
regulation in the financial sector. It was in May 1997 that the Thai
baht came under attack from currency speculators and was rapidly
put up for sale. By July, the Thai government had called on the IMF
to help bail it out, by which time the currency had devalued by

15–20 per cent. By the end of that month the Asian currency meltdown had begun and would contain severe shockwaves for the rest of the world. The immediate effect of the devaluation was a financial crisis that spread in contagion to the entire region. The crisis continued to plague the Thai economy well into 1999 even though the ruling coalition managed to hang on to power.

Thailand is classified as an NIC (newly industrializing country) with a free enterprise economic system, which puts it in the same category as countries like Malaysia and Indonesia. It has averaged more than 7 per cent annual growth since the 1960s (from the late 1980s to 1997 it was more than 8 per cent growth) prior to the economic disaster of 1997. In contrast to Singapore's state-managed intervention however, Thailand practises what has been described as a form of anarcho-capitalism. Some of the state institutions, such as the central bank, for instance, provide a central framework for economic activity; the private sector, on the other hand, explicitly ignores the legal framework of the state in its capitalistic enterprise. Individual economic interests are by and large protected and property rights respected, but like most developing countries the large majority of the population (nearly 65 per cent) still live in rural areas, and most people are largely dependent on agriculture for subsistence.

The income gap between town and country is still a major problem. In the demonstrations of April and May 1992, it was clearly the new emerging middle classes that dominated the protests. It was in urban Bangkok where most of these people showed their presence. The average GDP per capita in the greater Bangkok area was Baht 96,329 in comparison to the average per capita figure overall in Thailand which was Baht 32,026 (US$1,251) in 1989, or three times the amount.[4]

The economic results are similar for Thailand and Singapore; both have very high growth rates, but the contrast between the clean, orderly social management of Singapore and the frenetic chaos of Bangkok could not be more different.[5] The same applies to the application of laws and regulation, which in Thailand are carried out in a fairly haphazard and lax way, in contrast to Singapore's efficient and often overbearing system. Scenes of violence and demonstrations during the pro-democracy rallies in 1992 certainly had an effect on Thailand's ASEAN neighbours. In guarded responses in Malaysia and Singapore the press appeared to criticize notions of popular participation improving the undemocratic political system. The implications were clear; one Malaysian social analyst, Chandra

Muzaffar, argued that governments that are 'authoritarian should read the writing on the wall'. Such change had little impact in Singapore, where Lee Kuan Yew, Singapore's senior statesman, asserted: 'What will eventually determine the nature of Thailand's political system will be the interaction within Thai society itself', so clearly rejecting any idea that economic progress would lead to Western-style democracy.[6]

Thailand is clearly undergoing many changes, economically and politically. New forms of organization and politics have rapidly become apparent in the 1990s as a group of concerned citizens pointed out:

> In recent years Thailand's economy has become larger, more complex, and more closely linked to the world economy. Such an economic system can progress further only within a liberal economic and political framework, which permits everyone the freedom to participate and organise their economic rights ... Modern Thailand has become a complex, plural society. The democratic system ... provides every individual an equal opportunity to voice opinions and to participate in determining the future course of the country without domination by any one privileged group.[7]

Thailand is one of the most vulnerable countries in Southeast Asia because the Asian economic crisis had such devastating effects there. The economic crisis beginning in 1997 had severe effects on the social problems, which were already seen in the economy. Unemployment, for instance, became a major problem in 1998:

> The Department of Labour Protection and Welfare reported that 1,000 private companies closed down. Figures released by the Bank of Thailand showed that 670,000 people were laid off during the year, although it is difficult to get accurate estimates. Between January 1997 and February 1998, for instance, the IMF estimated from various sources that 54,000 workers had been laid off or made redundant. Unemployment (which has been typically low in Thailand) rose from 2.2 per cent of the labour force in February to 5.0 per cent or 1.61 million individuals in mid-year.[8]

Peter Warr also argued that:

> Whereas poverty afflicted around 8 per cent of the population in 1996, by the end of 1998, it could be 20 per cent, eliminating

almost all of the dramatic reductions in poverty incidence achieved since 1981. If growth remains below 6 per cent beyond 1998, poverty incidence can be expected to rise even further.[9]

These official statistics were conservative. The crisis had a major impact on education, forcing 800,000 school children and college students to drop out for financial reasons, while social problems (depression, mental disorders and large increases in suicide) were also noted. The social costs of the Asian economic crisis particularly affect the weakest and most vulnerable groups in society – migrants and refugees, for instance. Some societies that once welcomed the marginalized refugees and migrants have now decided they can no longer afford to sustain them. The trafficking in children and family members into prostitution will be more likely to increase in times of economic hardship. At the beginning of 1998, the Thai government announced it would be taking harsher measures against an estimated 800,000 illegal immigrants, most of them of Burmese origin. The Asian Development Bank in partial response to the situation earmarked US$1 billion to install a social safety net which might cover 300,000 people or roughly less than 10 per cent of the newly unemployed population. Such measures appear worthwhile but, until these systems are prepared to overhaul their financial management completely, they will continue to be prone to these crises.

Human Rights in Thailand

The problems affecting Thailand are those facing many developing nations. However, the adoption of a new constitution in October 1997 has signalled some real positive changes. This section deals in brief with some of the abuses committed under the system. These include extra-judicial killings, the misuse of police powers and mal-treatment of suspects, sexual discrimination against women and prostitution, and the use of child labour, among others. This section begins with what is usually regarded as a classical western right: freedom of speech and the freedom of the press in Thailand.

Freedom of Speech and the Press

The Thai constitution is fairly liberal when it comes to freedom of speech for its citizens, and observers familiar with western standards are quick to note how free the English-speaking press here is particularly in newspapers such as the *Nation* or to a lesser extent the *Bangkok Post*, which freely criticize government policies and politicians. Strictly off limits in Thailand are any criticisms of the monarchy, advocating communism or ethnic/racial and religious incitement. Press censorship is generally the rule when it comes to these subjects. Books, journals and the foreign media operate under similar guidelines. The electronic media are more tightly controlled than print because they are in the hands of the government and the military. Radio stations require a government licence and can be operated by government, military and private bodies. Government-produced newscasts on private stations must be played four times a day and military pronouncements once a day by law. Again, sometimes the application of these regulations can appear fairly lax; some stations that refused to play military commentaries were not closed down. There are internal censorship boards, which attempt to control the content of broadcasting, particularly politically sensitive issues and pornography. As in other parts of Asia (with the exception of Singapore) cable and satellite networks are beginning to develop at a rapid pace, allowing for a free flow of information.

Most foreign and domestic books are not normally censored unless they are critical of the royal family. A press law dating from 1941 allows the Director General of Police to stop the import of printed works deemed a threat to public order and morals; the last case of a foreign publication being banned was in 1989. In general academic research is allowed even on controversial issues such as corruption in political parties and among the police.

Overall, Thailand – certainly in comparison to its ASEAN neighbours such as Indonesia and Singapore – has a fairly good record in terms of rights that prioritize freedom of expression and the press.

Peaceful Assembly and Association

Another classical human right in the western tradition, which is generally accepted as a universal value, is the right to peaceful assembly. This is clearly a recognized principle in Thai law but in practice has not been fully adhered to, particularly in rural areas such as northeast Thailand. Inciting unrest is often used as an excuse in the countryside for arresting groups of more than ten peaceful protesters.

Perhaps the most famous example of violating this right in recent times was the Thammasat University massacre of October 1976, when armed police units and right-wing vigilante groups invaded the Thammasat University campus in Bangkok. Students on the campus were protesting against the return from three years' exile of the former Prime Minister, Field Marshal Thanom Kittikachorn, who was believed to be responsible for violent confrontations between army and students when he held office. Despite peaceful protests, the Border Patrol Police (trained and financed by the US) accused the students of insulting Crown Prince Vajiralongkorn. Although the protest was peaceful, the police responded with shocking brutality; students were burned to death, hanged from trees and shot at point blank range. The official number of deaths was estimated at 46, but observers argued that the true number was probably far higher; hundreds of casualties resulted from these actions and thousands were arrested. The same day a coup establishing a 24-man military junta was proclaimed with the consent of King Bhumibol, who appointed a civilian prime minister as a front. The latter was later replaced in a bloodless coup in October 1977 under General Kriangsak Chomanan. Thousands of students left Bangkok after the massacre, an estimated 3,000 were jailed and over 1 million books were burned in an event that ended the only period of democracy up to that point in Thailand's history.

In a smaller incident in 1993, thousands of farmers in Kamphaeng Phet province in northern Thailand blocked the main roads leading to the provincial capital in protest at the falling price of rice. The demonstration began peacefully, but violence ensued, with over 25 injuries and one death recorded as the police intervened. One farmer died from head injuries while in police custody, and his relatives were paid off with US$4,000 from the provincial administration.[10] In the end the case was hushed up, but instances of arbitrary violence like this are not uncommon. There are also reports of continued beatings in custody and extra-judicial killings on the part of the Thai police. In January 1999 there was a violent assault on protesting workers outside an auto parts factory, which led to renewed promises of improvement and disciplinary action to be taken against those involved. The police are also noted as being involved in various extra-judicial killings.

The fact that these are brought to the attention of the public through the print media does, however, represent some progress. Claims of police brutality, corruption and invasion of privacy rights have appeared as regular features within the newspapers.[11]

Freedom of association also precludes the operation of any type of Communist Party. The anti-Communist Act, initiated in 1933, and revised several times since makes it illegal to join, support or work for any Communist Party. If someone is arrested on communist charges they can be held for up to 480 days without trial. In general this law (which has been abused many times) gives enormous powers to the military and the police. Suspects can be arrested without warrant and held for longer than stipulated in the Criminal Procedure Code. A suspect's residence or vehicle can also be declared a restricted area; moreover, these powers are extended to occupy buildings. In February 1999, the Interior Minister, Sanan Kachorn-prasart, announced that the government was considering the abolition of this Act because it contradicted the new constitution and might be used to restrict citizens' rights.

Accusations of Abuse of Police Powers

Police in Thailand enjoy wide powers to arrest and hold suspects, but appear unaccountable in some ways to other institutions. Thai police are allowed to hold suspects for up to 48 hours without permission from other authorities. One MP argued that authority to issue warrants in criminal cases should be transferred to the courts.[12] The police have been accused several times of violating people's rights through the abuse of power. In January 1993, several parliamentarians called for a restructuring of the police department, arguing that curbs should be put on police officers' power of arrest and detention.

In April 1993, a former convict alleged on a popular television show that barbarous practices being instituted in jails in Thailand, including solitary confinement and unhygienic conditions. In March 1993 Somchai Panthepnimit claimed that he was beaten and tortured by the police after he was arrested for his alleged part in a parcel bombing that killed one person and injured five others. Somchai alleged that the police used torture and threats to his life to force a confession from him for a crime he did not commit. A lawyer from the Co-ordinating Group for Religion in Society (CGRS) stated that 'Physical and verbal assault is a common practice during police interrogation. It ranges from slapping on the face to beating and torturing.'[13] Despite the prohibition in the Criminal Code of cruel punishment or degrading treatment, there are credible reports that criminal suspects have been subjected to electric shocks and beatings to extract confessions. The poor conditions in prisons and immigration detention centres have also been widely criticized.

Reliable NGOs reported in 1993 that over 60 people died while in arrest or police custody in 1992, but these were incomplete figures and it is difficult to keep track of them. On 7 August 1993, five police officers from Ratchaburi Province were accused of killing a vegetable exporter who jumped a traffic light, but little progress has come of this.

In January 1994, a high-level panel was appointed to investigate an organized police racket, which was believed to be responsible for kidnapping, extortion and murder. Seven policemen were arrested after an initial investigation into 13 missing Chinese businessmen and the discovery of nine bodies in 1993.[14] Disappearances in Thailand are not as common as in the Philippines; but one case that has not been resolved is that of the former President of the Labor Congress of Thailand (LCT), Thanong Po-An, who has been missing since 1991. It is believed that he was kidnapped and killed because of his criticism of the military regime, which came to power in February of the same year. Overall, however, the number of disappearances reported appears to have declined.

The Refugee Problem

Thailand has always maintained fairly tough policies towards refugees. Between 1992 and April 1993, more than 385,000 Cambodians were voluntarily repatriated from Thailand, but 563 refused to return out of fear of persecution. The military denied them food and water for a week and then forcibly returned them to Cambodia. In mid-May, more than 10,000 refugees from Laos living in the camp of Chiang Kham were told they could no longer remain in Thailand indefinitely and were given warnings to leave.[15] Many of Thailand's problems with Burma were exacerbated by the various waves of refugees coming from different ethnic groups who suffered under the Burmese junta. The Karen and the Mon refugees have all posed various problems, which have not been handled effectively.

In 1990 there were almost 50,000 Burmese in Thailand without any legal documentation or legal status. The Thai response was to put pressure on international agencies to relieve this situation. Refugees were not recognized as such and were refused aid. Many of them were jailed or deported as illegal immigrants.[16] Several years later the problem had become much more severe; the numbers of internal refugees in Burma had reached nearly 500,000 and in Thailand 70,000 living in various Thai camps. While the Thai government allows various relief agencies to take care of the refugee problem on its own side of the border, it does not permit cross-border access to internally displaced people. In April 1993, a report stated that Thai soldiers had entered several refugee camps along the Burmese border and ordered those living there to leave the camps within 15 minutes and return to Burma, after which the camps were set on fire. The Thai press also reported the tough treatment meted out to Burmese student refugees who were forced into 'gulag'-like conditions in camps.

Immigration detention centres have also been criticized for their procedures, which do not fall under the regular prison system. Detainees can be held indefinitely if they fail to pay their bail or deportation costs, and are often prevented from leaving their cells. International observers have pointed out that the conditions at the Suan Phlu immigration detention centre, including extreme over-crowding and lack of medical care, can be seen as constituting cruel and unusual punishment.

To date, one of the most serious issues of human rights in Thailand remains the refugee problem, and particularly the huge number of Burmese in the country. A new constitution promulgated in October 1997 provided increased protection for citizens, but not for refugees or migrants. Thailand has still not signed the 1951 Convention on the Status of Refugees and there appears to be no real procedures that allow a person to be judged as a refugee who has a well founded fear of persecution. In short, this leads to arbitrary definitions of who is and who is not a refugee. Part of their aim is to repatriate many of the Burmese refugees (again something of a con-sequence of the economic crisis). The situation on the Thai–Myanmar border, where many of the refugees are based in camps, remains a precarious and particularly vulnerable one for the refugees. At various times ethnic Karen groups have been attacked. While we can hardly blame Thailand for the workings of dictatorial government in Myanmar, some of their policies have done little to alleviate the plight of these groups on their border. Migrants might expect similar harsh treatment: 'By July [1999], the Thai Labor Department reported that foreign workers had "vacated" 120,000 jobs to make way for Thai workers. Not all of those workers would have been deported, but deportations were clearly on the rise, and serious overcrowding in immigration centres had become an issue by the end of the year.'[17]

Social Problems

Thailand has some of the worst internal social and health problems of the Southeast Asian countries. It has a terrible reputation for being the sex industry's capital, with disturbing proportions of its population affected by the HIV virus and levels of exploitation which most western societies would consider unthinkable at the beginning of the twenty-first century. In part, much of the sex industry has been created and sustained by foreigners, but it remains a fact that a majority of Thai men also use prostitution as a form of recreation.

Perhaps the two main social problems that Thailand is facing today are those of child labour, and prostitution among both adults and children. In 1986 one estimate noted that 1.3 million children aged between 11 and 14 years old were in the labour force (70 per cent of this was in the agricultural sector). Employers at the time paid 2,000 baht (about US$74) a year to job placement agencies and roughly the same amount to the children's parents, who were forced to send their children to cities because of the scarce resources in rural villages; the same author noted that roughly 52,000 of these children were suffering from primary malnutrition.[18]

In 1984, several young prostitutes died in a fire at the seaside town of Phuket, provoking a public outcry. Other estimates say there are at least 1,000 child prostitutes in Bangkok (that is aged under 18, but many aged 11–14).[19] Many of these young girls are brought into Thailand from the northern hill tribe areas around Burma, southern China, Laos and Cambodia; Thai children are also sold on the international market for use in pornography and sexual services. The statistics vary; the more recent numbers which have been suggested for child sex workers varies from 13,000 to 800,000, a huge difference which illustrates the difficulty in obtaining reliable data on the problem. The figure of 800,000 prostitutes is from the Centre for the Protection of Children's Rights (CPCR). Various women's foundations in Thailand support this figure.[20] The exploitation has reached sickening proportions. The most well known cases involve foreigners, such as that of the 33-year-old Australian Bradley Pendragon, who was arrested in November 1993. When a Bangkok photographic shop processed pornographic pictures of him and several young women, it alerted a children's NGO and later police arrested Pendragon. The worst aspect of the affair was the description of the 'eight year old girl, sold to an agent by her grandmother, forced to perform oral sex on the Australian before he had intercourse with her 12 year old companion, sold to the same agent by her mother. She was crying. She had been beaten.' Similar incidents in the same period involved a Frenchman having sex with boys in Bangkok and a German couple in a Pattaya hotel having sex with two underage girls.[21] These are the common, sordid details of everyday life in the Thai sex industry.

CPCR has also estimated that there are about 2 million adult prostitutes, but other more conservative estimates have suggested these figures are really much lower. Whatever the true numbers, most agree that these are of major concern for Thai society and the rights of children in general in Asia.

The demand for the sex industry in Thailand also appears to have risen in recent years. Studies have shown that at least 50 per cent of Thai men's first sexual experience is with a prostitute. International sex tourism has become a major industry; 70 per cent of the tourists visiting Thailand are male and reports suggest that the majority of these are visiting for the sex industry.[22]

The implications of this problem for the development of HIV/AIDS is overwhelming; AIDS has reached epidemic proportions in Thailand, affecting over 500,000 victims; officials have noted that the number of children born with HIV is between 4,000 and 6,000 a year; by 1993, 36 per cent of the prostitutes in Thailand were estimated to have be HIV+ and Thailand now has the highest incidence of HIV/AIDS in Asia after India.[23] One writer, Vitit Muntarbhorn, Professor of Law at Chulalongkorn University, has conceptualized this problem as a violation of the individual human rights of the child. Many areas of Thai law and practice are in conflict with the International Convention on the Rights of the Child to which Thailand subscribes as a member of the International Convention on the Rights of the Child. The violations, in practice, include the differentiation in Thai law between Thai children and non-Thai children; the government's policy is to repatriate the latter, usually into the hands of repressive regimes like the Burmese, if they happen to be from there. Thais who are HIV+ also have difficulty gaining access to the formal legal system, and there is no real redress against discrimination by the authorities or services against people suffering from HIV.[24] The Asian economic crisis will have only served to make this problem worse.

In mid-November 1997, the Thai state enacted the Measures in Prevention and Suppression of Trafficking in Women and Children Act. This allows authorities to detain the victims (ironically) of the trafficking when they are caught in various searches of public places like airports, railway and bus stations and entertainment establishments among others. The law does not allow the authorities to detain the suspected trafficker often accompanying the victim.

In August 1998, the government enacted a new law in accordance with ILO standards which prohibits child labour and sex discrimination as well as outlawing sexual harassment, and allows for the standardization of working hours, overtime and benefits.

The Death Penalty

The death penalty is mandatory in Thailand for premeditated murder, the murder of an official on government business and regicide. It is an optional sentence for robbery, rape, kidnapping, arson and bombing that results in death. Insurrection, treason and espionage can also carry the death sentence. In 1979, new legislation made the death penalty optional for possession of more than 100 grams of heroin and mandatory for the production of drugs.

Between 1985 and 1988 at least 34 executions carried out in Thailand. There is no right to appeal against sentences imposed by military courts. The number of people under sentence of death in Thailand appears to be increasing. According to Amnesty International in May 1981, 121 people were under sentence of death; this figure had increased to 314 by February 1987.[25] The number sentenced to death appeared to decline in the 1990s.

Reactions by Thailand to the Debate on Human Rights

When the Prime Minister, Chuan Leekpai, opened the Bangkok regional preparatory meeting for the UN Conference on Human

Rights in March 1993, he argued that human rights should be developed within and not be imposed from outside. It was a position echoed by many of the countries in the region.[26] Thailand's former Foreign Minister in 1993 also argued that 'because of some weaknesses of our inner constitution, outsiders have taken advantage and try to make Asia a target practice ... for human rights to be valid, [the charges] should not emanate from international authorities.'[27]

In relations with one of its closest neighbours and one of the worst violators of human rights in the region, Myanamr (formerly Burma), Thailand has often played the 'constructive engagement' card. Anand Panyarachun, the interim Prime Minister, said as much when asked: 'We don't like what is happening in Burma ... We wish things were different in Burma ... But at the same time, in an Asian way, irrespective of my likes and dislikes for certain policies of certain regimes, it is none of my business to tell them what do with their country. If they decide to go down the drain, it is their decision.'[28]

When the government decided to allow the visit of eight Nobel peace prize laureates to Thailand in 1993, the military was adamantly opposed, arguing that the national interest would be compromised. The real issue they feared was that relationships between the Myanmar junta and the Thai military would be strained by the visit and that China would be offended by the entry of the Dalai Lama, the Tibetan leader in exile, and one of the proposed members of the visit. Noting the realpolitik of the scenario, one Thai political scientist concluded: 'Thailand has more to lose in terms of its strained relationships with its northern neighbours than to gain in terms of international prestige as a result of the visit.'[29] Despite this the Thai government bravely brushed aside objections and allowed the Dalai Lama to visit. More recently Thailand has called for flexible engagement in dealing with Myanmar, reserving the right to change their policies in the light of the recalcitrance of Myanmar to change.

Other writers have claimed that Thailand has bent democratic principles to accommodate bullying neighbours in ASEAN. This includes succumbing to pressure from Indonesia to forgo holding a conference on East Timor in Thailand and the handing over of the leader of a banned Malaysian religious sect to the Malaysian author-ities. Thai police and Malaysian agents forced vehicles belonging to the Kuala Lumpur-based sect, Al-Arquam, off the road in Thailand's northern Lampung Province in September 1994 and took the leader, Ashaari Mohamed, and ten of his followers into custody. Four members and Mohamed were thereafter handed over to the Malaysian Embassy in Thailand which transferred them to Kuala Lumpur, where they were held under the Internal Security Act. A *Bangkok Post* editorial was quoted as saying that the Thai government had granted a 'questionable request from a neighbour in the name of ASEAN solidarity' and the Thai Deputy Interior Minister, who was not informed of the action beforehand, stated that 'Malaysia has a special law on national security which is, by any words, a thug's law that allows the arrest of anyone.'[30]

More recently, in July 1999, Thailand attempted to change the ASEAN policy of constructive engagement to one of flexible engagement, which would enable them to raise issues about Myanmar, for instance, but in the framework of ASEAN. However, this idea fell through after the Thais could get the support of the Philippines only.

Attempts by the West to Influence Thailand's Policy

In 1993, at least five major American human rights groups and NGOs in Washington were lobbying to block all military aid to Thailand, including the provision of fellowships for Thai military personnel to study and train in the US. They were also planning to boycott visits to the US by members of the defunct National Peace-keeping Council who were actively involved in the May 1992 crackdown on pro-democracy demonstrations. The major concerns of human rights groups are with the continued involvement of the military in politics and their influence over foreign policy.

Human rights NGOs believe that the United States could promote democracy in Thailand by curbing the power of the Thai military.[31] In September 1994, a report stipulated that the Thai government and army were angry over a law linking US foreign aid to the former Khmer Rouge rebels including Pol Pot. The Thai military vehemently denied that it was selling arms or even offering shelter to the Khmer cadres along its eastern border who are trying to regain power in Cambodia. When the United States also showed concern over the lack of Thai support for democracy activists in Myanmar and refugees trying to flee to Thailand, the Thai government had a similarly defensive reaction. On 23 August 1994, the US President pushed forward the Foreign Operations Act which threatened to cut off aid to any country which supports the Khmer Rouge or 'impedes' support for Myanmar's democracy movement. The response of the Thai parliamentary budget committee was to freeze the US$480,000 allocated in the 1995 budget for the 40-year-old Joint US Military Advisory Group (JUSMAG), which organizes the annual US–Thai military exercises and helps US defence suppliers get orders from the Thai military.[32]

Conclusion

Thailand has had a fair degree of political violence in the twentieth century with many coups and internal bloodshed. In the 1990s it appeared to be coming to terms with its problems and moved towards a greater emphasis on democracy and human rights in its society. However, the past weighs heavily on Thai politics and we have seen that the Thammasat University massacre in 1976 will not easily be forgotten.

However, there has been some progress in instilling respect for individual human rights. Newspapers regularly let off political steam in their columns without repercussions, and a healthy climate of debate is engendered among academics and journalists, which is strikingly different from its ASEAN neighbours such as Malaysia and Singapore. Freedom of speech and the press is high on the agenda and this bodes well for the increasing democratization of Thai society.

Thailand is also faced, however, with other serious social problems including an HIV/AIDS epidemic, which threatens to eat away at the very social fabric of Thai society and destroy individual rights including those of innocent children. This is a classic example of where individual and community rights clash. Child prostitution and a thriving sex industry are problems that degrade and abuse the innocent and serve no dignified purpose in any society. This health problem will have devastating implications for the country. The use of child labour continues and has resulted in the abuse of the rights of young people.

Moreover, Thailand has still to promote fully the transferral of military to civilian politics. As one author notes, 'the military feels it has the right to intervene when they perceive that the government has lost legitimacy and civilian politics threaten military interests'.[33] Clearly, the army plays a large part in politics and their role needs to be tempered by the civilian government and the processes of democ-

ratization. The relationship between economic growth and democratization in Thailand is a complex one, however what happened in
Thailand during the economic crisis does lend some support for
liberal theories of democratization and human rights agendas in the
region. In response to a paper Kenneth Christie delivered at a
conference at Thammasat University, Bangkok, in June 1999, the
editor of the *Nation*, Kavi Chongkittavorn argued:

> Thailand is stuck in between the deep blue seas. What I mean is
> that Thailand has been in the past 67 years, since 1932, trying to
> instil the democracy and its institutions. We have gone through
> ups and downs. But finally we are getting there. Democracy is
> gradually taking root, although it is not yet very firm, with the
> promulgation of the new constitution in 1997. The democratic
> awareness has increased tremendously among the ordinary people.
> It is galvanised though a popular expression that is 'Khon jon koh
> mee sid na krab'. Literally, it means that the have-nots also have
> rights. In fact I would argue here that Thailand has successfully
> adjusted its position on both East and West interpretation of
> human rights and democracy. The reason why the human rights
> are respected here, ironically, it is due to the weakening of state
> power strengthening of public power. There are fewer abuses now
> by the state power. We need to improve on that.[34]

His comments help to elucidate what I would argue are the stronger
tendencies within Thai political culture, similar to the Philippines
in respect for improvements in democracy and human rights
progress compared to their neighbours. In July 1998, the Thai
Foreign Minister, Surin Pitsuwan, went much further than most of
his ASEAN colleagues in calling for change in the engrained principle
of 'non-interference' in the internal affairs of ASEAN members. He
argues that as a result of the economic crisis and its contagion-like
effect it may be 'time that ASEAN's cherished principle of non-inter-
vention is modified to allow ASEAN to play a constructive role in
preventing or resolving domestic issues with regional implications ...
When a matter of domestic concern poses a threat to regional
stability, a dose of peer pressure or friendly advice at the right time
can be helpful.'[35] Pitsuwan proposed a policy of 'flexible
engagement', suggesting a more ambitious role in some of the more
wayward and difficult members of ASEAN, and was supported by the

Philippines. The rest of ASEAN, however, maintained their usual opposition to any such ideas.

As the Thai economy becomes more global, it will be assessed by western standards of transparency and openness. The new constitution reflects this in some ways, attempting to adhere to and develop a more open and transparent system, moving away from the politics of patronage and corruption, which have characterized Thai politics. In this sense it is in the forefront of the ASEAN states as it moves towards more accountable practices of democracy and human rights standards.

Clearly, one of Thailand's problems as a NIC will be to improve the social and economic rights, reducing the gap between the rural and urban populations and managing these disparities while maintaining progress in democratization of respect for individual human rights. The social and economic costs of the Asian economic crisis have been substantial here. Resolving these will be one of Thailand most important tasks, and perhaps the major challenge it faces in the coming decades.

THE PHILIPPINES

The Philippines is a society that has had more contact and experience with the institutions of democracy and the notion of human rights than any other country in Southeast Asia. It is also one of the regions most underdeveloped and ill-regarded countries, and often seen as the 'economic basket case of the region'. The Revolution of 1896 was the first anti-colonial struggle in Asia, an incipient nationalism against imperial powers, in this case the Spanish. The idea was to establish a society along liberal and democratic lines with a degree of constitutionalism. The richness of tradition and diversity is again reflected in the political culture of the Filipinos; they are regarded as one of the most vibrant and colourful communities in Southeast Asia and the only Christian country in Asia with over 90 per cent claiming adherence. It is also seen as one of the most politically chaotic and unstable countries by many authoritarians who would prefer that democracy would not succeed here, because this might represent a precedent for their own discontented populations. In that sense the Philippines is a good example of how democracy and the processes that accompany democratization can be good for economic growth. Starting with

Corazon Aquino the new democratic dispensation had good reasons to reverse the dictatorial nature of the Marcos regime including instituting banking reforms, which benefited the Philippines when dealing with the Asian economic crisis.

Historical Overview

There is relatively little known about pre-colonial society in the Philippines because the Spanish, who controlled the 7,000 islands which comprise the archipelago for over 300 years, managed to eradicate most of what they felt was an uncivilized and pagan culture.[36] Originally, the Filipinos were of Malay stock closely related to the people of Indonesia and Malaysia; the Arabs arrived in the Sulu archipelago in 1380 and established a powerful Islamic influence over the next century, but their colonial history was to take a far different shape. In 1521, the Spanish explorer Magellan claimed the islands in the name of King Philip II at Cebu; where he was killed by local chiefs. Ruy Lopez de Villalobos, his successor, called the country Filipinos after Philip II of Spain. It was on Cebu in 1565 after conflict between the colonists and the locals that the first permanent Spanish outpost was set up in 1571. The Spaniards decided to consolidate this and moved their seat of control to Manila, gradually extending their control to the entire region. There were few indigenous institutions that had been established in any way before the onslaught of colonialism.

Following the defeat of the Spanish Armada in 1588 the Spanish Empire suffered a long period of relative decline and never managed to exploit their new acquisition. Eventually the colony became highly subsidized by the imperial treasury and up to the late eighteenth century was something of a liability. It was only with the introduction of tobacco crops in 1782 that Spain started to enjoy some profit. In the meantime other imperial powers were keen to take advantage of Spain's decline; the British even managed to take over Manila for one year. Competition from the imperial powers was a minor problem for the Spanish, however; over 100 revolts against colonial rule took place in the Philippines between the late eighteenth and nineteenth centuries alone. The final straw was the execution of the scholar, doctor and writer, Jose Rizal, in 1896, which pushed revolt to its ultimate stage creating a martyr in the process. The Spanish-American war of 1898 sounded the death knell of Spanish influence in the region. However, one colonial master was replaced by another, whose explicit aim was to civilize and evangelize the islands (the Spanish had already done the latter). The United States purchased the islands from the Spanish for US$20 million. Today more than 90 per cent of the population of 65 million are Catholics; in the extreme south of the archipelago, Islam is the religion of roughly 5 per cent of the population and has traditionally been seen as a force for resistance against the central government in Manila.

The Americans ruled for 48 years, but were subject to resistance from regular armies and then guerrilla forces. With the establishment of a colonial civilian government, the stage was set for the introduction of elections and institutions which attempted to replicate aspects of American-style democracy. The US was not a typical colonial power in the European mode; once institutions were established here and the people were regarded as ready for democracy, they would take their leave. The US colonial period attempted to impose democracy on the Philippines, however they were in fact superimposing democratic institutions on a system where the political economy was controlled by landed wealth and local family rule. The system was what one author called a *cacique* democracy, with so much influence from family patriarchs and local bosses.[37] Patrimonialism and patron–clientelism were the norms in the political and economic structure, and this has led scholars to question the depth and stability of Filipino democracy.

By 1935, the Philippines had been granted commonwealth status, with Manuel L. Quezon sworn in as President in a transitional phase pending full independence. In the meantime, the Japanese invaded and held the islands during the Second World War until the United States again intervened in 1944. Full independence was granted on 4 July 1946, and subsequently the Philippines was to be seen as a 'showcase of democracy' in Southeast Asia. It was a model few appeared to have adopted in the region. The United States left deep imprints on the political and economic shape of the country. Between 1935 and 1972, the country was governed under a constitution that was almost a carbon copy of the US constitution, including an elected president along American lines. The Philippines Congress has two chambers: a House of Representatives with roughly 260 seats and three-year terms, and a Senate, which has 24 members, elected usually for a six-year term. Both houses are elected in differing mixtures of single seats and proportional representation.

Between 1950 and the mid-1960s the Philippines experienced vigorous inter-party conflict, most importantly between the Nacionalista Party and the Liberal Party, experiencing fairly rapid turnover of governments. The politics of patronage and clientelism, a remnant from the Spanish Empire, was reinvigorated in this period.

In 1965, Ferdinand Marcos came to power and when re-elected in 1969, began to develop more than a taste for authoritarian rule. In 1972, Marcos declared martial law, which meant he could stay in office beyond the constitutional maximum of two terms. This developed into authoritarian control, random violence and large-scale corruption, which lasted until 1986. Civil and political rights fell apart under his misrule and the lack of any independent safeguards allowed his regime to arrest over 50,000 people, many of whom were held without trial while others simply disappeared. Human rights of any kind were abandoned during his dictatorship.[38] Both Muslim and communist guerrillas attacked his regime and there was widespread insurgency against his government. Marcos centralized political authority and favoured his cronies from his home base of Ilocos Norte, giving rise to the term 'crony capitalism'. He personally oversaw ballot rigging and fraud. In fact, Marcos represented the epitome of *cacique* politics, taking the system of patrimonial politics to the extreme and favouring his cronies and loyal supporters while deeply harming the overall Filipino political economy.[39]

The Philippines, already engulfed in human rights abuses, widespread corruption and political decay, was shocked by the assassination of opposition politician Benigno Aquino in August 1983 at Manila airport minutes after his arrival from overseas. A snap election in 1986 after several years of protests saw the opposition coalesce around his widow, Corazon Aquino. Despite both parties claiming victory, Aquino took the initiative and instituted a programme of non-violent civil unrest. Following this a constitutional democracy was restored after a mini-revolution based on 'people power'. Then Ferdinand Marcos and his wife, Imelda, fled the country for exile in Hawaii.

The Aquino period was hardly a peaceful interlude. Despite the approval of a new constitution which checks the president's power by a strong judiciary and single-term limit, there were still challenges from the military, including seven coup attempts in six years, and the challenges of a weak economy that had been overseen by crony capitalism hung over the administration. As one author argued:

Marcos' years of suppression, intimidation, corruption and cronyism had damaged the fabric of Philippine society. Not only did his dictatorship use political resentment, instability and stronger justification for communist-armed struggle and ethnic succession; it also brought about widespread poverty, economic disparity and social dislocation. In other words, the country was in a shambles – politically, economically and socially. Filipinos had lost confidence in the country's political and economic system, triggering further migration and flight of capital from the country. Philippine society was dangerously polarised, with the balance favouring Marcos' cronies. Restoring hope and confidence in the system was therefore crucial to efforts to normalise the country's political life. Such was the broad political context in which the 1987 Constitution was drafted.[40]

A second challenge was the Communist Party, which was still posing a military threat to constitutional government. Finally, there was an incipient Muslim rebellion in the southern provinces in this period.

Aquino failed to rejuvenate the Filipino economy, but did manage to sustain a constitutional democracy in the face of many hardships. In May 1992, General Fidel Ramos, her former Defence Minister, who won 23.6 per cent of the vote in a multi-party election, succeeded Aquino in office. Ramos was faced with a much easier task in many ways and he has managed to neutralize the Muslim and communist challenges, while generating fairly high economic growth. Ramos has argued that the military was a crucial element in the politics of transition in the Philippines, citing their role in the 1986 changeover from authoritarian rule under Marcos to constitutional democracy under Aquino.[41]

Politically, the period after 1992 witnessed a change in the relationship between the US and the Philippine governments; the US military presence was formally removed when they had to give up tenured installations at Subic Bay Naval Base and Clark Air Base. More than a century of colonial and postcolonial 'special relationship' had come to an end. Ramos provided the Philippines with a strong and stable basis for government allowing the country to adjust in this period. In September 1996, the government signed a peace contract with the Moro National Liberation Front, which ended in a formal sense the MNLF's struggle of over 24 years for the autonomy of the Mindanao Province and many of their forces were integrated into the Philippine army in 1997. A splinter group, however, still continues to deny complete peace to this section of the archipelago, the militant Moro Islamic Liberation front (MILF) has continued to oppose the peace agreement and a final solution remains out of reach for the time being. In fact, there were many who would have liked to see amendments in the constitution to allow Ramos to run for a second term, a process that developed in 1997, called charter change (cha-cha). Powerful figures, however, such as the former president Corazon Aquino and Cardinal Jaime Sin, both key players in the democratic resistance against Marcos, stepped in to oppose this, using people power techniques such as staging large rallies. The Supreme Court ruled that there could be no amendments to the constitution through signature campaigns.

In 1998, the vice-president, Joseph Estrada, was elected to power on a poll of 46.4 per cent, the remaining 54 per cent being divided between seven other candidates. It remains to be seen whether Estrada, who ran on a pro-poor platform, can fulfil the legacy of restoring and maintaining democracy. He has already been accused in some quarters of returning to cronyism and appointing favourites. He appears to play the populist card, something that Marcos was also keen on doing. In this sense his election is a testimony to the role of personalities in Philippine politics. Estrada was a film star with a Robin Hood-type personality, who positioned himself as the outside candidate determined to raise the living standards of the poor and underprivileged. Criticized by other groups, who see him as an uneducated, hard-drinking womanizer, it is nevertheless clear that he struck a chord among many people. The problems he faces are less ones of people's faith in democracy than the weakness of the Philippine state in combating corruption and violence. The so-called tradition of 'guns, goons and gold', which feeds into the elections in the Philippines, is pervasive in a culture that still contains many criminal and lawless elements.[42] In 1997, for instance, an estimated 200 people were kidnapped and 228 million pesos paid in ransom. Some of these offences have even been attributed to the police force. The Philippines in that sense will have trouble in establishing the correct balance between democracy on the one hand (which it has plenty of) and stability, growth and justice (on the other) which sometimes seem in short supply.

Political Economy

Economically, the Philippines is one of the weakest of the ASEAN countries, with its development and growth lagging well behind those of the other member states. Structural economic problems remain, including an oligarchic elite, which has a significant influence over the economy. One of Ramos's most difficult tasks (and now Estrada's) was to reform this situation, complementing political democratization with economic and social transformation. The 1980s were seen as the lost decade for the Philippine economy with annual growth rates reaching 0.9 per cent and real per capita income substantially declining. More recently it has started the movement towards economic modernization and appears to be sorting out its economic problems. Under Ramos the Philippines moved quickly to shrug off its image as the economic basket case of the region by attracting foreign investment, cleaning up corruption and expanding utilities. Unfortunately, this growth (like many of the other Southeast Asian states) has been stalled by the Asian economic crisis. By October 1998, more than one year after the crisis had begun, the Philippine peso was worth 40 per cent less against the US dollar than it was at the beginning of the crisis.

In 1991 the per capita GNP was US$730; the *Social Indicators of Development Report 1993* indicates an average annual 1.2 per cent growth rate for the 25-year period between 1965 and 1990. Signs of recovery in 1994 were greeted with optimism and renewed political claims that democracy and economic growth could go hand in hand; the economy grew 5.1 per cent in the first quarter of 1994, a vast improvement over the negative 0.5 per cent in 1991, 0.1 per cent in 1992 and 1.7 per cent in 1993.[43] Despite some growth, however, social conditions and poverty show little sign of improvement, with GDP growth lagging behind that of population growth. During martial law the gap between rich and poor widened significantly. In 1971 the poorest 60 per cent of Philippine households received only 25 per cent of national income and saw this share fall further to 22.4 per cent in 1979. The richest 10 per cent of the population, on the other hand, saw their share of income increase from 37.1 per cent to 41.7 per cent in the same period.[44] At the end of the 1980s one estimate showed that 75 per cent of the population of the Philippines (45 million people) lived below the poverty line.[45]

Of all the ASEAN nations, the Philippines has the lowest domestic savings rate; only 14.6 per cent of its GDP is saved in comparison to over 30 per cent for most of the other states and over 40 per cent for Singapore.[46] The effects of the weak economy were significant for large proportions of the population; consider this version of the 'Asian miracle' in the Philippines by a development expert:

> In the early 1990's there were some 3,000 families (20,000 people) making a living rummaging through, sorting, and selling garbage on Smoky Mountain. Everything has a value from broken glass (0.10 pesos/kilo), to rubber (1.5 pesos/kg), and bones (0.5 pesos/kg). Scavenging for 12 hours a day can earn the picker US$ 0.75–1.25.[47]

At least part of their problems is due to an entrenched oligarchic elite, which continues to dominate the economy and society of the Philippines; this is similar in some respect to the Indonesian situation. Since 1972 the Philippines national debt has risen from US$2.7 billion to US$29 billion, most of this the result of Marcos's drain on the treasury and his fraudulent activities. Despite the World Bank providing more than US$7.5 billion, the growth rate has fallen and poverty has increased in this same time period.

Nevertheless, there were signs of change in the 1990s that were very positive. Infant mortality decreased, with the number of deaths per 1,000 births falling from 72 in 1965 to 40 in 1995. At the same time, the percentage of illiterate people in the Philippines aged 15 and above was reduced by 10 per cent.

The revision of the relationship with multilateral financial bodies, with its implications for the rescheduling of debt and development assistance, after Marcos's fall from power, has boosted the economic potential of the islands. Investment in the Philippines has increased as well as net sales of major commodities. GNP, which started to grow under the Aquino regime, continued to expand steadily under the Ramos administration. In fact, the value of exports increased from US$4.6 billion in 1985 to US$7.1 billion in 1988.[48]

President Ramos also announced a larger vision for economic growth in the Philippines, similar to Mahathir's 2020 vision for Malaysia. This was called the 'Philippines 2000', and aimed to transform the Philippines into a newly industrializing country (NIC). The main question was whether such a goal could be achieved while sustaining a democratic political system, as most of the other countries in the region have generally achieved their success under authoritarian auspices.

The plan was based on three very important criteria: (1) restoring political stability, (2) opening up the economy by dismantling the monopolies and cartels, which are against the public interest; and (3) ending bureaucratic corruption and street crime. The plan sought to increase the growth rate to between 6 and 8 per cent in the period 1992–98, reduce poverty to less than 30 per cent of the population, keep inflation in single digits and increase exports and investments. In addition it planned to increase per capita income to $1,000.[49] One of the major aspects of this plan was to attempt to remove some of the stranglehold on the economy of the major families, long thought to hold too much power over key segments of the economy. The inefficient telecommunications industry, for instance, was one of the first for a complete overhaul.

Ramos's administration is also credited with ending the power crisis (crippling power shortages had plagued Manila and other urban areas for long periods of time because of the weak grid system).

By 1994 and 1995, the economy was achieving growth rates of between 5.1 and 5.7 per cent, a significant increase over that of the Aquino administration. The Philippines managed to avoid the worst fallout of the Asian economic crisis because it had already begun to reform its financial sectors and banking system; moreover, it had achieved a fiscal surplus by the mid-1990s. Despite the fact that growth slowed down after the crisis, it was spared the negative consequences seen in Thailand and Indonesia.

At the end of June 1998, President Ramos transferred power to his successor, Joseph Estrada. Ramos had delivered a powerful and positive growth rate during his presidency, which was only slightly marred by the arrival of the Asian economic crisis. The Philippines is no longer seen as the weakest economy. Ramos pursued policies of liberalization, deregulation and the privatization of key industries within the economic sector. During his period in office telecommunications, banking and some domestic transportation were placed in the hands of the private sector. Under Ramos, the Philippines ended over 35 years of IMF supervision. Some of the results were mixed; under his government the number of families living below the poverty line decreased by 7 per cent, but it also seems that the gap between rich and poor increased in the same period.[50] Nevertheless, given the history of the Philippines the economic atmosphere seemed ebullient, as it headed towards the twenty-first century.

Human Rights under the Marcos Regime

If ever there were a case against the development before democracy dictum that so many authoritarian leaders in East Asia relied on so freely, then a large part of that case would be represented by the Philippines under the regime of Ferdinand Marcos.

The Marcos regime saw some of the worst infringements and violations of human rights in the history of the Philippines. This began with the introduction of martial law on September 23, 1972, during which thousands of government critics and opposition politicians were arrested and detained. Habeas corpus was suspended, Congress was closed and the Executive ruled by presidential decrees. Over 50,000 people were arrested, including Benigno Aquino Jr, the leader of the Liberal Party. Military courts were initiated and personal arms were confiscated. Prior to this the Philippines constitution of 1935 had sought to provide guarantees of freedom and personal liberties. Martial law and the development of a new constitution in 1973 were supposed to liberate the country and act as a reform mechanism. The result, however, was dictatorship and widespread abuse of fundamental human rights. Marcos's declaration of martial law argued that the Philippines was in a state of rebellion and that this threatened to undermine the republic. People could now be arbitrarily arrested, searched and their property seized; their movements could be restricted; 'subversive' publications could be shut down; curfews imposed and rallies banned, along with a whole host of other restrictions passed in the name of safeguarding the republic.

The right to strike in 'vital' industries was disallowed and large-scale corruption followed in which Marcos and his close business associates, along with his family, amassed enormous personal fortunes at the expense of the masses. Martial law officially lasted eight and a half years, but it was to continue in spirit even after 1981. By the mid-1980s Marcos had already issued over 1,000 decrees and orders, most of which were highly repressive. One example of this was presidential decree 1836, which was apparently issued in January 1981, one day before the lifting of the martial law. It enabled the President to order the arrest of anyone who might undermine national security and public safety or, as one author argued, the 'full control over the freedom of every man, woman and child in the Philippines, since no charge or complaint was needed and no intervention of a court or prosecutor was admitted. All that was required was that the detention or arrest be ordered by the

President in his judgement.'[51] Another proclamation of Marcos, number 2045 of 1983, was that the writ of habeas corpus was to remain suspended in two regions in Mindanao and in cases involving national security crimes.[52]

Under Marcos, torture was widespread, with the preferred instrument the 'cranker dynamo'. Wires from a 90-volt, hand-cranked field telephone were attached to a person's sex organs and fingers. When the crank was turned, they screamed in pain. Of course, Marcos had a different view of martial law; he argued:

> Martial law, together with the New Society that has emerged from its reforms, is in fact a revolution of the poor, for it is aimed at protecting the individual, helpless, until then, from the power of the oligarchs. Martial law was therefore a blow struck in the name of human rights.[53]

The US Congress attempted in October 1977 to reduce military aid to the Philippine government, but the Carter administration opposed this, arguing that cuts in military aid 'would have a serious impact upon important programs with a treaty ally which allows us [Americans] the use of valuable military facilities'. Prior to this Secretary of State Cyrus Vance had already declared that 'whatever the human rights violations' in the Philippines, aid would not be cut off because of 'overriding security considerations'.[54] However, security aid provided by the United States to the Philippines was clearly used against the people. Cardinal Sin pointed this out when he argued that 'the United States should stop sending military aid to the Philippines because it only goes to slaughter Filipinos'.[55]

Human Rights under the Aquino and Ramos Governments

President Aquino had three main objectives in the first few years of her rule: national reconciliation, the reconstruction of democratic institutions, and economic recovery and reform. The Aquino government in itself was partly the result of the struggle against the dictatorship of Marcos and therefore a struggle against the abuses of human rights. As one author has argued:

> Even though it was the bankruptcy of the Marcos administration that precipitated the legitimacy crisis rather than any particular devotion to democracy by the people, the 'democratic idea'

promoted by Aquino and her followers captured the popular imagination, something the communists never understood. The widespread support she received represented both a popular perception that democratic reform could get the country out of its economic crisis and a growing consensus among the wealthy that Marcos's abuses of power had become so extreme as to undermine business prospects and threaten to send the country into political chaos. Aquino came to power in a situation that was ripe for far-reaching institutional and organizational reform.[56]

There is no doubt that there has been a positive change in the political system and the human rights situation in the transition from Marcos's dictatorship to the democracy espoused by Aquino. The Aquino administration established the 'Freedom Constitution' aimed at entrenching human rights through various international commitments such as ratifying international documents on human rights. Much of this was specifically designed to educate and provide training to Filipinos on human rights. Knowledge of human rights, for instance, became part of qualifying examinations for the civil service. Freedom of speech and the press were restored, along with an independent body to examine allegations of rights abuses. The number of extra-judicial killings declined both by government forces and insurgents. Six hundred political prisoners were released, habeas corpus was restored, a commission for human rights was established and the judiciary regained its independence.

One of the difficulties that remained was the strength of the insurgency movement in the Philippines; the communist guerrilla New People's Army (NPA) and the Communist Party of the Philippines (CCP) both flourished under the Marcos regime, gaining widespread support. In the wake of the People Power 'revolution' in 1986, which brought Aquino to power, both armed factions called for a cease-fire and attempted to negotiate a settlement with the new government. These talks, however, broke down due to differences over power-sharing and the conflict resumed in 1987. This left Aquino extremely reliant on the military to maintain stability and prevented her from making a complete break with the Marcos period.

Human rights ultimately suffered through efforts to combat communist insurgents. The role of the military in politics and in government increased, although not to the extent seen in Thailand or Indonesia. Consequently, violations by the military remained widespread and the campaigns to separate the NPA from it base areas resulted in the dislocation of thousands of refugees.

In addition, the NPA has been responsible for human rights violations, particularly by the two- to three-man 'sparrow units' that regularly seized firearms and ammunition needed by the guerrillas. One example of this is when the NPA clubbed to death a woman who refused to pay taxes to them. Thereafter, they hanged her body in her living room as a warning to other residents of the province of Davao del Norte.[57]

In 1992, the Philippine Congress approved an amnesty for 4,485 former communist guerrillas and Muslim secessionists (the Moro National Liberation Front, MLNF), it also endorsed the legislation of the outlawed Communist Party of the Philippines and agreed to abolish the country's anti-subversion laws in an attempt to reach political reconciliation and an end to the 23-year-old insurgency. The NPA reacted suspiciously, with one of their leaders declaring that this was 'deceptive'; other commentators were similarly sceptical as to whether those involved would receive a presidential pardon if they admitted their crimes. In August 1992, Ramos declared that the armed forces would continue to root out communists who rejected the amnesty.[58] By September 1996, however, the government had decided to sue for peace and an accord was signed formally ending the struggle for secession in Mindanao. Autonomy was theoretically granted to MLNF, but splinter groups, such as the Moro Islamic Liberation Front (MILF), opposed the agreement and tensions continue.

Disappearances

Amnesty International has reported that more than 50 people alleged to be opponents or critics of the government disappeared in the Philippines in 1990. There is some evidence that at least five of the disappeared were killed while in custody. The agents behind these disappearances were mainly government or government-supported security forces, including the Philippine Army (PA), the paramilitary Philippine Constabulary (PC), the official paramilitary auxiliary Citizens' Armed Forces Geographical Unit (CAFGU) and various semi-official 'vigilante' groups operating with the support or acquiescence of the military command.[59] Typical cases of 'disappearances' by the official CAFGU group involve leftists in various organizations. One person was abducted because he refused to join his local CAFGU:

Antonio Buenavista, aged 42 and a member of a fishing organisa-
tion in Bulacan province, Bangkalis, was abducted by a group of
armed men on January 7, 1990 in the village of Santa Cruz,
Hagonoy municipality ... He has not been seen since.[60]

It should be stressed, however, that these violations are not only
carried out by CAFGUs, but also by the various other private and gov-
ernmental-sponsored paramilitary, vigilante and insurgent groups.

Extra-judicial Killings

In the first half of 1993, the Commission on Human Rights (CHR)
noted 93 extra-judicial killings; a significant decrease from the 353
that took place in 1992. Numbers vary depending on what one is
counting. The Commission includes violations by both government
and insurgent groups including the CPP/NPA; some NGOs merely
count the figures for government-sponsored groups.

Regardless of the source, most reports agree that the majority of
killings are committed by the military forces and the police; in one
instance, William Rom, a researcher for Sildap-Sidlakan, an NGO for
tribal communities, was hacked to death, in July 1993, by *bolo*-
wielding CAFGU members who accused him of being an NPA
member. The Task Force Detainees of the Philippines (TFDP), a
prominent NGO, attributes 19 per cent of all the human rights
abuses in the first year of the Ramos presidency to CAFGUs.

The International Labour Organization, and various human rights
organizations concerned over the murder of trade union activists
and labour leaders, tried to persuade the government to disband the
CAFGUs; in October 1993, Ramos announced that 11,000 (out of
72,000) would be demobilized by the end of 1994. This, however,
was probably unrealistic given the opposition from within the
militia for any plans to make them unemployed. The NPA was also
active in this area of extra-judicial killings, and the most notorious
elements belonged to the Alex Boncayo Brigade (ABB), a ruthless
communist assassination squad controlled by the Manila-Rizal
Regional Committee of the Philippine Communist Party. This was
set up in 1984 after the death of a labour leader at the hands of the
security forces; it became more active following the downfall of
Marcos in the late 1980s, engaging in a campaign of urban terror
against government figures, the police and US military personnel.

Since mid-1994, however, the movement has been in some disarray following the arrest of Felimon Lagman, the leader of the Manila wing of the Brigade and the chief commander.

Arbitrary arrest, detention and exile are, in theory, illegal under the new Philippine constitution, but in practice they still occur. The CHR found that there were 42 cases of illegal arrest and detention in the first half of 1993 in comparison to 158 for all of 1992, while the TFDP found that 254 illegal arrests had occurred in the first half of 1993 compared with 938 in the previous years (again the figures being based on different measures). The new government of Ramos in September 1992 repealed the Anti-Subversion Law, which had provided for the legal basis of warrantless searches and arrests.

Despite the new provisions, the TFDP claims that there are roughly 350 political prisoners held illegally. And the CHR reported an increase in arrest and detention in the first year of the Ramos administration – 195 in the first half of 1993 compared to only 54 in the second half of 1992. Ironically, the committee attributes this increase to the new emphasis on economic development.

The Aquino legacy is a mixed one. Her government brought the country together, restored democracy and some freedoms and improved the economy. Others, however, criticized her on the grounds that she was more interested in the form rather than the substance of democracy; her approach to government, politics and social issues was in many ways a conservative one. Given the state of the Philippines in 1986, however, after the Philippines' disastrous flirtation with authoritarianism under Marcos, it may have been unwise and difficult to introduce radical reforms. Aquino's successor, Ramos, also came under criticism from exiled political parties for imposing a martial law situation akin to the Marcos period. The leader of the National Democratic Front accused him of 'following in the footsteps of Marcos by stepping up his total war against the people'. He also cited the influence of the army generals in the Philippine cabinet and the increase in the military budget which now stands at 30 billion pesos (US$1.2 billion), and the rebuilding of the CAFGUs to a strength of 8,000.[61]

In line with the Philippines' drive for democratization, the death penalty was abolished in 1987 at a time when there were 282 prisoners on death row; these sentences were commuted to life imprisonment. Increasing violence and the sensationalization of crime by the media led to calls for the reintroduction of capital punishment in 1987, although this was now confined to a list of 13 'heinous crimes'.

One senator, Francisco Tatad, who is in favour of abolishing the death sentence, argues that it is biased against the poor – most of the people on death row in 1987 had disproportionately low incomes. At the time Rogaciano Neberes, aged 62, was sentenced to die for the murder of a businessman in 1967. 'I never committed the crime for which I was convicted ... I am here because I was too poor to hire a lawyer', he maintained. Only three of the 84 people executed since the death penalty was introduced in 1904 were wealthy.[62]

Part of the problem is clearly that the rural areas of the Philippines are still largely run along feudal lines, with various landowners and dominant families holding power. Elections appear to be battles between charismatic personalities rather than the issues relevant to the day and have a distinctively Hollywood flavour. As one report put it: 'While the Presidential election appeared to be free and fair, some 17,200 other elections for parliamentary and local seats were marred by vote buying and intimidation, and new violence that killed at least 20 people by election day.'[63]

Corruption remains endemic and there is reported widespread discrimination against the Filipino Muslim population, who mainly live in Mindanao. A low-intensity counterinsurgency war still appears to be going on between the state and these groups, and part of the problem is that the police and the army themselves are involved in criminal activities. They have been accused of kidnappings and assassinations. When a society like the Philippines has a thin line between the forces responsible for state security and the criminals who are undermining it, it bodes ill for the country's democratic and peaceful future.

Conclusion

The Philippines faces an uphill struggle in the area of human rights, but one that has seen marked improvements from previous periods. It is difficult to imagine it backsliding to dictatorship given the level of awareness by people about their rights and the fact that Filipino political culture has embraced democracy. Moreover, it does not appear likely that some revival of cronyism as charged by the detractors from Estrada's government will make much impact on the system. Its transformation to democracy after bitter years of dictatorship and authoritarian government make it a target for attack for other authoritarian success stories in the region. It is a soft target for authoritarian regimes that advocate 'development before democracy' because it is perceived as the 'economic basket case' of the region.

Lee Kuan Yew, who has some familiarity with authoritarianism, has made several hard-hitting criticisms of its aspirations and launched thinly veiled attacks on its western-style liberal democracy. In a speech to Manila businessmen he argued that:

> The Philippines has an American-style constitution, one of the most difficult to operate in the world. There is a complete separation of powers between the executive, legislature, and judiciary ... But a developing country faced with disorder and under-development needs a strong, honest government ... The Aquino Presidency achieved the restoration of a democratic constitution. The Ramos Presidency will have to prove that this democratic constitution can be made to work and that development is achievable. Many checks and balances have been written into the constitution to guard against the abuse of power ... But they must not lead to a paralysis of government. At the end of the day, the discussion and debate, the legislature must allow the executive to take the hard decisions.[64]

Similarly, in an interview with *Time*, the same self-styled spokesman for East Asia condemned the Philippines for emulating the American 'gridlock' model:

> I don't see any of the Asian countries wanting to copy your gridlock system. I am aghast to watch the Americans. My God, how did you survive 200-odd years of this? The one Asian country, namely the Philippines, that modelled itself on America has become a negative example.[65]

However, the Philippines has shrugged off such criticism by pursuing with some success a strategy for a development-friendly democracy. The 'sick man of Asia' is gaining support by showing that a 'buoyant economy and a vibrant democracy' can go hand in hand.[66] Its view of democracy has been shaped most importantly by two recent historical experiences, one negative, the Marcos dictatorship, and one positive, the People Power Revolt of 1986.

Julius Caesar Parrenas has argued that the stability of authoritarian governments tends to be temporary; intangibles also matter in the decision by investors where to place money; Parrenas gives the example of Hong Kong businessmen who might logically prefer Singapore, but find that the regimented life there is not 'conducive to creativity' and opt instead for the advantages offered by the Philippines. And there is some argument that political rights are supportive of economic development and growth, as Amartya Sen, the Nobel Prize winner, has argued:

> Political rights, including freedom of expression and discussion, are not only pivotal in inducing political responses to economic needs, they are also central to the conceptualization of economic needs themselves. And this constructive role can be seen to be a central aspect of the importance of elementary rights that make it possible for citizens to interact and to form values and priorities.[67]

Democracy and human rights appear, particularly after the 1990s, to be conducive to economic growth and dynamism in the Philippines, countering the argument of authoritarians that development should precede democracy. Political order and stability were used as a justification under an authoritarian government led by Marcos that looted the country and reduced it to a shambles. It appears the Philippine people have no desire to return to that state of affairs. The most recent elections, in 1998, again have shown that the Philippine adherence to democratic values and efforts to instil human rights notions are resilient in nature. These turned out to be some of the fairest and most open elections in the history of the republic. The historical problems of widespread cheating, vote-buying and political violence were largely absent. The growth of NGOs such as the National Citizens' Movement for Free Elections (NAMFREL) ensured different vote tabulations and was a positive sign in maintaining openness and transparency in the elections.

However, there are still problems, which will take time to resolve. There is culture of lawlessness to some extent and corruption is widespread. In 1997 a member of the House of Representatives and a municipal mayor were convicted of rape, a positive note in the reinforcement of the rule of law in criminal procedures. As one writer notes: 'kidnapping and robbery cases abounded; an estimated 200 persons were kidnapped and 288 million pesos in ransom paid in 1997. The rise in criminal activities this year was attributed to the involvement of AFP and Philippine national police (PNP) personnel with various criminal syndicates in the country.'[68]

Some human rights NGOs have accused the police of torture and ill-treating suspects. Abductions and extra-judicial killings are also a problem. There have been charges against Estrada that he is undermining freedom of speech by attacking the press reports against his government. In February 1999, he threatened to sue the *Manila Times*, the Philippines oldest newspaper, after it printed a damaging report implicating him in corruption. Later he withdrew this.[69]

The political culture of the Philippines still remains highly personalistic; as one author notes, 'personal ties rather than ideology or issues determine most elections, especially on the local level. When it comes to getting things done, personal relationships are often far more important than institutions, laws or procedures.'[70] In this type of personalistic society the 'distinction between acts committed as public agents of the state and as private citizens is blurred'.[71] Patron–clientelism, engrained in the Filipino political culture, as well as the importance of populism, are forces that remain to be reckoned with. As one writer argued in 1999, 'Twelve years after the restoration, Philippine democracy remains a shallow and fragile one. Its biggest source of support could be said to derive from the illegitimacy of alternatives, with the experience of Marcos's authoritarian crony capitalism a significant disincentive to abandoning the democratic framework. However, each of the defining characteristics of democracy remains weak in the country.'[72]

The victory of Joseph Estrada was seen as a vote by the lower classes to improve their position. Estrada in turn promised to narrow the gap between the rich and poor. However, over the course of his first year in office, Estrada has been charged with returning to some of the crony capitalism so indicative of the Marcos period. The office of Ombudsman in 1998 dismissed eight criminal cases against Marcos's kin and some of his cronies. He has also tried to rehabilitate some of the cronies who benefited from corruption when the former dictator was in power.[73] Moreover, in the middle of August 1999, it was reported that some 50,000 Filipinos had marched in Manila in protest at the revival of cronyism, including key figures involved in the anti-Marcos movement. They were also protesting against proposals by Estrada to change the constitution; the protesters suggested that he might be trying to change the constitution to allow the incumbent president to stand for more than one term, a safeguard against the abuse committed under Marcos.

Nevertheless, the accusations of cronyism, well founded or not, will have implications for Estrada as he continues (rhetorically or otherwise) to oversee the democratic process in the Philippines.[74]

Abuses committed by the police and military personnel, including kidnapping, extortion and protection rackets, continue to impinge on the lives of individuals and the community. The role of the military in politics has increased and, despite the positive steps towards democratization, measures need to be taken to limit the opportunities for martial law to reappear. The guardians of democracy and the development of a human rights culture in the Philippines will be supported by the development and sustenance of the NGOs and the role they will play in Philippine society. As one scholar argues: 'active concern for human rights and wide accessibility to channels of orderly discourse are publicly asserted by an articulate civil society which enjoys and defends the conditions of democratic space, including the restoration of competitive elections, an energetic free press, and a plethora of well organized issue oriented groups. Community organizing and creative educational activities of NGOs contribute significantly to self-perceived efficacy of the citizens.'[75] It is clear in this respect that the Philippines is going through a period in which its democratic institutions and human rights values are being consolidated and entrenched. It is from such groups as these NGOs that we can hope for the best safeguards against intrusion into civil liberties and individual rights, particularly in the light of the overall impact of the economic crisis that developed in Asia from 1997.

6
Cambodia

Democracy means food for the people's stomach, shelter, education, medical facilities and basic amenities and the freedom of expression and free movement. This is democracy in the Cambodian sense ... It is easy to preach or advocate democracy when one has a full stomach, is living comfortably in a fully air-conditioned villa or mansion. But what about the poor rural people? The farmers who till the land for the day so that they will have food in their stomachs at the end of the day. To them, and there are millions like them in the Kingdom of Cambodia, democracy is just a phrase to be talked about in idle gossip.[1]

Throughout its turbulent and chaotic history, Cambodia has never experienced the ideas or practice of democracy and a human rights culture that respects individuals or groups. Democracy has had very little impact on society here. Despite the fact that human rights were included in the country's first constitution in 1947, they enjoyed no theoretical or practical prominence in any period afterwards. One of the reasons may be that Cambodia is one of the weakest states in Southeast Asia in the sense that sovereignty and legitimacy have been continuously contested in its history even after the UN-sponsored elections in 1993.[2] Gareth Evans, the Australian Foreign Minister at the time, noted the intractability of the conflict:

After the Middle East, the Cambodian conflict was possibly the most complex single diplomatic problem in the world to try and resolve, involving as it did not only four competing political factions within the country itself, but just about all the significant countries of the region and the major powers as well, each of whom had a direct relationship with one or other of the internal players.[3]

Cambodia is one of the few countries in Southeast Asia which shares a score of more than 40 per cent on the United Nations Human

Poverty Index with many African countries; 40 per cent living below the poverty line. In 1998, the UN Human Development Index ranked the country at 140 out of 174 states. With a population of 10 million, it has a very high infant mortality rate of 113 per 1,000 live births, which increases up to the age of five years to 177. It remains on the list of the poorest seven countries of the world with an annual GDP per capita of US$260. More than 80 per cent of the population are engaged in subsistence farming based on the cultivation of rice.

The political legitimacy of the regime continued to be disputed after an alleged coup by the forces of Hun Sen on 5 July 1997 against FUNCINPEC, the French acronym for the National United Front for an Independent, Neutral and Free Cambodia, the Royalist political party under the control of Prince Ranariddh, King Sihanouk's son. At least 60 people, civilians and troops on both sides, died in this naked power grab by the forces of Hun Sen.[4] After the coup, investors and financial institutions were reluctant to provide capital and international aid was cut. GDP fell to 2 per cent in 1997, compared to 6.5 per cent growth in 1996. Things appeared desperate at this juncture. The efforts to produce a democratic system, first presided over by the UN in 1993 were technically in ruins. Once Hun Sen consolidated power, he scheduled elections for the summer of 1998 which, despite accusations of being deeply flawed by human rights NGOs, have resulted in a fair degree of political stability given Cambodia's history of violence.[5] Hun Sen's party, the Cambodian People's Party (CPP), won with 64 seats and FUNCINPEC and the Sam Rainsy Party, the two main opposition parties, managed 43 and 15 seats respectively. To many people's surprise the elections were peaceful and there was very little violence. Polling proceeded with a large turnout of Cambodians – nearly 90 per cent voted. The election was seen as free and fair in the eyes of the international community, although 'free and fair' in Cambodian terms may not mean as much as it sounds and some local NGOs thought the electoral processes very unfair, with enormous voter intimidation in the month before the election.

However, there were other changes taking place; the Khmer Rouge rebellion ended and Pol Pot, the man who had been responsible for one of the worst blood-lettings in Southeast Asian history, died in April 1998. Some estimates argue he was responsible for the death of more than 1 million Cambodians in the Khmer Rouge reign of terror between 1975 and 1978. By the middle of the year many former top commanders in the Khmer Rouge had come over to the side of the government. The divisions between Prince Ranariddh and Hun Sen were eventually worked out after a cat and mouse-like game of court politics. Overall, there was some improvement in the political shape of the country. There was no massive conversion to democracy and the values it entails, but it seemed as if there was some effort to procure peaceful change. The situation certainly seemed an improvement on the negative events of 1997.

Historical Overview

Historically, Cambodia represents a very complex case in the Southeast Asian context. The 'golden age' of Cambodian civilization attained its height in the twelfth century under the self-styled rule of Khmer autocrats who claimed god-like status (*devarajas*). And in a similar way to other Southeast Asian societies, they imported ideas of governance, religion and political authority from outside, in this case the Indian subcontinent. From about the ninth to the fourteenth centuries, this empire built palaces and monuments (the much visited temple complex of Angkor Wat included) and established a degree of control over the region. After this the Khmers experienced relative decline, victims of imperial 'overstretch' and were subject to subsequent invasions by Vietnam and Thailand.

French incursions in Southeast Asia in the nineteenth century resulted in the establishment of a protectorate here which was overseen by the capital of French Indochina, Saigon. During the Second World War there was a period of Japanese occupation, but the French influence remained strong, particularly with the alliance of the puppet Vichy regime with Nazi Germany. Following the defeat of Germany and Japan, the country was given a form of 'autonomous' status within the French Union and remained on the sidelines of the Indochina wars. After the massive military defeat of the French by Vietnamese forces at Dien Bien Phu, these colonial possessions were granted independence in 1954 in line with decolonization in other Southeast Asian countries after this period. In a similar fashion to its neighbouring Indochinese states, other actors, including Communist Vietnam, China, Thailand and the United States, have also influenced Cambodia.

For much of its modern political history, Cambodia has existed under monarchical rule in the grip of King Norodom Sihanouk, who even today plays an influential role in the chaotic politics of Cambodia. However, there have been roughly four major changes in its history since gaining independence. In 1955, Sihanouk abdicated from the constitutional monarchy, giving the title to his father in order to enter Cambodian politics formally, establishing a broad coalitional political front, the Sangkum Reastre Niyum (Popular Socialist Community), which in turn gained all the seats in the elections held in September of that year. For over 40 years Sihanouk has with varied success dominated Cambodian politics with a paternalistic and charismatic brand of powerbroking and political manoeuvring, despite various periods in exile after first being overthrown by the US-backed Lon Nol dictatorship (1970–75) and during the brutal Khmer Rouge regime (1975–78). Even under Pol Pot he was reinstated as head of state, but resigned in 1976 when a new constitution was established for a republican Democratic Kampuchea. When the war in Vietnam spilled over into Cambodia, the US government embarked upon massive secret bombing of the Cambodian countryside.[6] The dramatic economic consequences and severe disruptions led to a further polarization between the Lon Nol government backed by the US and the Khmer Rouge forces backed by the Chinese communists.[7]

The Khmer Rouge ousted Lon Nol in 1975, establishing Democratic Kampuchea, which was less than democratic by any standards. This resulted in the massive reorganization of Cambodian society. Private property and money were abolished, the cities were emptied and rural collectivization was attempted on an unprecedented scale. If Communist Parties in other parts of the world desperately tried to adopt modern forms of industrialization and modernization, the Khmers deliberately went the other way, seeking to bring back the feudalistic period of Ancient Khmer empires in which reliance on forced slave labour was the norm. As Charles Twining has argued:

> To achieve this state, Cambodia must be self-contained and self-reliant to the point of autarky. Essentially, it must pull itself up by its own bootstraps to achieve a greatness exceeding that of even Angkor, in which everyone would benefit equally and from which Cambodia could deal with the outside world from a position of strength.[8]

In the process so-called impure elements, including foreign educated intellectuals based in urban areas, were to be done away with. This amounted to nearly 20 per cent of the population or nearly 1 million people. Buddhism was all but eliminated. If medieval Cambodia was the golden age in its history then the years of Khmer rule (the 'zero' years) represented the nadir.[9] It became, in the words of one scholar, 'the most radically altered country in the world' and, as Phnom Penh Radio declared, 'Two thousand years of Cambodian history have virtually ended.'[10] It was to be an experiment that Cambodia will probably never forget. In an effort to create the classless, agrarian (almost pre-feudal) society, executions, overwork and starvation caused as many as 2 million deaths during the regime of terror that the Khmer Rouge inflicted upon Cambodia.

One of the key aspects of the genocide was the systematic nature of the killing signified by the existence of mass graves. Although Cambodians were the majority of victims, the ethnic Vietnamese in particular were singled out (an aspect that has recurred in human rights violations since the 1993 elections). When Cambodia was invaded by Vietnam in December 1978, they installed the Kampuchean People's Revolutionary Party (the KPRP) in an effort to bring the murderous regime to book, and Sihanouk was again forced into exile in North Korea. The People's Republic of Kampuchea was declared the official name of the new state on the 8 January 1979, after Phnom Penh fell to the Vietnamese forces and the composition of the state now reflected the invading forces. The new leader of the now People's Republic of Kampuchea, Hun Sen, was formerly a Khmer Rouge commander, and was installed by the Vietnamese, a legacy that remains part of the opposition's arsenal of attack against him to this day. He ruled through the vehicle of a Marxist-Leninist Party, the Kampuchean People's Revolutionary Party, the only political organization allowed, comprised of a mix of Khmer Rouge defectors and Cambodian communists who had long been associated with the Vietnamese regime. At the age of 33, Hun Sen was the world's youngest prime minister at the time. The Khmers still remained an active force, however, controlling sections of the Thai border and pursuing a campaign of guerrilla warfare against the Hun Sen regime; there was, in effect, incipient civil war. The state remained as weak as ever and Cambodia suffered from international economic isolation, which did nothing to improve its shattered economy. In an effort to procure political legitimacy (because he was viewed as a puppet of the Vietnamese), Hun Sen decided in 1989 to legalize Buddhism which had been outlawed by the Khmer Rouge, and again changed the country's name to the State of Cambodia, altering the national flag and anthem to remove any offensive symbolism.

At the beginning of the 1990s the external supporters of the various contenders to power decided to seek political accommodation and a cease-fire, with arrangements for the first democratic elections in 1991, was signed by the four warring factions. This followed an international conference held under the auspices of the United Nations in Paris in 1991. The Paris Accords, signed in October 1991, allowed for a period of normalization in Cambodia and laid the basis for peace. In its final section it stressed:

> The primary objective of the reconstruction of Cambodia should be the advancement of the Cambodian nation and people, without discrimination or prejudice, and with full respect for human rights and fundamental freedom for all.[11]

The signatories of the treaty acknowledged the special role human rights would play in the troubled country and sought to oblige others to promote and respect these. At the same time the ruling party (KPRP) had changed its name to the Cambodian People's Party (the CPP) and abandoned its Marxist identity in an effort to read the new political winds of change sweeping Cambodia. Because this was a negotiated settlement there was no mention of the genocide inflicted by the Khmer Rouge; nor was there any mandate offered to the UN to punish Khmer Rouge crimes. Not only did this reflect a strategy of peace and reconciliation over retributive justice, it also adhered to norms within the Cambodian political and social culture. The level of disorder in recent Cambodian history provides us with some continuity but little change in the rules of governance. Such was the scale of anarchy and civil strife in the country that on 28 February 1992 the UN Security Council approved by a unanimous vote of 15 to 0, the 'biggest, most expensive, and most ambitious peacekeeping operation in UN history'.[12] As such, the UN Transitional Authority in Cambodia (UNTAC) was an 'internal' peace-keeping operation with a specific mandate to achieve 'a comprehensive political settlement of the Cambodian conflict'. Those goals, however, were not as comprehensive as the rhetoric and included elements such as the restoration of human rights, developing a civil administration, the maintenance of law and order through a civilian police component; the repatriation and resettlement of over 370,000 Cambodian refugees on the Thai side of the Thai–Cambodian border; disarming and demobilizing the four factional armies, controlling the cease-fire agreement, verifying the withdrawal of foreign forces and organizing and supervising the general elections held over 23–27 May 1993. Human rights were seen as a central element in this supervision. UNTAC, with 22,000 personnel, were placed in charge of supervising elections and monitoring the cease-fire in March 1992 and generally establishing the peace in the troubled and divided land. It had an enormous and complex task:

> Obstacles to the elections were daunting: a legacy of twenty-two years of brutal war, autogenocide, and the massive destruction of almost all aspects of a civil society; the refusal of the well armed and unforgiving Khmer Rouge faction to abide by the Paris peace agreements; armed banditry by soldiers; and organized suppression of the political opposition by the incumbent regime, which led to the death or injury of hundreds of persons in the months leading up to the elections.[13]

Before and during UNTAC's presence, Cambodia signed ten international human rights instruments which guaranteed (among others) women's rights and the rights of the child. A document published by UNTAC in 1992 concerning human rights in Cambodia was republished by the Khmer Institute for Democracy in 1995 in which they provided a brief history of rights since 1947. It also drew parallels between the mass killings in Cambodia in the late 1970s and the Nazi Holocaust. It refers to the internal Cambodian problems of corruption in every regime since this period, quoting the French Declaration of the Rights of Man and the Citizen of 1789: 'Ignorance, forgetfulness or contempt of human rights are the sole causes of public misfortune and government depravity.'[14]

The UN-supervised elections proved highly successful and had a large turnout. The Cambodian People's Party (CPP) under Hun Sen came second in the polls with 38 per cent of the vote after Norodom Ranariddh's nationalist, anti-Communist FUNCINPEC which gained 46 per cent, a fairly narrow margin. Under the threat of a new civil war a new assembly was established which restored the constitutional monarchy and a form of power-sharing in a coalitional government providing the prince with the title of First Prime

Minister and Hun Sen Second Prime Minister. This coalition comprised the two main parties mentioned and the smaller Buddhist Liberal Democratic Party (BLDP), which had links to FUNCINPEC. It was a compromise that appeared to offer Cambodia some semblance of stability and hope for the future. The greatest obstacle to the peace plan was the Khmer Rouge. In fact, throughout the 'transitional' period the Khmer Rouge have resisted the implementation of the Paris Agreement, and have continually made life difficult for UNTAC, which they regard as a 'colonialist force'.

The State of Cambodia under Hun Sen was equally critical of the UN. Their cease-fire violations were described as defensive acts to protest the rice harvest, to regain hold over productive lands and to help provide some semblance of security in the country prior to the elections. The fact that a peace-keeping mission was installed in Cambodia did not prevent human rights violations; many ethnic Vietnamese residents of the country were killed in this period and politically motivated murders became more common in the run-up to the 1993 election. Moreover, the Khmer Rouge were not involved in the elections despite signing the Paris Peace Accords; they simply failed to implement any of these measures. In the aftermath of the elections they continued to wage a low-level, guerrilla-type war.

The important point here is that elections do not in themselves produce peaceful settlements, particularly if one or more of the factions involved in the conflict find that their political aspirations are not met or are even undermined by the election results. There is a world of difference between electoral democracies (as many of the states in Southeast Asia appear to be) and liberal democracy, which implies not just elections but participation and the opportunity to choose between alternatives.[15]

Despite some electoral success, the country was back in the thick of civil strife even before the last peace-keepers had left, with government pitted against the Khmer Rouge. Abuses from the latter group, on the one hand, and the Cambodian armed forces, on the other, exacerbated the environment of conflict. Human rights groups documented murder, rape, hostage-taking and the Khmers' use of a 'scorched earth' policy. The government also carried out measures against civilians such as secret detention, extortion and the death of many at the hands of military intelligence. The difficulty in assessing the extent of state violations as opposed to extra-state actors such as the Khmer Rouge makes the task of human rights collation all the more difficult.

Despite some optimism for the future we have to understand that the Paris Peace Accords were a political compromise between the various warring factions; there were no plans to assume any retributive or punitive sanctions against the genocidal Khmer Rouge, for instance. In fact, in 1994, the coalition government decided to offer an amnesty to thousands of these soldiers. In August 1996, a further 2,000 Khmer defectors were provided with amnesty for the crimes committed between 1975 and 1979, including the former Foreign Minister, Ieng Sary, who was responsible for many atrocities. No mention of the Cambodian genocide was made in the Agreements and the focus was primarily on looking towards the future while avoiding discussion of the past. As a result there were no calls for truth commissions as in other countries with traumatic pasts. In some ways the result was that the conflict was put on hold and the poor results are a consequence of failure to deal with these basic issues.

The resulting political coalition was always a shaky compromise between political partners; after UNTAC pulled out of Cambodia, the stage was set for renewed tension. At the beginning of July 1997, Hun Sen's forces finally attacked Royalist troops loyal to Prince Ranariddh and the former declared himself the sole legitimate leader on 7 July. Three days later ASEAN decided to postpone the entry of Cambodia to its organization, which had been planned for some time to coincide with the 30th anniversary of its founding.

Many Cambodian traditions support an acquiescent 'subject' culture marked by emotional reserve. The prevailing form of Buddhism also promotes avoidance of anger and revenge. Therefore there was little sense of actively seeking justice against the genocidal leaders. A noted Cambodian scholar has assessed accurately this culture of fatalism in his analysis of Cambodian poems from the nineteenth century. He argues that:

> The attitudes which the poems foster and reflect may explain in part why the French often spoke of Cambodians as 'asleep', and why governments and demagogues since independence were unable to draw people away from their families to pursue supposedly higher frames of reference. The world picture transmitted by the *Chbap* is one where deference and fatalism take up more space than rebelliousness or hope. The same values that made so many Cambodians reluctant to struggle for their 'rights' under the French, Sihanouk, and Lon Nol has preserved many survivors of the 1970's from revolutionary transformations.[16]

It seems that even Pol Pot and his grand experiments with social change could not undermine or alter this conditioning type of cultural behaviour.

However, this may be changing. When Pol Pot died in April 1998 he had not been brought to justice, but at least that was part of the horrific past over. The national election of 1998, which was the first since the UN-sponsored election of 1993, was regarded as a success by most, although there were some serious problems in the initial stages. Hun Sen had already given out guarantees of safety for returning political leaders to Cambodia to contest in the elections; however, through the first part of 1998, the CPP was the only party able actively conduct political campaigns throughout the country. It was only in May 1998 that the opposition parties were legally recognized and only in June that they were allowed to register to participate in the election. In the final two months before the elections the Office of the High Commissioner for Human Rights in Cambodia received several hundred complaints of intimidation against voters, threats of death, acts of violence against and illegal arrests of individuals, plus the confiscation of voter registration cards by local authorities and coercion by the CPP to join their party, among other grievances. Moreover, the human rights office detailed at least 22 murders in which they argued political motivations played a part.[17] Thirty-nine political parties were to compete for the 122 seats in the National Assembly; the majority won by the Cambodian People's Party (CPP), controlled by Hun Sen. They gained 64 seats, the two major contenders in opposition (FUNCINPEC) 43 seats and the Sam Rainsy Party received 15 seats. The Joint International Observer Group (JIOG), which is run by the United Nations, concluded that the election went well, although others, notably the opposition and at least one human rights group, seemed to believe there were widespread irregularities in the voting procedures. They also pointed out that the JIOG had completed a very superficial job of election monitoring. They issued a statement saying the election had been free and fair before the counting was finished and only sent 250 pairs of observers to cover more than 11,000 polling sites and 1,600 centres. The logistics of their operation were, in short, questionable with many observers arriving there just before the election and leaving very quickly afterwards. The counting of votes continued several weeks into August after JIOG had issued its approval on 27 July.

The main opposition parties in turn organized a series of protests based on their complaints, which concluded with a grenade attack on Hun Sen's residence. Provoked by this, Hun Sen demanded the arrest of the opposition which led to further rioting and political violence in which at least 18 people were killed. By the middle of November, the political situation had calmed down sufficiently to allow a new coalition, comprising Hun Sen as Prime Minister and Ranariddh as Chairman of the National Assembly with amnesty offered to military who had served under the latter. Rainsy was excluded from this coalition. However, it was and is clear who is really in charge of Cambodia and that was Hun Sen, who in reality had managed to consolidate his grip on power through his effective manipulation of and manoeuvring within the political system.

Political Economy

The economic situation in Cambodia is extremely poor and in many respects it can only be compared to Burma among Southeast Asian nations. After the coup in 1997, it looked certain that their socio-economic conditions would worsen and many thought the country after struggling with the aftermath with its first democratic elections of 1993 would slide back into an economic abyss. There was almost no economic growth in 1997 despite prior targets of 7–7.5 per cent; in fact, the economy was constantly attempting to break free from negative growth, sometimes reaching highs of 2 per cent. Like many states in Asia, natural disasters play a hand; there was heavy flooding in 1996, which severely affected much of the agricultural sector. According to a local newspaper in this period, more than 20 people were killed, over 1.3 million internally displaced and hundreds of thousands of hectares of crops wiped out in the floods.[18] Various strikes in the textiles industries also played a part in the poor growth record. However, the main blow to the economy in this period was the coup in July 1997, which dramatically increased inflation rates and cost millions in damage to the economy. Over 7,000 foreign nationals left the country and tourism declined dramatically. When I visited Angkor, Cambodia's beautiful temple complex in June 1998, this incredibly rich archaeological site was more or less empty of tourists.

The proportion of military spending, although slightly less than 1997, was still a very significant portion of the state's budget; this amounted to 45 per cent of total spending (or roughly US$397 million).[19] Combined with the system of corruption in the illegal logging business where there was almost no collection of revenues, there remained little doubt that the government was either too inefficient or corrupt or both to provide an effective development strategy in Cambodia.[20] Between 20,000 and 40,000 service workers became unemployed as a result and the drain on public resources increased as the government starting spending more on security and defence.[21]

After the coup there was also a decline in foreign aid, much of which brought needed foreign exchange into the country. The IMF, for instance, which previously had agreed to release the remaining portion of the enhanced structural adjustment facility (which was another $40 million out of $120 million) suspended its loans. Its other donors (including the United States) suspended in different ways non-humanitarian aid, but the economy was kept afloat in part by the humanitarian money which flowed in. There was no massive collapse of the economy because Cambodia was not really integrated into the Southeast Asian currency system. The economy was based on the US dollar; the most common form of banknote in circulation. Therefore there was no currency to fall.

Rice shortages, the ineffective management of agriculture, low levels of investment (as in Burma) and still slow growth in the tourist industry together have ensured that Cambodia has continued to remain a weak state economically. The fact that landlessness and poverty have increased in rural areas is another issue which feeds into this destructive cycle. Cambodia is caught in a cycle that needs to be broken if it is to break free of the development versus democracy debate that it faces. Its poverty and the dire economic conditions for its people will not, as Ranariddh rightly points out, foster conditions conducive to democracy and a human rights culture. The land question will come to dominate a significant discourse in the future of Cambodian politics.[22] People in Cambodia are still seeking to realize very basic concerns such as adequate food, shelter and security. It appears that these economic concerns will continue to dominate the agenda for some time.

Human Rights since the UN Elections

The efforts by the UN to solve the political chaos were initially impressive. In many ways Cambodia represents the most difficult and problematic case among the Southeast Asian countries by virtue of its status as the weakest, subject to grave internal conflict that shows no end in sight and by the history of genocide inflicted under the Khmer Rouge. In fact, human rights violations reached their peak in the Khmer Rouge period. How could anything that came after be compared to the slaughter they inflicted on Cambodia society? And it appears that on an international scale, memory of atrocities is short-lived. As Kundera points out:

> The bloody massacre in Bangladesh quickly covered over the memory of the Russian invasion of Czechoslovakia, the assassination of Allende drowned out the groans of Bangladesh, the war in the Sinai desert made people forget Allende, the Cambodian massacre made people forget Sinai, and so on and so forth until ultimately everyone lets everything be forgotten.[23]

Progress in human rights in general since the elections has been slow, halting and at times abandoned altogether. Any progress was significantly retarded in the wake of an aborted coup in the aftermath of the election. Former repressive practices crept back into Cambodian politics, the government became more intolerant from 1994 onwards. The judiciary is weak and there appears little effort to act independently of the government. An immigration law passed in 1994 fails to meet international human rights standards. This allows for the possibility of detention and expulsion of non-nationals who may have a legitimate claim to residence within Cambodia. The idea of 'Cambodian nationality' does not have a specific legal definition which opens it up to arbitrary violations. Since September 1993, the human rights situation appears to have deteriorated according to reports released by Amnesty International. They accused members of the police and armed forces of acting with impunity and the government appeared intolerant, violating the rights in particular of ethnic minorities such as the Vietnamese.[24]

There appears to be a culture in Cambodia which is characteristic of war-torn states in stages of transition, but also has deeper roots in Cambodian history. Security forces appear to act without the usual reversion to justice and redress.[25] This has been documented by an Amnesty International report released in 1995 which found evidence of major human rights violations in Battambang by the S-91 military intelligence unit, including abductions, illegal detention, extortion, forced conscription, rape and extra-judicial executions of civilians in the province. In this sense the situation might be comparable to the role of the military in Burma which carries out similar violations. In their report Amnesty International noted that there were

> at least 19 people who were held captive in the environs of Wat Cheu Kmau between November 1993 and July 1994. The organization believes that S-91 was responsible for the extra-judicial execution of at least 35 people from August 1993 to November 1993. Further Amnesty International believes that this same military unit carried out a series of killings in Battambang between July 1992 and August 1993.[26]

When the government ordered an inquiry, the investigation was criticized on the grounds that it was not impartial in terms of its composition and methods. Politically motivated killings, intimidation of the courts and widespread attacks on ethnic Vietnamese constituted some of the serious violations. In the case of the latter, between 1991 and 1993 (the UNTAC period), more than 100 ethnic Vietnamese Cambodians were killed and more than 80 injured in violent attacks. In October 1994, seven ethnic Vietnamese including three children were killed in the fishing village of Peam Charalai in Kampong Chhnang Province by forces of the PDK (Party of Democratic Kampuchea, aka Khmer Rouge).[27] According to a US report:

> One of the most serious incidents occurred in June (1996), when a group of 37 KR guerrillas abducted approximately 50 woodcutters in Kampot Province. Although 31 of the workers were later released in exchange for ransom money, the KR reportedly murdered 14 of the hostages. In July Khmer Rouge forces abducted 25 villagers in Siem Reap province; they later killed 21 of them. The KR also targeted ethnic Vietnamese, killing 25 citizens of Vietnam in August.[28]

The judiciary in particular, at the end of 1996, remained weak and arbitrary. There appears little dividing the executive and judicial branches and there is a lack of efficiency, a shortage of resources and a great deal of corruption. Citizens still continue to be denied the right to a fair trial. Again hostility towards the ethnic Vietnamese marks a general feeling of antagonism in Cambodia. Some have even accused Hun Sen of being a Vietnamese puppet, and in the aftermath of the election at the beginning of September 1999 at least four ethnic Vietnamese were killed by mobs in Phnom Penh after a rumour had spread that more than 70 people had died as a result of poisoning by the Vietnamese people. It appears to take little here to stimulate xenophobia and hatred against their closest neighbour.

Freedom of Speech, Religion and Civil Liberties

These tenets of western human rights doctrines are all virtually unknown quantities in Cambodia. No ruler or regime has ever respected basic rights enjoyed in other societies at any time in this country's history. Concepts like the rule of law and an independent judiciary have virtually no history in their society. Under the monarchical rule of Sihanouk, civil liberties were ignored and political opponents jailed. Opposing the monarchy was seen as treason. Elections were held, but the situation was reminiscent of the theory of the 'divine right' of kings (which reached its apex in the seventeenth-century debates around the civil war in England) where power descended from the monarch to the people, not the other way round. In this sense Cambodia was still a feudalistic pre-modern society.

Similarly, the military dictatorship of Lon Nol was one of repression of human rights. Elections were meaningless and political opposition disallowed. By most other Southeast Asian standards in the postcolonial period, Cambodia had no real human rights. That is why in some ways it is almost impossible to discuss human rights during the Khmer Rouge period where genocide was the prevalent mode of government.

There have been some disturbing trends in the post-UN period, including continued incursions on freedom of speech by repressing the press and media. A press law passed in 1992 provided the Cambodian government with the ability to shut down newspapers critical of policies and to jail journalists and editors. In the last four months of 1994 at least two journalists were murdered in extrajudicial executions, according to Amnesty International.

During 1995 the Cambodian government unleashed a campaign to silence critics; it targeted independent newspapers and various political figures for intimidation and harassment. There were more than twelve occurrences of the suspension, closure or confiscation of newspapers as well as criminal charges brought against journalists. A new press law was introduced to allow for such measures to continue.

Initially, this law appeared to contain a number of positive features, including prevention of pre-publication censorship and right of access to government held information. These concessions were undermined, however, by the use of criminal law to prevent publication of material that could affect national security or political stability. In 1995, five Khmer-language papers and the English bi-weekly, the *Phnom Penh Post,* were under investigation and prosecution. One Khmer editor, Thun Bun Ly, was found guilty of disinformation and defamation and fined 10 million riel (US$4,000), for publishing articles and cartoons which were critical and satirical of government figures. His newspaper *Odom K'tek Khmer* (Khmer Conscience) was closed down. Thun Bun Ly was shot dead by two men while riding a motorcycle taxi in Phnom Penh in May 1996.[29] The regime also arrested six men for distributing leaflets during US Secretary of State Warren Christopher's visit to Phnom Penh. In the leaflet there was some criticism of the FUNCINPEC party, alleging corruption among other aspects. Despite the fact that none of these tracts provided incitement to commit criminal or violent acts, they were charged under criminal law. Up to the time of writing there were no arrests made in connection with Bun Ly's death. Newspapers continue to be tightly controlled although many of them expressed criticism which belied a climate of fear and self-censorship.

In 1996, the government refused to allow the KNP (Khmer Nation Party) to have its own television and radio stations; any form of media which was overtly critical of the media, in fact, was subject to state intimidation. Since 1991, many journalists have been threatened and intimidated and at least half a dozen killed. In June 1998, the editor of *Koh Santeheap* (Island of Peace) was shot after he had published articles which showed the government were involved in drug trafficking.[30] In general many of the newspapers are funded by politicians in order to criticize and insult their political opponents but without any real substance.

Conclusion

In August 1997 the leader of Cambodia, Hun Sen, stated that his government was setting up a body to monitor human rights and called on UN officials to be replaced. The latter estimated that some 40 supporters of the ousted Prince Ranariddh were killed in the aftermath of Hun Sen's takeover in 1997. Part of the problem in the Cambodian human rights situation is the lack of solid institutions which will defend the rule of law. Impunity against human rights violations is widespread; a 1994 Law on Civil Servants established that unless state officials are caught red-handed, they cannot be prosecuted unless the government provides advance permission. There is no real, independent judiciary, legislature, army, police or civil bureaucracy. There appears to be rule by law instead of rule of law. Once its institutions are entrenched Cambodia is likely to head towards an illiberal form of democracy. Factional politics continue to plague the murky waters of Cambodian democracy with many politicians and officials having difficult pasts, diverse affiliations and engaged in widespread corruption.

There are some positive signs, however. Following a fairly peaceful and non-violent election by Cambodian standards in 1998, the country appears to have settled into new phase of transition. Denied access to ASEAN in the aftermath of the 1997 coup, it has now been admitted and will seek to benefit from regional cooperation instead of isolation. Cambodia is a country that has had far more of its share of suffering, human rights violations and misery than most other countries. Surrounded by antagonists, it appears weighed down and a victim of its past and acquiescent political culture where deference comes naturally and rebellion remains an anomaly. It appears straddled between fault lines of Indochinese civilization, between Theravada Buddhism and Confucianism, and it appears subject to the negative influence of the latter as various invasions serve to testify. It is to some extent a victim of its geopolitical location. Social and political change appears as chaos compared to the rest of Southeast Asia. There has been a fair amount of criticism particularly from US politicians. Dana Rohra Bacher, a Californian congressman, stated that Hun Sen was comparable to a 'communist dictator' and 'war criminal' with Pol Pot-like tendencies, who would destroy any basis for Cambodian democracy.[31] Certainly prior to and in the aftermath of the Cambodian elections of 1998, he did himself no favours by continuing a pattern of violence against opposition party members and workers. A memorandum from the Special Representative of the Secretary General for Human Rights in Cambodia detailed 42 killings and six long-term disappearances in the aftermath of the 1997 coup. Following the 1998 elections hundreds of opposition activists fled their homes in the provinces in fear of death threats and reprisals from local officials.[32]

Cambodia's history and human rights situation have invariably been termed 'tragic' and the term 'powerlessness' applied to most of the population. However, in recent years there have been signs that Cambodia could stabilize and the human rights situation might improve. The last election was marked by the notable absence of strife, and long-awaited plans to bring the former Khmer Rouge leaders to justice are finally materializing. There is a great deal of discussion about the different methods of justice which might be applied, from truth commissions to courts of law. Effectively, the situation no longer appears one of incipient civil war. There has been a growth of NGOs since the democratic 'moment' of the UN elections in 1993; now there are more than 300 NGOs campaigning on everything from human rights to ethnic minorities to children's rights.[33] A fairly vibrant and determined political opposition is emerging, something not seen in some of the vastly more developed countries of Southeast Asia. This in itself is a positive sign in developing a civil society which will respect and nurture human rights. This situation does not appear likely to change dramatically; the country remains outside the mainstream of the Southeast Asian miracle in the sense that economic growth will not make a serious impact on the majority of the population for some time to come. The quest for the balance between economic growth, political stability and justice is more relevant than ever to a society which has never experienced much of any of these commodities and it is clear that the present government will focus on the economic development before democracy given the dire situation of the country's position. However, there are positive signs which hold hope for a country plagued by violence and gross human rights violations.

Part 2

Northeast Asia

Denny Roy

7
China

Most of the human rights issues China struggles with today stem from the great inertia of Chinese traditional attitudes, a product of the country's great age, size and pride. The largely western 'international' norms by which foreigners often evaluate China are relatively new to a country that emerged as a fully-fledged member of international society only in the 1980s. Even where the state accepts and codifies certain human rights protections, effective enforcement throughout the country is often difficult. The leadership's responsibility for managing such a populous empire has perhaps created the expectation of policies that are sometimes callous, imposing suffering on part of society in the interest of some greater good. And the authoritarian tradition inevitably results in abuses of power and intolerance for challenges to the authority of the ruling regime.

Citizens of ancient China enjoyed the benefits of having a place in what they understood as the world's pre-eminent civilization. Threats to the physical and economic well-being of individuals, which in modern parlance might be termed 'human rights', were thought to stem primarily from disorder and warfare (either civil war or foreign invasion). Most Chinese saw hope for protection against these threats not in expanded individual liberties and a weakened state, but in members of society fulfilling their obligations and in a strong government that ruled righteously. Confucian philosophy prized social harmony and taught that this was best achieved by individuals conforming to the ideals associated with their particular role (father, son, friend, farmer, official, etc.). Rulers would be most effective, said Confucius, if they ruled virtuously, inspiring lawful and responsible behaviour through moral example rather than through compulsion and punishments.

Thus, both state and society had their respective obligations. The Confucian system required deference of subjects toward their rulers. The civil service examination system, through which, in principle, a Chinese male from even a peasant background could qualify for a high-ranking job in the government, assured the populace that officials were men who had earned their posts though outstanding merit, justifying the power society implicitly trusted to these officials. Rulers, for their part, were expected to take a benevolent interest in caring for their subjects. Pre-modern Chinese governments usually made some effort to meet their people's basic survival needs, maintained emergency grain reserves, undertook large public works projects to improve transportation and irrigation, and provided military protection in the event of invasion. The eighteenth-century Manchu Emperor Yongzheng even made several decrees intended to halt discrimination against groups of Chinese outcasts who seemed to be trapped in undesirable occupations. At the same time, however, the Chinese governments of antiquity had minimal protections for what are known in modern parlance as civil and political rights, although many Chinese intellectuals demanded increased political privileges, usually without success. Criminal suspects of all types were routinely tortured, dissent was not tolerated and execution was the typical fate of political offenders. Many of the rural masses lived on the brink of starvation. Attempts by the monarchy to improve living conditions in the countryside were frequently counterbalanced by the avarice of local officials and landlords. Women were traditionally limited to domestic roles, had little access to education and were subjected to footbinding.

Confucian thought recognized the possibility of an unjust government being overthrown from below. A successful rebellion would indicate that a ruler had lost the 'mandate of heaven' due to a lack of virtue. In practice, of course, the state's broad powers to repress and punish its opponents made revolution difficult and extremely risky.

Concern for the well-being of the general population and the narrower interest in protecting the ruling regime's power and status overlapped in the strong emphasis Chinese rulers placed on maintaining stability within the empire. Several insurrections throughout China's long history contributed to a legacy passed on to modern Chinese governments: a near-obsession with national unity and a conviction that internal and external security threats are linked: '*nei luan wai huan*' (disorder within, peril without).

THE GOALS AND PROGRAMME OF THE CHINESE COMMUNIST PARTY

The arrival of emissaries from western countries in Asia marked a transition from the long era of China as the 'Middle Kingdom', the centre of the known universe, to the 'Century of Shame', when China fell prey to intrusion and exploitation by technologically and industrially advanced foreign powers. This profoundly traumatic period saw the strength and authority of the Chinese central government severely damaged, important economic and legal concessions coerced from Chinese officials by foreign pressure and large tracts of Chinese territory handed over to foreign control. The Chinese also consider this a disastrous period for human rights, as the Chinese people suffered continual exploitation and turmoil due to the avarice of foreign invaders and the ineffectiveness of their own government to protect their interests. The population suffered socioeconomically through the draining of their national wealth and loss of privileges to foreigners. Worse, many suffered more direct physical abuse as a result of lawlessness or cruelty – the infamous 'Nanking Massacre' of Chinese civilians by Japanese troops being only one example.

The events of the 'Century of Shame' imbued modern Chinese nationalist leaders with the conviction that to reverse its dire predicament, China needed strengthening from within –through unity, stability and economic development – in order to uphold Chinese sovereignty against foreign molestation. Both the Nationalists, of whom Chiang Kaishek would emerge as leader, and the Chinese Communist Party (CCP) under Mao Zedong saw an authoritarian, patriotic government as part of the solution.

The CCP, which proclaimed victory over the Kuomintang (Nationalist Party) forces and sent the remnants of Chiang's regime fleeing to Taiwan in 1949, faced immense challenges. The great majority of the population was poor, most desperately so. Tens of millions of Chinese had resorted to living in caves. There were frequent cases of families unable to provide one set of clothing for each family member – 'one-trouser families' – and whole villages whose inhabitants blackened their bodies with charcoal in lieu of clothing. To establish a foundation for security and prosperity, China desperately needed to close the gap between its own level of modernization and industrialization and that of the developed countries that were China's potential rivals. Its national construction efforts were impeded by the losses incurred during the Japanese invasion and the civil war against the Nationalists. In its early years, Mao's regime faced residual opposition at home and the possibility of attack from the United States and later the Soviet Union.

Preserving North Korea as a buffer between China and the American bloc cost the Chinese nearly 1 million casualties in the Korean War.

Under these circumstances, the CCP insisted on national unity, stability and total societal support for the party, while its leaders pushed ahead with programmes designed to raise living standards and strengthen national defence. The party implicitly offered enhanced socioeconomic rights for the masses of China, while reserving strong political powers to the state, that is, holding back the civil and political rights most Chinese had never possessed anyway. The CCP argued that the interests of the revolution, which would bring unprecedented benefits to the Chinese working class, required that the state had every advantage in its ongoing struggle to root out and subdue opponents of the revolution. CCP ideologues maintained that while the West claimed to be the champion of civil and political liberties, in the inherently unjust capitalist system the working masses had no real rights, either political or economic. Conversely, since the party (in theory) guards the interests of society as a whole, the rights of the citizenry are best protected by giving greater power to the state. From the standpoint of human rights, the CCP's monopoly of political power has allowed it to block opposing political forces whose agenda would undermine the safety and prosperity of China's people. Chinese officials often warn that a multi-party system would open opportunities for unpatriotic or self-interested politicians to pursue policies that would unleash chaos, destroy the gains made under the CCP's guidance in recent decades, and potentially turn the clock back to the 'Century of Shame'. High-ranking Chinese continue to express wariness about foreign plots to soften up China for neo-colonial style exploitation by enfeebling the central government through 'bourgeois liberalization'.

Accordingly, in early 1949 the CCP regime abolished the legal system of the previous regime, which it said could be used as a refuge by capitalist holdovers to protect their interests. Instead, the CCP ruled according to a handful of legal statutes combined with a series of 'campaigns' targeting specific groups of domestic enemies. The CCP also set up an intricate and highly intrusive system to monitor the populace. During the 1950s, the internal security and surveillance network grew to an estimated 1.7 million spies and police.[1] Untold numbers were punished under the broad label of 'counter-revolutionary activity'.

The concentration of authority within CCP officialdom has also given rise to abuses with ramifications for human rights. Corruption, widespread among high party cadres, has often led to unjust treatment of Chinese citizens or embezzlement of funds that would otherwise have benefited the public. Another problem is the public's inability to protect itself from harmful government policies. This point is illustrated most dramatically by events such as the Great Leap Forward of 1958–59. With nearly unchallenged power and authority, CCP Chairman Mao Zedong mobilized China's population in a programme of intensive collectivization and amateur steel production that he hoped would propel the country into rapid economic development. Rural Chinese wasted their energy producing low-quality, useless steel instead of tending their crops. The resulting poor harvest, combined with a series of natural disasters, led to massive famine and starvation. Another example of the cost of unchecked power unwisely employed was the Cultural Revolution, which began in 1966. Fearing he was being politically marginalized by other high CCP leaders appalled at his economic policy failures, Mao publicly called for mass criticism of the arts, then of the party itself. University and school students responded enthusiastically, calling themselves the Red Guards and forming large mobs that ran rampant throughout China looking for signs of 'bourgeois revisionism'. Uncontrolled and often undisciplined mobs were soon attacking all semblance of authority, from high-ranking Communist Party officials to school teachers. Victims were tortured, publicly paraded, beaten, sometimes killed, and their property stolen or destroyed. Those who died in the violence, although impossible to quantify, probably number in the millions.

If the new regime's authoritarianism was a point of continuity with the past, the CCP's welfarism broke with tradition. The new government sought to guarantee economic necessities such as food, employment and housing, a responsibility that previously rested with families and local communities. The Communists promised their system would cater to the masses, including land redistribution in the rural areas and an end to the exploitation of industrial labour in the cities. Improving the socioeconomic lot of poor rural Chinese required forced sacrifices by some of their fellow citizens. Under CCP policy, landlords and wealthy peasants lost all their land without compensation. Not surprisingly, many resisted, suffering the fate of 'class enemies'. Probably hundreds of thousands, perhaps more, died in purges and 'struggle sessions' (public trials) in the 1950s alone.

POLITICAL AND CIVIL RIGHTS ISSUES IN THE PRC

A one-party dictatorship leaves limited scope for political rights in China. None of China's paramount leaders has tolerated challenges to the CCP's authority to rule China. Indeed, one of the Party's 'Four Cardinal Principles' makes criticism of the government illegal. There are countless documented cases of peaceful dissenters suffering persecution and stiff punishments, both individually and in groups. One of the best-known recent examples was the Tiananmen Square incident of May–June 1989, which began with peaceful protests by students and their supporters against corruption among party officials, and ended with a violent crackdown by soldiers of the People's Liberation Army and official denouncing of the demonstrators as subversives encouraged by foreign enemies of China.

Chinese have traditionally emphasized the protection of society against criminals over the protection of suspected criminals from erroneous prosecution. Defence lawyers have been expected to work towards an outcome most beneficial to society as a whole, not merely to focus on upholding their client's interests; thus the defence lawyer may act as a liaison between the defendant and the prosecution or help persuade the defendant to confess to the alleged offences. Guilt or innocence has largely been determined by the investigating police. The primary purpose of a trial has been to determine the appropriate sentence, which depends heavily on the defendant's attitude.

The Chinese legal system has undergone important reforms in the 1980s and 1990s. The authorities are clearly making an effort to improve the system; the Chinese press reported that in 1998 the government disciplined 5,000 prosecutors and judges and overturned 8,110 judgments, and in 1999 the Ministry of Justice ordered 500,000 judicial officers to undergo additional legal training.[2] Reforms implemented in January 1997 provide greater privileges to accused criminals. Detainees are now entitled to earlier and more frequent access to legal counsel and the police are required to inform the detainee's family of his/her arrest. The new Criminal Procedure Law also increases the possibility of a defendant winning an acquittal, including giving greater scope for defence lawyers to argue their clients' cases. In recent years, a few victims of abuses by public security personnel have sought and obtained compensation by working within the system. Although routine trials are now open to the public, exceptions are still made for certain types of cases, including those the government says involve state secrets. Thus, the state still can, and often does, try dissidents *in camera*.

China ratified the United Nations Convention against Torture and Other Cruel, Inhuman, or Degrading Treatment or Punishment in 1988, and the Chinese constitution expressly forbids torture. The problem is enforcement of prohibitions against torture. Chinese officials say several hundred cases of alleged torture by police are investigated each year, and that the guilty are punished as the law provides. A small number of police and prison staff is jailed for unlawful torture annually. Nevertheless, the torture of criminal suspects is a deeply rooted practice that remains widespread. Even the Chinese press occasionally complains about the prevalence of torture. The most common forms of torture are beating, sometimes with a cane; shocking prisoners with electric cattle prods; and tying or chaining prisoners in painful positions, such as binding their arms behind their backs and hanging them by their wrists. Electric cattle prods are now standard equipment for police and prison guards, and reports indicate that official guidelines limiting their use to certain exceptional situations seem to be frequently ignored.[3]

Chinese prisons are spartan and often insanitary, and in many parts of the country the institutional protections against abuses of prisoners by guards and fellow inmates are weak. Convicts with shorter sentences usually man the labour camps located in rural areas. Some camps are large and sprawling, small towns in their own right. The work in these camps is hard and the living conditions poor. Among the harshest critics of China's prison camps is Hongda Harry Wu, who spent 19 years in labour camps for a few remarks critical of the party, emigrated to the United States and later returned to research China's 'reform through labour' process. Wu estimates that at least 50 million, most of them political offenders, have served in labour camps during the PRC's history, with as many as 20 million currently incarcerated. 'China,' says Wu, 'has the biggest slavery enterprise in the 20th century.'[4] Wu's estimates are exceptionally high, and therefore controversial. Other foreigners estimate the number of inmates at around 200,000.

The Chinese press reports about 1,000 executions per year, but the actual number, unknown outside official circles, is probably several thousand.[5] Executions are generally made public only if the authorities believe the story will serve a beneficial social or political function. In recent years, the government has expanded the scope of capital punishment, so that there are now 45 crimes for which civilians may be executed (ten additional offences apply to military personnel), including several crimes that do not involve physically harming another person: theft, bribery, embezzling, smuggling, export of forbidden cultural relics, and so on. A high official in Guangdong has even suggested the death penalty for people who make cellular telephone calls using other people's code numbers.[6] Corruption under 'market socialism' has reached such crisis proportions that executing white-collar criminals has become common. Former Hubei Province official Jin Jianpei was given a death sentence in 1999 for embezzling and then losing $188 million through gambling and poor investments, but Zhao Binyi of Tianjin was executed in 1997 for fraud involving only $6,000.

If applying the death penalty to non-violent crimes is disturbing, critics also raise the alarm about the possible links between capital punishment and trafficking in human organs. Again, the issue is proper enforcement of Chinese law. Chinese officials admit to harvesting the organs of executed criminals. The government says prior consent of the prisoners and their families is required in these cases, but the process remains opaque. Although the Chinese Ministry of Health says the buying and selling of organs is officially forbidden, wealthy foreigners willing to pay huge sums for replacement body parts reportedly find a ready source in China, which supplies 2,000–3,000 organs per year. If the judicial authorities know that each execution is worth thousands of dollars in revenue, it is not difficult to imagine this becoming an important consideration in the passing of death sentences.

The era of 'market socialism' inaugurated by Deng Xiaoping and maintained by his successor Jiang Zemin has seen changes in the character of the Chinese press, which historically has been tightly controlled by the party. Its primary function has been to explain and praise party policies and provide the official interpretation of the news. Throughout the 1990s, however, the state found it increasingly difficult to manage the media, which has presented the authorities with challenges of regulation similar to those associated with the other burgeoning aspects of Chinese society. The press has freely reported many instances of corruption, even among officials, which supports the state's objective of deterring further offences. Political reporting that creates pressure to clean up the present system is generally tolerable, in contrast to suggestions that the present system be changed. Some periodicals have recently flirted with the latter by discussing topics such as democracy and the role of dissent and opposition parties. These remain subject to bans. In mid-1999, for instance, the *Renmin Ribao* boasted that police had destroyed 120,000 illegal political publications for the year.[7] Nevertheless, the authorities seem unable to block them all. The internet presents a similar challenge. The government attempts to filter out objectionable web sites, such as those operated by foreign news media, but has been unable to deny computer-literate Chinese access to these sites.

In China's past, religion often developed into a rival to the authority of the state, sometimes stimulating insurrection. Furthermore, Marxist ideology extols atheism and denigrates religion as a tool of elites for suppressing the working class, an 'opiate' to placate them in their undeserved poverty. Not surprisingly, therefore, the CCP is often accused of either persecuting religious groups – from Tibetan Buddhists to Muslims to Christians – or of attempting to hijack religious organizations and turn them into vehicles for promoting loyalty to the party.

The fate that befell Falungong, a nationwide society that combines Buddhism, Taoism and traditional Chinese breathing exercises, clearly illustrates the government's fear of religion not only as an impediment to building the ideal socialist society, but also as a potential rival for political power. After a Tianjin magazine printed a disparaging article about Falungong, an estimated 10,000 Falungong supporters stood outside the walls of Beijing's Zhongnanhai, the compound containing the residences and offices of the PRC's top leaders, in a silent protest. Alarmed by the unity and power of mobilization this protest demonstrated, the central government launched a campaign to suppress Falungong, labelling it a 'cult' that brainwashes and blackmails its followers and has caused 1,400 deaths by forbidding medical treatment. By November 1999 the authorities had arrested over 100 Falungong leaders, charging some with stealing state secrets and threatening public order. If Falungong previously had no political, let alone anti-CCP agenda, as its supporters claimed, the government's reaction threatened to create a powerful new enemy.

MINORITIES IN THE PEOPLE'S REPUBLIC

China's 55 ethnic minorities make up just 8 per cent of the population. The CCP's national vision welcomes these minorities as citizens of the People's Republic. Being 'Chinese' has historically had more to do with culture and political allegiance than with ethnicity per se, in contrast to countries such as Japan and Korea. Yet China remains in some respects an empire, and that means that self-determination for minority regions is out of the question. The CCP's treatment of national minorities has therefore been a mix of paternalistic assistance and harsh suppression. The central government has made significant efforts to benefit minorities through employment and education quotas and through construction of infrastructure in some minority-populated regions. In general, the standard of living of Chinese minorities has improved under CCP rule. While discrimination against minorities by Han Chinese prevails, this may have more to do with traditional Chinese attitudes than with government policy. Some minority groups complain, however, about government hostility towards some aspects of their culture, particularly religion. Organized opposition to Chinese rule, sometimes violent, persists among Muslims in the western province of Xinjiang. Friction between the CCP regime and local society has been even stronger in Tibet.

The CCP defined Tibet as an integral part of the new Chinese state, and soon after the foundation of the PRC sent a military expedition to enforce Beijing's control. The official Chinese position is that before intervention by the CCP, 'Tibet was under a feudal serf system' in which 'the broad masses of the Tibetan people suffered from unbearable political oppression, economic exploitation and mental enslavement'. The lamas, the ecclesiastical authorities of Tibetan Buddhism, were repressive, parasitic and widely hated. The local people therefore welcomed entering Chinese troops as saviours. CCP officials implemented 'democratic reform' and as a result Tibetans enjoy the same 'personal and religious freedom' as their Han countrymen.[8] Tibetan nationalists dispute this version of history, asserting that there was no feudal system in Tibet before the Chinese takeover, that even peasants who worked on large estates owned land and were under the jurisdiction of the state rather than that of local aristocrats, and that Tibetan society in general had a relatively high degree of social mobility.

Tibetan nationalism has suffered heavy and determined Chinese repression because it represents two forms of threat the CCP views as serious: religion (Tibetan Buddhism), as a rival to the party for the loyalty of PRC citizens, and national separatism. Since the 1950s, the Chinese government has sought to weaken the authority of Tibetan

Buddhism and struggled, often ruthlessly, to repress Tibetan nationalism. Numerous reports from foreigners and from the Tibetan community exiled in India suggest the Chinese have killed, imprisoned and tortured hundreds of thousands of Tibetan activists, guerrillas, monks and nuns and destroyed thousands of Tibetan temples. Remarkably, Tibetan resistance to Chinese rule remained strong throughout the 1990s, fuelled by the participation of younger Tibetans who had never known anything but CCP rule. The People's Liberation Army was forced to station as many as 200,000 troops in the region, and there were continued reports of torture and other abuses perpetrated against proponents of Tibetan independence or Tibetan culture. But with the influx of Chinese settlers (encouraged by financial incentives provided by the state), Chinese and cosmopolitan culture, and wealth and materialism into Tibet, the long-term vitality of Tibet's independence movement is uncertain.

SOCIOECONOMIC ISSUES

The 1982 constitution explicitly guarantees Chinese women 'equal rights with men in all spheres of life, political, economic, cultural and social, including family life'. Nevertheless, as in most societies worldwide, women in China tend to earn less money and hold less influential positions than men. Females seeking high-status employment are disadvantaged by deep-seated traditional attitudes and by the expectation among employers that hiring women may mean paying the additional costs of maternity leave and benefits. Women continue to be kidnapped and trafficked in China, especially in rural areas, despite what most observers agree have been serious counter-efforts by the central government.

Mao's development and defence strategies emphasizd the advantages of China's large population, and he encouraged women to have large numbers of children. Consequently, China's population doubled during his tenure. In 1979, the new post-Mao government announced the one child per couple policy, a drastic attempt to slow the trend and cap China's population at around 1.2 billion. China's population reached that number in the 1990s and is still growing. It is now projected to level out at around 1.6 billion in the middle of the twenty-first century.

The one child per couple policy is supported by a combination of education, monitoring, incentives, intervention and punishments.

The policy is most stringently enforced in the urban areas of China's eastern half. In practice, a two-child policy has become the norm in rural areas, and there are few if any restrictions on ethnic minorities in sparsely populated areas such as Tibet and Xinjiang. Couples that adhere to the one child policy enjoy preferential access to medical care and education. Women who have not obtained permission to have a child are required to employ birth control measures and to be monitored by regular physical examinations. If a couple has a second child, one of them is required to undergo sterilization, and the family is subject to a fine that may be as high as several times the household's annual income. Violators of the policy often suffer additional disciplinary action as well, including, in some cases, losing their jobs. Forcible sterilisation or abortion are officially forbidden, but numerous reports point to the conclusion that even through the end of the 1990s, health workers under pressure to achieve state goals have sometimes resorted to these extremes.

Economic reform and development, designed to stimulate economic development and higher living standards, have themselves spawned new socioeconomic challenges. Beginning in the 1980s, Deng Xiaoping and his protégés rejected the principle of economic egalitarianism. Instead of striving to maintain equal (and necessarily low) living standards among the entire population, the leadership would allow those capable of getting rich quickly to do so. Although this competitive approach would create a gap between the wealthy minority and the impoverished majority, it would encourage entrepreneurship, with positive effects for the Chinese economy as a whole. Eventually, the leadership hoped, the income gap between the rich and the poor would correct itself. Government welfare policy has moved gradually from the 'iron rice bowl' social security system toward laissez-faire. Relatives, instead of the state, have been given increasing responsibility to care for the elderly and the unemployed. These reforms have created opportunities resulting in tremendous wealth for some Chinese, but the new conditions yield losers as well as winners. Many urban workers face a difficult transition from the security of a centrally planned economy to the competition of the capitalist marketplace, a shift China's entry into the World Trade Organization will accelerate. A large percentage of the workforce is employed by state-owned industries, which are largely unprofitable and act as a drag on economic growth. The government is moving to privatize these industries, which means bankruptcy and liquidation for many, while managing the numbers of former workers who lose their jobs and benefits as a consequence. This has been a difficult balancing act for the state. The party has faced increasing attempts to organize independent trade unions, which the CCP has always vigorously opposed. Although illegal, strikes have proliferated in the troubled waters of China's recent double-digit economic growth. A CCP report revealed that over 5,000 protests took place in China in 1998, some involving thousands of people and many leading to violence. In that year, 442 policemen died in the line of duty. Beijing also reported that China endured 2,500 bombings in 1998, an average of eight a day.[9]

Under Deng's reforms, farmers obtained greater property rights and are allowed to sell their crops for personal profit, but they get much less state subsidy. Rural areas have also been inordinately hard hit by decreases in state funding for services such as education and unemployment benefits. Many farmers cannot compete successfully in the new market economy. Unhappy with employment opportunities in the countryside, tens of millions of rural Chinese looking for work have migrated to the cities, where they often end up living in shanty towns or sleeping on the streets. Rural unrest has reportedly increased dramatically in recent years. Even the farmers efficient enough to survive under the new conditions are bedevilled by high taxes, corruption among local officials and the inability of the government to pay for the crops it purchases. Many of the poor peasants who travel to the booming cities in search of work are cheated and abused by the new bosses who circumvent regulations designed to protect workers. China has therefore suffered in recent years some of the conditions that were widespread in the industrializing West a century or more ago: increases in industrial accidents, illegal child labour, workers toiling for less than the minimum wage, and scores of workers killed in fires and collapsed buildings in Chinese boomtowns.

China under economic reform is also experiencing increasing levels of the kinds of problems familiar in developed capitalist nations, but which the Chinese have prided themselves on avoiding: homelessness, unemployment, stress on traditional family relations and rising crime rates.

CONCLUSIONS

Despite the obstacles it inherited, CCP has largely kept its promises to the Chinese people. Living standards have greatly improved. CCP programmes have promoted not only economic development, but also education, medical care, welfare services and campaigns to improve opportunities for women and minority groups. Between 1949 and 2000, China's population saw dramatic improvements in important areas such as average income, literacy and life expectancy. The government points out with pride that unemployment is low, hundreds of millions have been lifted out of poverty, and that China manages to feed 22 per cent of the world's population with only 7 per cent of the world's arable land. China is recognized as a regional great power and an important global player, and it is militarily more secure than at any time in the modern era. China started from a low base, but the CCP can truthfully claim that the average Chinese is better off than before the establishment of the CCP regime, and indeed the total human rights situation (that is, including socioeconomic as well as civil/political rights) today is the best in China's history.

Serious problems, however, remain. Many human rights abuses in China stem from difficulties of enforcement or from lingering traditional attitudes, areas in which the government has demonstrated considerable openness and willingness to improve. A more intractable problem is the PRC's political system, which inherently restricts some political rights that are widely accepted internationally. The CCP does not hesitate to crush challenges to its exclusive political authority, and certain kinds of peaceful politically oriented expression and activity are severely punished. Party officials have frequently asserted that China is presently unable to provide the full spectrum of desirable political privileges. The country is too vast, too poor and too populous to sustain political *and* economic rights. The former would destroy the latter: permitting citizens to challenge the regime would lead to chaos; allowing workers to strike and demonstrate would destroy the nation's prosperity; uncontrolled births would render the country unable to feed itself.

Some Chinese, however, reject this position. 'No country or society can dispense with legal protections ... if it is to upgrade its economy', says Wei Jingsheng, a former Red Guard who was later imprisoned for criticism of the regime. 'As the standard of the authority and the justice in the legal system ... is improved, the rights of the people will be better guaranteed, and their economic capabilities will be enhanced.' Dissident Wang Juntao adds: 'Maybe there are some cultural differences [between China and the West], but there is no big difference in the simple principle, "If you speak, let me also speak." I also do not think it is necessary to persecute those dissidents in order to develop economically.'[10] Granted that the well-being of Chinese generally improved under CCP rule, might China also have progressed equally quickly, or perhaps more quickly, under a more liberal political regime? And might this have also precluded some callous or misguided policies by powerful party officials that caused massive but perhaps avoidable waste and suffering?

The future holds the promise of political liberalization and greater civil liberties for PRC citizens. China's legal system is evolving, albeit slowly, in the direction of more liberal international norms. Chinese authorities have sought the advice of legal experts from democratic countries on possible reforms. Limited democratization is being implemented at the local government level, with elections held for some leadership positions. The path blazed by neighbouring states South Korea and Taiwan, which evolved from authoritarian to democratic systems, suggests that economic development creates irresistible pressures for political reform. Continued progress in human rights will be challenged by the regime's paramount concern with preserving 'stability' amid the turmoil created by China's rapid growth. At some point, it is likely that further reforms will be impossible without political liberalization that allows for greater accountability of the government to its citizens and permits the legal participation of alternative political parties and trade unions as well as those sanctioned by the CCP. If and when this occurs, human rights in China will reach an important crossroads of potential crisis and potential opportunity.

8
North and South Korea

Korea has been an important focus for human rights activists since it gained widespread notice in the West as a result of the Korean War. In the 1980s, South Korea became famous as battleground between a conservative state and a restive society, vividly illustrated by the perennial street fights between riot police and student demonstrators. Political conflict in postwar South Korea is partly fuelled by some of the same issues involved in the debates between advocates of 'western' and 'Asian' models of human rights. North Korea, on the other hand, is notorious as a totalitarian police state, the closest thing to the nightmarish regime in George Orwell's *1984* the world has yet produced. Here, debates on human rights and other political matters remain suppressed or controlled by a government that allows no challenges to its legitimacy. Different though they are, modern North and South Korea evidence clear links to a common past.

TRADITIONAL KOREAN STATE AND SOCIETY

Life in Korea has never been easy. Isolated by seas on three sides, the Korean peninsula is highly mountainous, leaving only 25 per cent of the land arable. The climate is also rather harsh, with hot summers and cold winters, especially in the north. Man-made hardships have been even more severe; the dominant theme in the history of Korea's foreign relations is continuous invasion and harassment by foreigners. In the past, these included the Chinese, Kitan, Mongols, Manchus, and Japanese. Remarkably, in spite of these encroachments, Korea has been a unified state throughout most of its long history.

At the beginning of the twentieth century, Korea became one of the principal objects in the rivalry among would-be regional hegemons China, Russia and Japan. The Japanese, newly invigorated under the Meiji modernization programme, won the prize by defeating China in 1895 and Russia in 1905. Tokyo formally annexed Korea in 1910, an arrangement that ended only with Japan's defeat in the Pacific War in 1945. Koreans hoping the end of the war would bring self-determination were disappointed when the United States and the Soviet Union replaced Japanese rule with a superpower trusteeship, under which the North and the South established competing and irreconcilable governments that went to war with each other soon after their sponsors' military forces withdrew. The war, which eventually ended in a stalemate, resolved nothing, and North and South Korea still live in fear of attack from each other. Ironically, although non-Korean foreign powers are now far less threatening than in ancient times, security still eludes the Koreans.

Korean culture and philosophy bears profound Chinese influence. The Chinese controlled the region around present-day Pyongyang for four centuries. Later, during the succession of three dynasties (Silla, Koryo and Yi) which began in AD 700 and lasted until the Japanese annexation, the central government adopted the Chinese model and made Chinese-style Buddhism and later Confucianism the state religion. The Korean monarchy adopted the Chinese examination system for entry into the civil service, a vehicle for acquiring status and wealth. But unlike the comparatively egalitarian Chinese system, the Korean examinations were open to the sons of aristocrats only. Government officials also won their posts through inheritance or as a reward for supporting the monarch against his enemies. Chinese was the language of government officials and the Confucian classics the source of their ethics. Koreans paid tribute to the Chinese emperor and generally acquiesced to the status of 'younger brother' to China.

The strong Confucian influence from China was also visible in the tendency of Koreans to understand social relationships in hierarchical terms. People generally saw themselves as superior or inferior to their fellow beings, not equals. Indeed, egalitarianism was associated with disorder, an indication that the proper hierarchical organization, the glue that bound society together, had been lost. Each person's age, gender, occupation and position within the family and society prescribed a particular set of responsibilities. Children were supposed to obey and respect their parents, disciples their masters, and citizens their rulers. This sense of hierarchy extended to the Korean language, which has developed different levels of politeness, allowing speech itself to reaffirm the relative social standing of the speaker and the listener. Peace and harmony would prevail only if individuals learned and fulfilled their appropriate places within society, even if this meant suppressing personal aspirations for something different.

Such a system was not amenable to challenging officialdom or to criticism of superiors by inferiors. The central government was traditionally authoritarian, monopolizing power and outlawing or suppressing competing groups.[1] For most of Korean history, state power was centred in a king, whose decrees had the force of law. These rulers exercised their power over life and death arbitrarily – sometimes compassionately, but often cruelly. In the case of political crimes, the entire families of offending individuals were often slaughtered by the state; alternatively, the government might blacklist the convict's relatives and their descendants, leading to generations of discrimination. Certain Korean kings also persecuted Buddhism, fearing it had become a rival political force (which was often true). Later rulers saw Christianity as a threat to the age-old Confucian order. The nineteenth-century regent Taewon'gun, for example, massacred 8,000 Koreans who refused to renounce Catholicism.

The state could take over any citizen's property, and was under no obligation to pay fair compensation. Citizens were not free to travel within the kingdom without permission from state officials. Dissent against the authorities, their policies or the prevailing social and political order was forbidden, and offenders were sometimes executed. Intrigue and coups were frequent, and usually led to a massacre of the losers and their supporters. Judicial and law-making functions were closely connected to the executive. Corporal punishments were cruel and public, as this was thought to maximize their deterrence value. These punishments included decapitation, dismemberment, flogging and confinement in the stocks.

The distribution of wealth in pre-modern Korea was highly unbalanced. At the top of the economic pyramid were the *yangban*, the Korean aristocracy. While these landowners supplied officials to man the Korean bureaucracy, they also continually struggled (often successfully) with the central government for control of agrarian revenues. The *yangban* were generally conservative and largely parasitic, growing wealthy from the surplus of peasant production while keeping the peasants themselves at subsistence level. Membership in this class was perpetuated by inheritance. From Yi dynasty times up to the Korean War, the *yangban* class comprised virtually the same group of several wealthy families. In the hands of the *yangban*, the rigid Confucian codes of appropriate conduct for one's position in society became a means of suppressing the lower classes.

The sociopolitical elite had many privileges; peasants and other members of the lower classes had few. Peasants had very little upward mobility, rarely owned the land they farmed, and were subject to heavy taxation and conscription for military service or government construction projects. The status of the smaller merchant class was lower than that of peasants because Confucian elites considered commerce a dishonourable occupation. Below the merchants were the *cheonmin* ('lowborn'), including slaves and workers in jobs considered unclean or dangerous, such as butchers, tanners, entertainers, miners, gravediggers and mortuary workers. Slaves were convicted criminals, prisoners of war and their children. The Korean government was a major slave-owner, employing thousands in its factories, until 1800. Private slavery continued thereafter for another century.

Periodic uprisings by common people and slaves, usually triggered by their desperate economic circumstances, were brutally crushed. A sixteenth-century rebellion fomented in the southwestern Cholla Province by a disgruntled former official convinced the central government, controlled mainly by natives of Kyongsang Province, that the Cholla were untrustworthy and prone to rebellion – a stereotype that persists in present-day South Korea. Another major uprising, perhaps the most famous in pre-modern Korean history, was the Tonghak Rebellion of 1894. Tonghak ('Eastern Learning', known today as Chondokyo, 'Church of the Heavenly Way') was a mixture of Christian, Buddhhist, Taoist and neo-Confucian doctrines. Its supporters consisted mainly of peasants seeking better economic conditions. The Tonghak agenda included egalitarianism and expulsion of foreigners, but its adherents affirmed support for the government.

This rebellion, too, began in Cholla, where Tonghaks took over the provincial capital of Chonju and then attacked cities in neighbouring provinces. Unable to cope with the insurrection, the central government asked for a truce and promised amnesty and concessions to the Tonghaks. Their leader accepted, and then made further demands, including the elimination of *yangban* privileges, redistribution of land, reduction of peasant taxes and debts, destruction of slave records, recruitment of civil servants based on merit rather than heredity, punishment of corrupt officials and the right of widows to remarry. These demands, of course, were never realized. While negotiating with the Tonghaks, the Korean government had called for reinforcements from China, and soon moved to quash the rebellion. The Tonghaks were beaten in early 1895 with help from Japan, which had sent troops of its own to counter the influence of its Chinese rivals.

By the time of the Tonghak Rebellion, the external forces that would destroy the *ancien régime* – and introduce new elements into Korean thinking on human rights – were already becoming apparent. The Japanese had intimidated the Korean government into signing a treaty in 1876 providing for greater economic and diplomatic ties between the two countries. Worried that relative technological backwardness made Korea vulnerable, many Koreans advocated importing western technology, an echo of the Chinese Self-Strengthening Movement. In the 1880s, Korea established diplomatic relations with many western countries and invited in western missionaries to establish schools. As western ideas became more accessible, some Korean intellectuals began to espouse western-influenced political philosophy. Backed by the Japanese legation, Kim Ok Kyun unsuccessfully attempted a coup in 1884, the stated aims of which included eliminating the privileges of the upper classes, ensuring equal rights for all Koreans, expanding opportunities for education and promoting Christianity (which Kim believed would speed Korea's modernization). Four years later, Pak Young Hyo sent a long memorandum to the Korean king which referred to western social contract theory and the American Declaration of Independence and called for equal rights for all citizens (including women), popular elections, and freedom to criticize the government. So Jae Pil (known in the West as Philip Jaisohn) and Yun Chi Ho organized a pro-democracy movement called the Independence Club and published a newspaper that extolled such principles as government accountability to the public, the rule of law and equality under the law. Their activities flourished briefly until 1898, when the Korean King Kojong decided the movement was subversive and outlawed it.

KOREAN HISTORY EARLY IN THE TWENTIETH CENTURY

Japan annexed Korea in August 1910. Although the Japanese claimed this move would be mutually beneficial, their objective was to extract and exploit material and human resources in Korea for the building of the Japanese empire. In the process, Japan also sought to Nipponize the Korean population by destroying the native culture. As a result, Koreans were made second-class citizens in their own country. Japanese colonists reserved for themselves the best schooling and jobs, while Koreans were forbidden from speaking their own language or studying their own history and were forced to adopt Japanese names. (Even those Koreans who took on Japanese names had their ancestry noted on their family records and on applications for jobs and schools, making them easy targets for discrimination.) Koreans were required to pledge loyalty and obedience to the Japanese emperor and pressured to pray at Shinto shrines for Japanese victory in the Pacific War. Many Christians went to jail for refusing to participate in Shinto rites. Japanese authorities also forced hundreds of thousands of Koreans to work in Japanese mines and factories or serve in the Japanese military. The Japanese strictly controlled all political activity, forbidding spoken and written dissent against colonial government policies. Thousands who resisted died at the hands of Japanese police or were imprisoned as 'thought criminals'.

The political plight of Koreans under Japanese occupation was epitomized by the March First Movement. In 1919, thinking that the end of the First World War and the promulgation of President Woodrow Wilson's Fourteen Points had created a favourable international atmosphere, a group of Korean activists composed a declaration of Korean independence to be sent to the Paris peace conference and to the Japanese government. The leadership of this group included a strong contingent of Christians, and another from Chondogyo, the modern descendant of Tonghak. The public heard the declaration on 1 March and immediately rallied around it. In the weeks that followed, 1–2 million Koreans participated in demonstrations and protest marches throughout the country. The Japanese reacted predictably, claiming the March First Movement was an 'uprising' (although fewer than ten Japanese and policemen died in all the demonstrations) and brutally crushing it. The authorities killed over 1,000 Koreans, wounded 16,000, imprisoned nearly 20,000 and destroyed hundreds of houses and churches.

The Japanese occupation's impact on the postwar Korean state is difficult to overestimate. It is also a complex legacy, a mixture of both positive and negative elements. The Korean economy semi-industrialized, and Korean rice production modernized, under Japanese rule. In the short term, the benefits for Koreans were few.

Korean workers earned, on average, less than half their Japanese counterparts. In the private sector, management was thoroughly dominated by expatriate Japanese, as only a handful of Koreans rose to positions higher than labourer or petty clerk. Despite dramatic increases in rice production, the surplus was exported to Japan, leaving much of the peasantry on the brink of starvation. Nevertheless, the long-term benefits of this Japanese-built economic infrastructure would become manifest in North Korea's rapid progress in the mid- and late 1950s and South Korea's economic 'miracle' in the 1960s and 1970s.

Many Koreans studied in Japanese universities, where some of these students gained their first instruction in liberal western political philosophy. But the Japanese occupiers also strengthened the bureaucracy and security apparatus, establishing the model of a repressive, quasi-military state government to which future South Korean regimes would bear great resemblance.

As part of their perceived project to modernize and 'civilize' Korea, the Japanese colonial authorities implemented or attempted certain reforms that were arguably pro-human rights. These included outlawing punishment of the families of convicted criminals, giving widows the legal right to remarry and forbidding discrimination against illegitimate children or against the Paekchong. Ironically, such measures often failed due to opposition from the Koreans themselves.

After losing the Pacific War, the Japanese were stripped of their Asian-Pacific empire. But instead of gaining the autonomy they yearned for, Koreans saw their country divided between two new groups of foreign interlopers. American and Soviet planners originally agreed to a temporary occupation of Korea, with the Soviets taking the half north of the 38th parallel and the Americans the southern half, in preparation for peninsula-wide United Nations-supervised elections that would yield a single Korean government. But as the two divided Koreas moved in radically different political and economic directions, efforts to coordinate these elections failed, and each half formed its own government.

In the southern half, US military authorities backed Syngman Rhee and other conservative politicians with ties to the *yangban* and former Japanese collaborators. In the early Cold War atmosphere, the Americans, ignorant of local history, language and culture, had difficulty distinguishing Korean 'communists' from Koreans with legitimate demands for self-government or land reform, and right-wing politicians did their best to exploit the confusion. Although US officials came to dislike Rhee's heavy-handedness, pursuit of political vendettas and unwillingness to root out inefficiency and corruption, Rhee convinced them he was their best hope of avoiding a communist government in Seoul. Frustrated, and goaded by communist agents, many Koreans in the south turned to armed rebellion, resulting in an effectual guerrilla war in some areas of the South prior to and during the Korean War.

In the North, Soviet occupation forces sponsored Russian-trained Kim Il Sung as interim ruler. Respected as a former anti-Japanese guerrilla leader, Kim redistributed land and raised the social status of the peasants, but his policies also promised to make life miserable for Christians, professionals, landowners and other traditional Marxist class enemies (about 1 million of whom fled into the South during the Korean War). Behind the scenes, Kim began the ruthless campaign that would eventually establish him as North Korea's absolute autocrat.

Perhaps the most profound effect of the US–Soviet occupation of Korea was to institutionalize the sociopolitical divisions created by Korean history up to that point: while the North's programme emphasized socialism, land reform, Korean independence from outside powers and the leadership's record of anti-Japanese resistance, the regime in the South was capitalist, pro-*yangban*, largely Japanese-trained and relatively dependent on American aid, advice and approval.

POSTWAR SOUTH KOREA

The Rhee government was authoritarian and heavily penetrated by corruption. Rhee used his powers to ensure his repeated re-election, angering Koreans who favoured democratization. But Rhee's failure to produce satisfactory economic progress was also a major source of his unpopularity. Anti-Rhee sentiment climaxed after the March 1960 election, which exhibited clear evidence of tampering. In protest, students marched on the presidential palace. Security troops shot and killed about 200 of them. This sparked further nationwide rioting, finally forcing Rhee to resign and leave the country. Significantly, the regular army units called into Seoul to maintain order during the anti-government protests remained apolitical, refusing to fire on the demonstrators or to attack Rhee's palace.

In the wake of Rhee's ouster, an interim government made extraordinarily liberal reforms. The new Prime Minister, Chang Myon, and President, Yun Po-sun, oversaw what was by far the most democratic Korean government in history. But the new regime's tolerance invoked many of the forces that historically have limited democratization in Korea. Freed from Rhee's authoritarian grip, factionalism ran rampant, creating a sense of near-chaos in the government. Relaxed controls on organized labour led to an increase in strikes. Inflation and unemployment grew. A softer line on relations with North Korea worried the military. Conservatives in general feared communist sympathizers were taking advantage of the Chang government's political liberalization to make inroads into keys areas of South Korean society. Thus, there was widespread assent when a military coup overthrew the Chang regime after only ten months.

Pak Chung Hee had been an officer in the Japanese army, and later graduated from the Korea Military Academy after the liberation from Japan. During Rhee's tenure, he and other younger generals were frustrated by the privileges and inefficiency of the older officers who filled the high command, limiting the promotion opportunities of the ambitious men below them.

Pressured by the US government to show progress toward democratization, Pak retired from the army and ran for president as a civilian in 1963. The election was generally clean and Pak won. He oversaw the introduction of a new constitution, written with American advice, which weakened executive power and allowed for a stronger opposition party. But he also laid the groundwork for reasserting his presidential power, founding the Korean Central Intelligence Agency (KCIA), the name of which reflected the American version that served as its model, and establishing a powerful, well organized political party.

In the 1971 presidential election, after Pak barely defeated Cholla Province native Kim Dae Jung despite widespread government cheating, Pak returned to outright authoritarianism. Pak's 1972 reforms gave him broad, almost dictatorial powers, including the means to stay in office indefinitely. The regime suppressed dissident journalists through imprisonment, harassment and prior censorship. As part of his strategy for economic development, Pak kept wages low and discipline tight for urban workers. Strikers were likely to be beaten and tear-gassed. Pak justified strengthening these measures on the grounds that South Korea's precarious security and economic circumstances required strong, decisive leadership.

Kim Dae Jung left Korea but continued his campaign against Pak's regime. In 1973, KCIA agents kidnapped him from a hotel in Tokyo, brought him back to South Korea and placed him under house arrest.

By the end of the 1970s, as economic reforms began to bear fruit and the wealth gap between industrialists and their workers widened, labour unrest grew to levels the police could no longer control. In late 1979, while Pak considered cracking down hard on threats to internal stability, his KCIA chief shot him dead.

As was the case after Rhee's resignation, Pak's assassination led to a brief interregnum of wide-ranging political debate, followed by a military coup. The new leader was General Chun Doo Hwan, who had been head of the Army Security Command during the investigation of Pak's assassination. Chun first carried out an intra-military coup, assisted by his Korea Military Academy classmate Roh Tae Woo, purging many of the army's older generals to create room for the younger officers of Chun's generation. Then, in May 1980, he declared nationwide martial law, outlawed criticism of the government and dissolved the National Assembly (Korea's legislature), which was preparing to vote on ending the pre-existing limited martial law. Kim Dae Jung, who had been released a few months earlier, was again arrested along with another future president, Kim Young Sam, and hundreds of other politicians, activists and students who had advocated greater democratization. A few months later he retired from the army and an electoral college named him as South Korea's president. His government bore a close resemblance to that of his recent predecessor: a highly powerful executive, weak legislature and judiciary, tight controls on organized labour and the media, and ruthless suppression of dissent.

News of Chun's takeover enraged South Cholla Province, the historical hotbed of dissent. In the provincial capital of Kwangju, hundreds of students demonstrated in May against the extension of martial law restrictions. Violent overreaction by a Special Forces unit of the South Korean Army sent to reinforce riot police outraged Kwangju's citizens, who drove out the troops and took over the city on 22 May. The Chun government declared that communist agitators were behind the Kwangju 'uprising' and sent a regular army division to recapture the city on 27 May. At least 200 Kwangju residents were killed and several thousand arrested. Although he was under arrest at the time, Kim Dae Jung was blamed for the affair, convicted of sedition and sentenced to death. (In the more liberal Korea of 1996, the retired generals and former presidents Chun and Roh Tae Woo were brought to trial for their roles in the Kwangju incident; Chun was sentenced to death, and Roh to a lengthy prison term.)

Aware of unfavourable comparisons with Rhee and Pak, Chun had promised not to seek a second term as president. Negotiations were also underway between the government and the opposition on revising the constitution, including the procedure for electing the president. The opposition wanted direct presidential elections, absent since 1971. In April 1987, Chun snubbed the opposition by announcing that since negotiations had yielded no agreement, there would be no reforms before the next election. Shortly thereafter, Chun's ruling Democratic Justice Party (DJP) named Roh Tae Woo, Chun's former army ally and then party chairman, as its next presidential candidate. This further angered dissidents, who expected Roh would follow in the authoritarian footsteps of his fellow former generals, Chun and Pak.

Chun's attempt to avoid constitution reforms sparked widespread protest, not only among students, but also journalists, academics, religious leaders, and much of the middle class. The reaction revealed the depth of the public's desire to curtail the military's involvement in politics. With the country seemingly headed towards civil war just a few months before Seoul was to scheduled to host the Olympic Games, the DJP relented. In an historic announcement, Roh declared support for political liberalization, including direct presidential elections, greater freedom for the press and amnesty for over 2,000 political prisoners, including Kim Dae Jung.

Ironically, Roh won the 1987 election, aided greatly by disunity among his opponents – both Kim Young Sam and Kim Dae Jung also ran for president, splitting the opposition vote. In his first speech as president, Roh said, 'The day when freedoms and human rights could be slighted in the name of economic growth and national security has ended. The day when ... torture in secret chambers [was] tolerated is over.'[2] During Roh's tenure, former President Chun was forced by public pressure to apologize for his misconduct, testify before a National Assembly investigative committee during televised hearings and send himself into temporary exile in a Buddhist temple. Roh also made the promised institutional changes that decentralized governmental power, strengthening both the opposition and the National Assembly, and allowed the press more freedom to question and criticize official policies. But arrests for political crimes continued, and at a rate even greater than when Chun was President.

Kim Young Sam's 1992 victory in South Korea's first direct presidential elections since quasi-military rule seemed to herald a new, unambiguously democratic political era. The new President covenanted that 'Justice will flow like a river throughout this land', and his government soon declared that South Korea was no longer an abuser of its people's human rights. Kim was himself a former political prisoner, and he marked his tenure by freeing 144 imprisoned dissidents. Former President Chun was convicted and sentenced to death (later commuted to life imprisonment) and his successor Rho given a prison term of 17 years for their actions in the coup of 1979–80. Yet Kim left the strict National Security Law on the books, and Amnesty International reported that 'the human rights situation has not substantially improved under the new government'.[3]

South Korea's journey toward liberalization appeared near its end with the election of former political prisoner Kim Dae Jung as President in December 1997. Kim promised to heal the lingering political wounds dividing the country and to pay particular attention to strengthening human rights and the rights of women. Kim indeed oversaw notable progress in these areas, but he too found it difficult to fulfil his promise to do away with the National Security Law.

SOCIAL AND ECONOMIC RIGHTS IN SOUTH KOREA

South Korea's overall standard of living has increased dramatically since the country's turbulent inception. Per capita GNP has grown from $675 in 1960 to $7,250 in 1994. Opportunities for education have greatly expanded; South Korea boasts over 100 universities, and the national literacy rate is now 96 per cent, higher than that of the United States. The average Korean life expectancy has risen from 58 years in the early 1960s to 72 years in 1994.[4] These statistics demonstrate admirable progress in South Korea's campaign to provide for its people's basic survival needs. But because most of this progress took place under the country's most authoritarian postwar regimes, it came at a high cost.

Authoritarian elites consistently maintained that tight controls on organized labour were necessary to prevent their manipulation by communist agitators seeking to foment national disorder. Pak, far more interested in economic development that his predecessor Rhee, also saw a low-paid, disciplined workforce as an important factor in his country's developmental strategy: in effect, this cheap, efficient and obedient workforce was to be South Korea's comparative advantage. Chun tried to continue Pak's approach. The Fifth Republic's constitution granted workers the freedoms to strike, form unions and bargain collectively, but then took these rights away in a clause giving the government the power to restrict any activities by organized labour detrimental to the national interest. Consequently, union leaders, like dissident journalists and other political activists, were frequently subjected to extra-legal coercion, including detention, beating and torture by police and assault at the hands of thugs employed by management or state authorities.

Just prior to the 1987 election, Chun's government relaxed these controls. As a result, the late 1980s saw a dramatic increase in labour disputes and a doubling of the average wage for labourers. But South Korea has also lost the comparative advantage of cheap labour that once attracted foreign manufacturers in droves and helped fuel the country's high economic growth rates of the 1970s. Indeed, with their economy's less than spectacular performance in the early 1990s, many South Koreans are looking back with nostalgia to the Pak years, willing to overlook his authoritarian excesses as part of the price that must be paid for major increases in the living standards of the country as a whole.

Workers' rights expanded as Presidents Roh, Kim Young Sam and Kim Dae Jung enacted their broad political reforms. Since 1997, more than one trade union is permitted in a given workplace, and unions are allowed to engage in political activities. Workers in the public sector were previously forbidden to organize, but workplace councils for government workers were approved in 1999.

Somewhat ironically, recent efforts to conform to liberal international economic norms have also aroused discontent among Korean workers, leading to mass strikes. The South Korean government has moved to reform its labour and business practices to qualify for admission to the Organization for Economic Cooperation and Development, the prestigious economic club of the industrialized democracies. Korean unions have complained, however, that these reforms undertaken in 1996–97 did much to help Korean management make their firms internationally competitive, while providing too few additional rights and benefits for workers.

Two groups in Korea have suffered widespread social discrimination: women and members of the *paekchong* caste. For Korean women, existence in a traditionally patriarchal society has meant that for most of Korean history, females had very limited opportunities beyond child rearing and household duties. Worse, the outright exploitation of women has deep roots in Korea. In ancient times, the monarchy gave women as tribute 'gifts' to China and Mongolia. During the Yi Dynasty, Confucian philosophers described the ideal woman as one who sacrificed her happiness or life for her parents or her husband. Both written and unwritten law reflected this attitude. Women were generally confined to their homes, did not have rights to divorce or inheritance, and were expected to be chaste and faithful. A *yangban* woman traditionally carried an ornate dagger, with which she was supposed to kill herself if touched by a man other than her husband. In contrast, men had primogenitor inheritance rights, could legally divorce their wives on a minor pretext and freely partook of extramarital sexual relationships.

The recent publicity concerning the tens of thousands of Korean 'comfort women' conscripted as prostitutes by the Japanese Army during the Pacific War largely overlooked the fact that in many cases, Korean families gave their daughters to prevent their sons from being drafted into the Japanese armed forces.

Women obtained greater legal protection with the foundation of the modern South Korean state. The US-sponsored 1948 constitution, for example, gave women the right to vote. But exploitation and discrimination, particularly in the workplace, continue in postwar Korea. Cheap female labour was a key factor in the South Korean 'economic miracle' of the 1970s. Women make up about 40 per cent of the workforce and earn, on average, only about half as much as men.[5] A 1997 survey indicated that nearly a third of Korean households had experienced domestic violence. The government addressed this issue by classing domestic violence as a serious crime in 1998, earning the praise of women's advocacy groups. There are still complaints, however, that rape and sexual harassment are underreported and inadequately punished.

The *paekchong* are the Korean counterpart to the *burakumin* of Japan (see the next chapter). Originally nomadic tribesmen, they took up the 'unclean' occupations of butchering and leather tannery. Later their duties expanded to include other dirty jobs, such as catching rabid dogs and removing and burying corpses from the sites of executions or autopsies. The rest of society treated them with contempt; most Koreans took it for granted that *paekchong* were subhuman. By the time of the Chosun Dynasty, their social status was below even that of slaves. Some stories from pre-modern Korea indicate that *paekchong* were required to yield the right of way on the roads to all non-*paekchong*, and that a non-*paekchong* could kill a *paekchong* on the slightest pretext with little or no legal retribution.

Well into the twentieth century, government records routinely applied the notation 'butcher' to the names of all Koreans of *paekchong* descent, regardless of their actual occupations.[6] Systematic discrimination against *paekchong* continues in modern Korea. In a society that tends to attach great importance to ancestry, many consider *paekchong* to be of inferior stock – a prejudice that can affect opportunities for employment, education and marriage.

CIVIL AND POLITICAL RIGHTS IN SOUTH KOREA

Until recently, South Korean did not generally recognize the right of their citizens to criticize the government. Dissidents faced imprisonment, torture or death. Scores of reports from the Pak era suggest that the government perceived few restraints on its authority to punish and neutralize dissenters. Guarantees of due process and fair trials for accused political offenders did not hinder South Korea's authoritarian governments from pursuing their vendettas, and the judiciary was hardly more than a compliant tool of the President.

In a notorious 1974 case, the government made a mockery of its own legal system in its determination to punish a group of alleged communist revolutionaries accused of conspiring to overthrow the government (charges Amnesty International later concluded were false). The press pronounced the 22 defendants, who were tortured into confessing, guilty before the trial began. The proceedings were closed to the public and to foreign journalists. The defendants' lawyers were kept incommunicado under house arrest while witnesses for the prosecution testified, and the court barred any witnesses for the defence. Eight of the accused were given the death sentence. Before their rights of appeal, which the government pledged to honour, were exhausted, they were hanged. Some of the bodies were cremated, apparently to hide signs of torture.[7]

The right of dissent greatly expanded beginning with the liberalization of 1987. Still, perhaps 200–300 remain incarcerated for their activities during the 1970s and 1980s. These cases are controversial because many of those officially charged with treason or sedition may actually be guilty only of peaceful expression of dissenting political opinions. Kim Dae Jung freed 103 such detainees in August 1998 on the condition that they promised in writing to be loyal citizens of South Korea and to obey its laws.

Police torture of suspects of political and other crimes has been a black hallmark of the South Korean justice system. Frequently reported techniques include electric shock, near-drowning and burning. Women have often been subject to rape or sexual torture. Convictions often rely on confessions obtained through torture. Kim Young Sam's government outlawed torture of state detainees, and several policemen have gone to jail for using torture during interrogation. The most cruel types of physical torture by the police and the Agency for National Security Planning (which enforces the National Security Law) appear to be declining, but complaints indicate the persistence of police torture, especially milder forms of coercion such as verbal abuse, rough handling and sleep deprivation. Korea's Supreme Court recently ruled that evidence obtained from a suspect who was subjected to sleep deprivation was not admissible in court. Continuing cases of abusive interrogation of detainees stems largely from the traditionally heavy emphasis placed on obtaining confessions from criminal suspects. In general, however, the number of such cases seems to be declining.

Conditions in South Korean prisons are traditionally harsh, and the government has in recent years taken steps to rectify potentially abusive and health-threatening practices such as lack of protection against extremes of weather, poor food, inadequate medical care and unduly rough handling of prisoners by guards.

The Rhee, Pak and Chun regimes all sought to control the press. An important turning point came during the dying days of the Chun administration. In September 1987, a few months after Roh's declaration of the DJP's plans for political liberalization, and shortly before the scheduled presidential election, the government tried to suppress an article in an issue of the monthly journal *Shin Dong A*. Intellectuals and much of the rest of the public rallied behind the journal's editor, saying this attempt at prior restraint on political grounds called into question the sincerity of Roh's promises. The government eventually caved in, lifting its restrictions against *Shin Dong A* and apologizing publicly. Soon thereafter, Chun's restrictive Basic Press Law was repealed, replaced by much looser regulations that inaugurated an era of unprecedented press freedom in South Korea that prevails today.

OBSTACLES TO THE EXPANSION OF HUMAN RIGHTS IN SOUTH KOREA

Perhaps the greatest impediment to greater civil and political liberties in South Korea is the country's external insecurity. Since the Korean War, Seoul has consistently maintained that stern measures are justified by the imminent threat of military hostilities with North Korea. While denying any aggressive designs on South Korea, Pyongyang has provided plenty of fodder for Seoul's position. For a small, relatively poor country, the North maintains an extraordinarily large and well equipped army, much of it deployed near the inter-Korean border. The North Koreans say this is to guard against a South Korean/US attack, but Seoul says Pyongyang plans to invade at the first sign of weakness in the South. Small groups of North Korean troops have been known to infiltrate the South, most notably a commando squad that attacked the presidential palace in an unsuccessful 1968 attempt to assassinate Pak. In October 1983, while much of the South Korean government was visiting Yangon, Myanmar, a bomb blast killed several members of Chun's cabinet. Chun himself escaped injury because he arrived at the scene behind schedule. Seoul immediately blamed North Korean agents, and an investigation by the Myanmar government reached the same conclusion. A North Korean defector confessed to the bombing of a South Korean airliner in 1987, saying the order came from Kim Jong Il, Kim Il Sung's son and anointed successor. The risk of another Korean War seemed particularly high during the crisis over North Korea's suspected nuclear weapons programme in 1992–95; one North Korean official publicly threatened that Seoul would be turned into a 'sea of fire'. Even when North Korea was weakened and forced to beg for international assistance by a famine in 1996, 13 North Korean soldiers infiltrated South Korea from a beached submarine and eventually killed 13 ROK security personnel and civilians.

External insecurity has worked against political liberalization and, consequently, limited the development of civil and political rights. At the heart of this problem lies South Korea's National Security Law (NSL), the ostensible purpose of which is to protect the country from internal political activities that might encourage or facilitate a North

Korean attack. Under quasi-military rule, the NSL was also a convenient tool for repression, and officers of the Agency for National Security Planning, the body that enforces the NSL, are still frequently accused of illegal and abusive treatment of dissidents, including arrests and searches without warrants, beating of prisoners and depriving suspects of sleep during interrogation.

Critics say the NSL is a catch-all law authorities can use to prosecute any and all political challengers. The law prescribes penalties for supporting 'anti-state' organizations, a vague category that includes anything from North Korean terrorists to slightly left-of-centre political activist groups. Since the Pyongyang government is the ultimate anti-state organization, expressions of sympathy for North Korea's leaders, policies or even interpretation of sensitive historical events (e.g. the Korean War) are criminal offences. The Kim government, for example, arrested students who publicly praised North Korean President Kim Il Sung after the 'Great Leader' died in July 1994. Some 200 dissidents were jailed under NSL auspices in 1996, including a singer and publisher who produced a book containing songs that allegedly lauded North Korea. Amnesty International reports that two former North Korean soldiers captured during the Korean War and later convicted of espionage are still in jail after over 40 years because they have refused to sign renunciations of communism.

The NSL forbids South Koreans from unauthorized travel to North Korea or meetings with North Koreans or their agents abroad. Violators are subject to conviction even if there is no evidence of treason or espionage. The law leaves no room for South Koreans who simply want to observe conditions in the North first hand, discuss the possibilities of reunification with people in the North or visit their relatives cut off by the national division. Several cases in 1989 demonstrated the implications of the proviso against unauthorized fraternizing with the enemy. Im Su Gyong, a 21-year-old female student, travelled (via Europe) to North Korea to attend Pyongyang's International Youth Festival. The Reverend Mun Ik Hwan, then 71, went to Pyongyang and met Kim Il Sung. Chung Ju Yung, head of the Hyundai conglomerate and future presidential candidate, also met with Kim in Pyongyang, in this case to discuss joint economic ventures. Im, Mun and a Catholic priest who escorted Im, were arrested and imprisoned upon their return to South Korea, but Chung, who travelled with the Seoul regime's blessing, was not.

Government prosecutors have gained convictions using extremely broad interpretations of the NSL. In 1992, for example, Lee Kun Hee was sentenced to three years in prison for passing 'state secrets' to a friend later accused of being a North Korean spy. In his defence, Lee pointed out, to no avail, that the 'secrets' in question were taken from an article in a journal published by the South Korean government for the general public. Lee worked in the office of the opposition Democratic Party, and his conviction came shortly before a presidential election. Cases like his fuel the argument that the National Security Law provides the government with an irresistibly tempting tool for silencing or discrediting political opponents. Critics also question whether it is still necessary for the South Korean government to punish all discourse on North Korea that is not negative, now that it is so abundantly clear that South Korea has decisively won the contest between the two systems. In 1997, for example, Duksung University Kim Eun Hee was convicted under the NSL for posting a greeting from North Koreans on a campus bulletin board. In another case, a Catholic priest, Moon Kyu Hyun, who had received the government's permission to travel to North Korea, was prosecuted in 1998 because he had made a complimentary statement about former North Korean President Kim Il Sung during his visit. Several hundred are still charged under the NSL annually.

The question of whether or not North Korea continues to pose a credible military threat to the South is highly controversial, the hard-line argument having been rejuvenated by Pyongyang's suspected nuclear weapons programme. As long as this argument remains persuasive to a sizeable portion of the South Korean population, the NSL, and its potential for abuse, will likely remain in force.

Other forces that have limited the expansion of human rights in South Korea include the country's authoritarian tradition, Korean nationalism and inter-regional animosity.

Traditionally, Koreans have not subscribed to the western notion that individuals possess rights as a 'natural law'. Rather, the state grants the people whatever rights they enjoy. Opposition to authority has never been among these rights. Donald S. MacDonald, a respected scholar of Korean affairs, notes, 'Any challenger of the official orthodoxy, now as in the fifteenth century, tends to be viewed as a heretic for whom tools like those of the Spanish Inquisition are appropriate. The quality of mercy toward persons not within one's own group is not a part of the Korean culture.'[8]

One manifestation of this authoritarian tradition is the difficulty South Korean governments have had accepting the concept, imposed on them by the US government, of a legal opposition party. Another is the degrading treatment of suspected criminals, which remains a deeply ingrained aspect of South Korean law enforcement. Suspects in police custody are considered to have forfeited the usual claims to respect and dignity, let alone a presumption of innocence. They assume subhuman status, which their captors may reinforce by forcing them to kneel on the floor with their heads bowed while they await questioning. Compared with their western counterparts, Korean police have a greater responsibility to determine the guilt or innocence of suspects. If they think a suspect is guilty, the police must obtain a confession. If the suspect refuses to confess voluntarily, the police use coercion.

Korean nationalism has often supported arguments and policies that strengthened the power of the state government and thereby undermined the political rights of Korean citizens. On the other hand, proposed liberal or egalitarian reforms have sometimes met additional opposition because they were perceived as alien in origin. A principal reason for the failure of Kim Ok Kyun's 1884 bid to take over the government was lack of public support. While his proposed reforms focused on improving the lot of ordinary Koreans, the public took greater notice of Kim's alliance with the Japanese legation, which convinced them he was a traitor.[9] Some of the constructive legal reforms promoted by Japanese occupation authorities were also tainted by their association with foreign imperialist interference. Pak's temporary capitulation to US pressure in the early 1960s produced a more democratic constitution, but also brought accusations within Korea that he was serving the interests of a foreign power rather than those of his countrymen.[10]

As we suggested in the opening chapter, a government should not necessarily be held accountable for every case of discrimination against members of despised groups among its population. Despite reasonable efforts by governments to outlaw and otherwise discourage such discrimination, it may still occur. But if the government acquiesces to the discrimination, or is itself actively involved, this may properly be considered a violation of human rights. Although legal protection for women and *paekchong* has improved, critics argue the state should do more. Similarly, natives of the Cholla provinces claim systematic discrimination by a government filled predominantly by men from the Kyongsang region. During Pak's presidency, for example, the government invested heavily in his native Kyongsang, while Cholla enjoyed few of the benefits of the Korean economic miracle.

HUMAN RIGHTS IN NORTH KOREA

The human rights story is much simpler, if grimmer, in North Korea. Instead of the lively battle between state and society that has characterized postwar South Korea, we find in the North that all institutions, all forms of social organization, all activities of every kind are harnessed to serving the Kim regime (now presided over by Kim Jong Il, since his father's death in 1994). Inevitably, human rights get in the way of this totalitarian project, and are consequently crushed.

Kim Il Sung and his inner circle of trusted comrades were veterans of the anti-Japanese guerrilla war in Manchuria. To become the Great Leader, Kim had to triumph over several rival factions: a domestic faction of communists who stayed in Korea during the Japanese occupation, a pro-Soviet faction with ties to the USSR and a pro-Chinese faction with ties to China. Kim accomplished this within about a decade, then sought to consolidate his position, partly by building a personality cult that all but deifies him, and partly by maintaining a ruthless and efficient internal security apparatus designed to nip dissent in the bud.

Like its former mentor the Soviet Union, North Korea is highly secretive about its internal problems. Moreover, opposition to the government officially does not exist. What little information is available provides grounds for believing execution and imprisonment for political purposes is commonplace in North Korea. The number of victims is unknown, but probably extends at least into the tens of thousands, and 100,000 is often ventured as a working estimate.

The North Korean government has made a considerable effort to research and record the family and social background of its citizens. Based on this information and on current political dossiers, the government has established a kind of political caste system that separates the population into three general categories: the core class (loyal citizens), the wavering class (citizens whose commitment to the regime is suspect) and the hostile class (people with a record of opposition to the government or descendants of class enemies such as western-trained intellectuals, collaborators with the Japanese,

Christians, landowners, industrialists, etc.). Members of the latter group, who make up as much as 20 per cent of the national population, are given the most difficult and undesirable jobs. These general categories are further divided into 51 sub-categories. Besides employment, a person's ranking determines his or her access to a host of other goods and services affecting the quality of life, including education, housing, food, medical care, electricity and consumer goods.

In 1988, Asia Watch published a damning report of human rights in North Korea. Pak Gil Yon, head of Pyongyang's Permanent Observer Mission to the United Nations, responded that 'violations of human rights do not take place and are unthinkable' in North Korea.[11] North Korea has resisted attempts by the United Nations and Amnesty International to investigate its protection of human rights. Pyongyang is a signatory to the International Covenant on Civil and Political Rights (ICCPR), but has refused to submit the reports required as part of its membership in the ICCPR.

The North Korean constitution guarantees its citizens the usual political liberties: a free press, free and fair elections, freedom of speech, petition, assembly and religion, and guarantees against arbitrary arrest and searches. In practice, implementing these guarantees is the perquisite of the ultimate recognized state authority, the Korean Workers' Party (KWP), which is in turn controlled by the paramount leader.

The result is a virtual absence of civil and political rights. The press is under strict government control, and all media present the same message: extreme praise for the Kim regime and its policies, and con-demnation of its enemies. Travel and access to outside information by ordinary citizens are restricted. North Korean radios, for example, are built to receive only local stations. The North Korean judiciary and legislature are wholly controlled political tools of the KWP. The North's elections are patently meaningless; the government consis-tently claims incredibly high (up to 100 percent) voter turnout, and voting for the proposed slate of KWP candidates is invariably 'unanimous'.

Criticism and dissent are forbidden on pain of severe punishment. Essentially, any act considered by the authorities a threat or challenge to the party, its leaders, its policies or its ideology is illegal. Imprisonment for purely political and non-violent offences is com-monplace. Family members of North Koreans who defect may be locked up as a reprisal. People may be imprisoned even for unintentional acts suggesting disrespect for Kim Il Sung, such as stepping on or tearing a photograph of the Great Leader printed in a newspaper or on a postage stamp. Penalties include imprisonment with hard labour and forfeiture of political privileges. Extraction of confessions through torture appears to be standard procedure.

Some observers have estimated that the Kim regime held tens of thousands of political prisoners in twelve or more prison camps throughout the country. Attempting to rebut these reports, the North Korean government told Amnesty International in 1991 that there were only about 1,000 such prisoners and three such camps.[12] Defectors have described conditions in these 'detention centres' as brutal. Prisoners are reportedly given insufficient food, little clothing and no medical care. Inmates who violate rules may spend weeks in tiny 'punishment cells' in which the prisoner is unable to stand up or lie down.[13]

Some prisoners are also placed at work sites, where they do harsh jobs such as mining and logging and endure harsh living conditions. Here, as well, reports indicate overwork, torture, disease and malnutrition are common, often causing deaths among inmates.

North Korean law provides for the death penalty, executed by shooting or hanging, for murder and for serious political crimes against the state, such as treason, conspiracy to overthrow the government or sabotage. Executions are often public, and some are apparently summary. A 1993 letter to Amnesty International from a North Korean government official mentions an accused murderer who was executed 'at the request of the crowd'.[14] The government claims the death penalty is rare; reports from defectors and other observers suggest executions are frequent.

Many ethnic Koreans in Japan have complained that some of their relatives, lured by Pyongyang's propaganda, emigrated to North Korea, only to be executed as 'spies' or imprisoned to extort money from family members overseas.[15] Although the North Korean government promised it would allow the 6,637 Japanese women who had emigrated to North Korea with their Korean husbands regular visits to Japan, Pyongyang blocked these visits until 1997, and in the interim their relatives in Japan received no correspondence from them. Two small groups of Japanese women residing in North Korea were allowed to visit Japan in 1997 and 1998, but the North Korean authorities cancelled a planned visit by a third group in June 1998 on the pretext of 'inhuman acts on the Japanese side'.

In line with conventional Marxist ideology, North Korean offi-cialdom severely criticizes religion (except, of course, for Kimilsungism, which has effectively been the state religion, and remains so even after the elder Kim's death). Presumably, North Koreans who attempt to maintain their practice of mainstream religions such as Buddhism and Christianity (which established a significant presence in the North before the communist takeover) are persecuted. The government allows a few Christian and Buddhist places of worship to remain in operation, apparently as showpieces to substantiate the claim of religious freedom.

In the area of socioeconomic rights, North Korea's constitution promises the 'material well-being' of its citizens. The government therefore guarantees each citizen food, housing, clothing, basic education, employment and health care. That is the good news.

The bad news begins with the inescapable fact that Kim Il Sung's economic development policies have proved to be a massive failure, undermining the project of building a 'socialist paradise'. Located in the heart of the world's most economically dynamic region, North Korea has recorded negative economic growth in the 1990s, a phenomenon exacerbated rather than caused by the country's recent natural disasters. Its factories reportedly operate at only 30–40 per cent of their full capacity. The prevalence of rationing and government-sponsored campaigns encouraging the population to eat less attest that food was not plentiful even prior to the famine of the late 1990s. With the worsening conditions created by several seasons of disastrous weather, North Koreans suffered both socio-economically and politically, as indicated by reports of severe punishment of those making desperate attempts to get food.

Although the North Korean political system professes a devotion to serving the workers, their lives are generally bleak and arduous. Labourers are constantly hectored by government campaigns designed to generate greater productivity: diggers being required to hoist 1,000 shovelfuls of dirt before taking a rest, soup eliminated from meals for female factory workers to reduce work time lost on visits to the bathroom, and so on. While the constitution guarantees the right to 'rest', North Korean workers have precious little leisure time. Workdays are long, and workers are required to attend evening indoctrination sessions. These consist inevitably of reading and discussing the works of Kim Il Sung and his son. (Given the mediocrity and tedium of these works, being forced to read them for two hours a day must itself constitute some kind of human rights violation.) Those who fail to attend these meetings risk a drop in their political ranking and consequent loss of privileges. The state provides some entertainment for the masses, such as television programmes, cinema and theatre, all of it designed to reinforce party ideology and policies.

Because of the party's pervasive control over North Korean society, a person's occupation and compensation are essentially political decisions made by local party representatives; 'loyal' citizens have better opportunities for desirable work and promotion. Any semblance of labour organization outside party auspices is, of course, impossible, and workers who complain openly about working conditions or mistreatment by the authorities risk imprisonment and 're-education'.

CONCLUSIONS

Throughout most of Korean history, there has been little if any tradition of 'human rights' in the classical western sense, and only a small minority of Koreans has enjoyed the legal, political and economic privileges of the kind typically included in international declarations on human rights today.

In this light, South Korea's recent progress in human rights perhaps rivals its 'economic miracle'. In both the social/economic and political/civil categories, South Korea's human rights situation today shows great improvement over both the pre-modern period and the era of postwar quasi-military governments. There is room for continued improvement, particularly in the treatment of women, dissidents and accused criminals in police custody. The resolution of South Korea's still-precarious security situation will be a major variable affecting the scope and speed of future political liberalization. The North Korean threat is perhaps the last refuge of opposition to further reform.

The case of South Korea supports the theory that economic development creates pressures for democratization.[16] Progress in political and civil rights was virtually suspended during the period of South Korea's most rapid economic growth. With prosperity, however, demands for political liberalization increased. One can imagine the unrepentant ghost of Pak insisting that without his tough policies, South Korea would not have developed the economic strength that allowed it to contemplate political liberalisation. As in the China case, It remains arguable whether the absence of press censorship, systematic torture and illegal executions would have significantly hindered the country's admirable economic development.

North Korea has failed to uphold even the most basic civil/political rights, and its record on socioeconomic rights is also poor. The regime's political oppression of its citizens is clearly unjustifiable beyond the most narrow form of regime self-interest. But although it undermines the state's ability to provide for the basic well-being of its people, economic mismanagement per se does not constitute a violation of human rights. The Kim regime may have made honest mistakes arising from its values and perceptions. Like other authoritarians in Asia, the Kims have evidently worried that political liberalization will corrupt and weaken their society[17] – that is, the familiar 'Asian values' argument that democracy causes drug abuse, homelessness, family breakdown and violent crime. The regime also claims to prize *juche* (self-reliance), which would steer it away from the strong links with international capitalism that have promoted rapid economic growth in South Korea, Japan, Taiwan and China. If anything positive can be said for Kim Il Sung, it is that he has protected his people from the ugly side-effects of capitalist prosperity, such as the materialism and conspicuous consumption that are now prevalent among wealthy East Asians.

But it is fair to blame the North Korean regime to the extent that economic progress has been sacrificed to maintain the legitimacy of Kim Il Sung and Kim Jong Il's rule. Despite the example set by its neighbours and firm advice given by the Chinese, Pyongyang has resisted meaningful economic liberalization. Apparently the regime fears free market reforms and greater economic contact with the outside world will reveal to North Koreans what the rest of the world knows already: that Kim Il Sung's greatness is a myth, and that his strategies have retarded rather than accelerated national development.

South Korea's relative openness has tended to draw attention to human rights abuses away from the secretive North. This is unfortunate, because North Korea's human rights situation is worse than South Korea's has ever been. A complete reckoning, and deliverance for the surviving victims of the vindictive North Korean state, must await the demise of the Kim Jong Il regime.

9
Japan

The cliché of Japan as a land of contradictions (western-style political institutions built upon an age-old Asian culture, *The Chrysanthemum and the Sword*,[1] and so on) extends to Japan's human rights record as well. During the Pacific War, the Japanese government repressed and exploited its own citizens, while at the same time exhibiting unparalleled brutality throughout the region: massacring civilians, abusing prisoners of war and enslaving conquered peoples. From this experience, however, emerged within a generation a democratized Japan whose protection of both political and socioeconomic rights has been admirable by any standard, and arguably superior to the performance of its postwar mentor, the United States.

The cultural context of this remarkable development includes several attitudes prevalent throughout Northeast Asia. One is groupism, in which 'members of the group as individuals are neither free nor equal', the price paid in exchange for the security of belonging.[2] At the same time, group leaders tend to prefer consensus-building to domineering, recognizing that the success of the group as a whole is in endangered if individual members are dissatisfied. Open conflict is usually avoided if possible, and criticism indirect.

Strong Confucian influence from China via Korea has given Japanese society a hierarchical structure. Among the consequences are a comparatively high degree of respect for and trust in authorities, including government officials; and the general expectation that superiors will take care of those in their charge. Subordinates, of course, are expected to be deferential and loyal in return.

These cultural influences have laid the groundwork for the Japanese tendency to address the problem of human rights from a broad, society-wide viewpoint – that is, human rights violations are problematic because they undermine social harmony, not necessarily because they infringe upon the rights of individuals.[3] This may help explain why the Japanese government demonstrates a stronger commitment to protecting political rights, but a weaker approach to combating violations of socioeconomic rights, such as discrimination against socially disadvantaged minorities: unfair treatment of these minorities causes disharmony, but so would harsh punishments against the offending majority.

HISTORICAL BACKGROUND

The emphasis on social harmony was a logical reaction to Japan's unfavourable physical circumstances: a large population crowded into an archipelago with little arable land, few resources and frequent natural disasters, including earthquakes and typhoons. The Japanese islands were also relatively isolated, but this had the advantage of protecting them against foreign attack (the first successful invasion was the postwar occupation by the United States).

Although nominally under the authority of a single monarch since antiquity, Japan was internally divided until a group of warlords unified the country in 1192. For the next seven centuries, Japan was ruled by a *shogun*, the ranking warlord, although the emperor remained titular head of state. Civilian political institutions remained undeveloped during this period. The post of *shogun* went to the general who could win and maintain it through military strength. The cultivation of personal loyalties among commanders and between commanders and troops was critical to this enterprise. Later in the *shogun* age, centralized political control weakened, and Japan settled into a feudal system of rule by petty warlords. At the top of the social hierarchy were the *shogun* (warlord) and his administrators, the *daimyo* (aristocracy) and the *samurai* (warriors). Below them were the peasants, merchants and artisans. As in China and Korea, rulers and ruled had reciprocal duties; subjects owed their rulers security and taxes, while rulers were supposed to provide security. In practice, however, the relationship was exploitative. The elites enjoyed political and economic privileges, the working classes did not (peasants were forbidden, for example, from owning land), and there was virtually no governmental accountability to the public. Ever-increasing taxes led to frequent peasant revolts in the later part of the Tokugawa shogunate (1603–1868).

The Tokugawa regime resisted modernization and struggled, ultimately in vain, to prevent Japanese contact with westerners. Many younger *samurai*, lacking high positions in the *shogun* administration and impressed with western military technology, joined disgruntled aristocrats in armed rebellion against the shogunate, overthrowing it in 1868. What followed became known as the Meiji Restoration. The new government rejuvenated the position of the emperor as the symbolic head of state; established a centralized political apparatus; instituted a crash programme of industrialization; declared a desire to acquire foreign learning and harness it in strengthening Japan; and wrote a constitution.

The Meiji Restoration was more a capitalist than a social revolution. To facilitate modernization, the Meiji reformers implemented land reform and a degree of political liberalization, although the political system remained on the whole authoritarian and oligarchic. An elected, bicameral parliament, the Diet, was established, but it gave representation to only the wealthy minority (about 5 per cent of the male population could vote). Criticism of the government by the press and fine arts was highly restricted, and dissidents were subject to imprisonment. In 1880, the government blacklisted books that dealt favourably with the subject of democracy, forbidding their use in schools.[4]

Inevitably, however, the receptivity to knowledge from foreign countries led to an influx of western political philosophy, including the notion of natural rights. One of the side-effects was an increase in demands for economic and political rights by newly wealthy groups not traditionally part of the social elite. Indeed, it was only in this period that the word 'right' (*kenri*, literally 'power to gain') appeared in the Japanese language. Many Japanese intellectuals rejected the state-as-father view, arguing instead that the government's only legitimate role was to protect citizens' right to pursue their self-interest.

Demands for empowerment by the workers, peasants and a growing middle class continued into the twentieth century, culminating in a series of democratic reforms in the 1920s, including the granting of universal male suffrage. But this period of relatively liberal politics was short-lived. Throughout the 1930s, conservatives successfully counter-attacked. Several factors aided them: the worldwide economic crisis, the effects of which in Japan were often blamed on liberal politicians; Japanese military victories against Russia and China, which enhanced the prestige of military men seeking a greater voice in domestic politics; and the Japanese public's growing fears of internal political instability and of leftist subversion. By the end of the decade, Japan was under the control of a fascist quasi-military government.

The exigencies of the Pacific War made human rights expendable. Military men dominated the government, and in the army's view, 'The protection of individual life and property are not inviolable goals. On the contrary, they will often have to be sacrificed for national defence.'[5] By law, dissidents could be arrested and imprisoned indefinitely without trial. Arbitrary arrests of suspected troublemakers, including political offenders, were common. Many of these detainees were tortured, and some killed, by civilian and military (*kempeitai*) police. The press was strictly controlled, with negative reportage about the war or government policies forbidden. Communist and liberal literature alike was banned. Education was geared towards promoting 'patriotism' – support for the military government, the war effort and the emperor cult, and denigration of the people of enemy nations. A jingoized Shinto became the effectual state religion, leading to the persecution of Christians and other non-believers.

The Japanese military represented perhaps the worst aspect of the system. Here, millions of loyal, law-abiding Japanese were treated with remarkable brutality by their own government. Saburo Ienaga writes that 'the officer class in general had the status and authority of feudal lords. The privates, especially the new recruits, were at the miserable bottom of the pyramid. They had no human rights. They were non-persons. Military education, training and the daily routine of barracks life at the squad level was an unending stream of humiliation and rough treatment.' In this light, writes Ienaga, the atrocities of Japanese soldiers against enemy prisoners of war and civilians are not difficult to understand. 'Individuals whose own dignity and manhood had been so cruelly violated would hardly refrain from doing the same to defenceless persons under their control. After all, they were just applying what they had learned in basic training.'[6]

After Japan's defeat, American occupation authorities under General Douglas MacArthur made sweeping institutional and procedural reforms. Japan became a parliamentary democracy. The US-written constitution, never seriously challenged since its implementation, guarantees 'fundamental human rights' as 'eternal and inviolate'. These specifically include the freedoms of thought, assembly, petition, the press and religion; the rights to work and to own property; and equality of all citizens under the law. The only limitation is that the exercise of these rights must 'not interfere with the public welfare'.

Political prisoners were released and many civil liberties restored. State sponsorship of Shinto was abolished. The education system was completely changed, with the fascist agenda removed. Land reform made 90 per cent of Japan's farmers landowners. To investigate alleged human rights abuses, a Civil Liberties Bureau was established. The Bureau's enforcement powers, however, are weak; its self-professed mission is 'educating' rather than punishing violators.

CIVIL AND POLITICAL RIGHTS

While scholars debate the nature and depth of Japanese 'democracy',[7] Japan's political system offers a range of civil and political rights comparable to the democratic nations of the West. In accord with the constitutional guarantee of a free press, the government does not forcibly stifle political debate. But the Japanese government has been more effective than many other democratic states in 'managing' the news. To get access to information controlled by the government, journalists must maintain a good relationship with public officials. To maintain such a relationship, journalists must avoid writing negative stories about the government. Consequently, there is little serious investigative reporting in Japan, and a striking homogeneity in news coverage among the major media organs.

Religious freedom is observed, and many religions other than the former state religion of Shinto are freely preached and practised. Japanese citizens are free to change their place of residence and occupation within Japan and to travel abroad. Political protest assemblies are allowed, provided they are not considered a danger to public safety. In the past, punishment has often been lenient even for highly destructive demonstrations. Organization and collective bargaining is allowed for all workers except the military, police and fire fighters. Trade unions are independent and active, particularly at election time and during the yearly 'spring wage offensive'.

It should probably be taken as a positive commentary on the climate of civil and political rights in Japan that the *yakuza* (Japanese mafia) crime boss Takumi Masaru complained that a 1992 law aimed at organized crime 'violates [gangsters'] constitutional guarantees of freedom of assembly, equality under the law and freedom of expression'.[8]

Since the postwar democratization, the police force has not been abused as a political tool by the government. Cruel or degrading treatment by police or prison guards is forbidden by law, but isolated cases of police brutality occur, usually involving violence of verbal abuse of criminal suspects in order to obtain confessions. Amnesty International has concluded that the mistreatment of detainees in police custody is widespread and that procedural safeguards are inadequate.[9]

The Japanese prison system remains a holdover from the country's more authoritarian past. Prisons are administered by a relatively autonomous bureaucracy according to statutes that date from 1908. Prisoners endure a tough, highly constrained regimen that borders on cruelty. Not only the activities, but the very freedom of movement of prison inmates is limited by strict rules. Prisoners are not allowed to speak or make eye contact with guards during the prison workday (typically eight hours). Only certain movements are permitted during washing and eating periods, and these must start and stop according to the commands of the guards. Prisoners who commit even minor infractions of these rules may lose their bathing privileges, have their hands bound by handcuffs attached to a leather belt or be placed in solitary confinement. Prison cells and workplaces, moreover, are often unclean, unheated in winter and uncooled in summer, conditions that contribute to poor health among the inmates. The fruits of this tough system are not impressive; the recidivism rate is 45 per cent.[10]

Japanese law forbids arbitrary searches, seizures and arrests, and there is no evidence of systematic disregard of these protections. By law, the maximum period a suspect may be held without being charged and given the right to legal counsel is 23 days. This rule is sometimes circumvented through the practice of *bekken taiho*: arresting people on a minor charge and using the time allowed for detention to investigate the more serious charge the police are really interested in. If something turns up, the police can then arrest the suspect again on a new charge and get another 23 days.

Criminal suspects have less power relative to the state than in the West. The suspect has no right to legal counsel during the first few days of detention, when interrogation takes place. If indicted, however, suspects are entitled to legal counsel, at government expense if necessary. In accordance with the constitution, trials are public and reasonably speedy. Generally, trials are held within two months of an indictment. Suspects and their lawyers cannot confront witnesses for the prosecution. Defence lawyers are cooperative, even sympathetic, with the state's interests. Verdicts are determined by judges rather than juries, and these judges have broad leeway in determining what evidence is admissible. Yet Japanese legal authorities tend to employ their considerable powers with restraint. Only about 2 per cent of convicted criminals are jailed.[11] As in China, the attitude of the defendant is important; those who appear more penitent are likely to get lighter sentences, or to avoid prosecution altogether. Despite this generally gentle handling of convicts, Japan practises capital punishment, executing a few criminals yearly.

SOCIAL AND ECONOMIC RIGHTS

In the main, Japan is a highly prosperous country in which the wealth is widely shared. Over 90 per cent of the Japanese population regard themselves as 'middle class'.[12] Affluence is spread relatively evenly throughout Japanese society, partly through conscious efforts such as high inheritance taxes and a steeply progressive income tax rate. One Japanese writer calculates the wealth inequality ratio between the poorest 20 per cent and the richest 20 per cent of the population at 2.9:1 (the figure for the United States is 9.1:1, and for Britain and France over 10:1).[13] Beggars are rare (and not because police have rounded them up). Unemployment is under 3 per cent. The Japanese enjoy the world's longest average life spans: 81 years for females, and 76 years for males. Japan's violent crime rates are among the lowest in the world. Private ownership of firearms is illegal, although a recent spate of shootings suggests that the number of guns being smuggled into Japan is increasing[14] and the sensational subway gas poisonings of 1995 shook the sense of security of many Japanese. The relatively low crime rate has more to do with culture than an intrusive or rigorous law enforcement system. Louis D. Hayes observes, 'In Japan obedience of the law is ingrained, a product of social expectations to conform, rather than the threat of punitive retribution imposed by agencies of the state.'[15]

Literacy and primary and secondary school attendance are close to 100 per cent. The quality of life of Japanese secondary school students, however, leaves something to be desired. To gain admission into high school and college, students must take standardized examinations. The higher the student scores, the better the school he or she will be eligible to attend. Because educational background is so critical to future employment opportunities, the pressure on students to perform well is intense. The run-up to these exams, held twice a year, is known as 'exam hell'. Students sleep little and spend nearly all their waking hours studying. Many parents pay thousands of dollars to send their children to special courses designed to prepare them for the high school and college entrance exams – and some of these cram schools have their *own* entrance exams. Says one Japanese observer, 'Our children are being robbed of their childhood.'[16] For the 10–15 per cent who fail to do well enough to get into any college, the usual reaction is severe disappointment and shame, contributing to the comparatively high rate of teenage suicide in Japan.

Ordinary Japanese have other complaints about their living conditions, including exorbitant property prices, cramped housing, long commutes to work, and excessive prices for some agricultural products resulting from the government's protection of inefficient domestic producers. It would be far-fetched, however, to classify these as human rights abuses.

LABOUR

In keeping with the traditional importance of patron–client relationships, employees tend to place high value on maintaining a good personal relationship with their superiors, rather than banding together with co-workers in open confrontations with management, as their most effective means of career advancement. Employees even accept guidance from superiors in their private lives. For their part, Japanese firms consciously cultivate a harmonious relationship between the worker and the company. As a consequence, workers' loyalty and identification with the firm is high, and even with the flurry of strikes typical during the 'spring offensive', work stoppage in Japan is relatively low for an industrialized country.

Many Japanese companies guarantee their employees lifetime job security. As in Japanese society as a whole, the distribution of income between the highest- and lowest-paid employees of Japanese firms is far less unequal than in, for example, the United States. Japan's rate of industrial accidents is comparatively low. Minors under the age of 15 are prohibited from working, and workers in jobs considered hazardous must be at least 18. Laws stipulating minimum wages, maximum working hours and reasonably good working conditions are evidently well enforced.

The largely favourable circumstances of Japanese workers help compensate for a lack of social mobility. It is common for families to maintain roughly the same economic level through several generations. For those outside the elite, it is difficult to break in. Most current political and business leaders are sons of men who held similar positions. Family background dictates educational opportunities, a highly important determinant of one's socioeconomic destiny – about half of Japan's top executives and politicians are graduates of Tokyo University. 'In Japan', concludes Louis D. Hayes, 'there is no chance for someone with a working-class background to make it to the top and very little chance for anyone from the middle class.'[17]

DISCRIMINATION AGAINST MINORITIES

Despite the constitutional pledge that 'There shall be no discrimination in political, economic, or social relations because of race, creed, sex, social status, or family origin', discrimination against socially disadvantaged groups is a probably Japan's most serious internal human rights problem.

Ethnically, Japan is highly homogeneous. Japanese generally consider their homogeneity as a strength, sparing them the destructive racial and religious conflicts that afflict many other countries. Accordingly, they have resisted the growth of a non-Japanese minority. Even with a labour shortage and a host of foreigners eager to take on the low-paying jobs few Japanese will accept (there are some 100,000 illegal immigrants in Japan), the Japanese have been reluctant to admit foreign workers. The fear of an influx of non-Japanese also explains Japan's treatment of foreign refugees and asylum-seekers, which has moved Amnesty International to contend that the Japanese government has not fulfilled its obligations as a signatory to two relevant UN documents. From August 1995 to August 1996, for example, Japan's Ministry of Justice received 93 applications for asylum and approved none of them.[18] According to Amnesty International, would-be applicants are often made ineligible by technicalities or deterred by complicated procedures; others who request consideration as political refugees apparently do not receive it; and many applicants with strong evidence that they would suffer political persecution if they returned to their home country are turned down.[19] Tokyo agreed to harbour about 10,000 Vietnamese 'boat people' refugees only after strong international pressure. (By comparison, Britain, a poorer, more distant, non-Asian country, has taken in nearly twice as many Vietnamese refugees.)

Ethnic homogeneity and the belief of Japanese in their own uniqueness have bred a racism that appears broad-based and officially condoned. Japanese politicians are notorious for periodically making racist statements that find their way into the international press, irritating other countries such as the ethnically heterogeneous United States. At the highest levels, the relatively cosmopolitan Prime Minister Yasuhiro Nakasone once said publicly that the average intelligence level in the United States was lowered by 'blacks, Puerto Ricans and Mexicans'. At lower levels, there is the example of a police staff manual that said Pakistanis 'have a unique stink', 'do nothing but lie in the name of Allah' and that police should wash their hands after interrogating Pakistani suspects to avoid disease.[20] Japan seems less embarrassed by the views these gaffes represent than by the fact that such statements were carelessly uttered within the earshot of outsiders. While the Japanese do not have a monopoly on racism, the widespread acceptance of certain racist assumptions in Japan helps explain the permissive attitude observers have noted among Japanese officialdom towards many discriminatory practices: while laws protecting minorities exist, they are rendered nearly ineffectual by a lack of prescribed criminal penalties.

Minority groups that endure some form of negative discrimination include the *Burakumin*, the Ainu (an indigenous group of about 50,000 who reside mainly in the northern island of Hokkaido), Okinawans, descendants of atomic bomb survivors, Japanese who have lived abroad, Japanese citizens of mixed race and permanent resident foreigners, the largest group being ethnic Koreans.

Burakumin literally means 'village people'. The name is a great improvement over *eta* ('much filth') or *hinin* ('non-human'), as *Burakumin* were previously known. Like the Paekchong of Korea, these are the descendants of families consigned to 'unclean' jobs involving animal carcasses or dead human bodies. In the past, they were severely stigmatized. Ordinary Japanese refused to associate with or even touch them. *Burakumin* were required to wear clothing identifying them as outcasts. In a famous nineteenth-century court case, an Edo judge exonerated a mob on trial for killing an *eta* who attempted to enter a shrine. The life of an *eta*, ruled the judge, was worth only one-seventh the life of an ordinary person; therefore, unless at least seven *eta* were murdered, there was no basis for assessing punishment.[21]

Burakumin obtained legal equality during the Meiji Restoration, and many have long since abandoned their traditional occupations, but over a century later they remain segregated in several thousand ghettos, their socioeconomic level considerably lower than that of mainstream Japanese. Although *Burakumin* do not look or speak differently from other Japanese, many, perhaps most, Japanese continue to harbour the negative stereotype of *Burakumin* as physically unclean, intellectually inferior, and morally incontinent.

Despite the government 'guidelines' forbidding discrimination against *Burakumin* seeking jobs, prejudice is clearly a factor. One *Burakumin* lamented, 'Nowadays no company or local government is going to come right out and refuse someone a job because they are *Burakumin*. Employers are more subtle than that. They are adept at finding excuses for not hiring us, such as schooling or aptitude. It's the same old game, but they have become much better at playing it.'[22]

Discrimination against them is perpetuated by family registry records. A lengthy book of *Burakumin* genealogy was banned in 1980 for this reason, but the information reportedly continues to circulate underground among prospective in-laws and employers.

In contrast to typical urban Japan, the slums where *Burakumin* reside are often filthy, dilapidated and infested with rats and disease. Many live pathetic, desperate lives, indulging in gambling and heavy drinking, worsening their poverty.

Yoshio Dan, a union officer in Osaka's Airin slum, largely inhabited by *Burakumin*, says, 'this area is like a concentration camp in an open space. When we're not getting beaten up by the police, we're getting fleeced by the *yakuza*.' Police in the area are notorious for roughing up drunks and homeless people, whose complaints carry little weight with the authorities. The *yakuza* exploit down-and-out *Burakumin* through loan sharking or by hiring them as temporary labourers and then skimming their wages.

Rioting occasionally breaks out in *Burakumin* neighbourhoods, as occurred in Airin in 1990. Residents attacked the local police and train stations and burned several other buildings. Two hundred rioters and police were injured in a week of mayhem. Significantly, the Japanese media gave the incident only minimal coverage.[23]

Burakumin pressure groups have successfully lobbied for new legislation to provide special social services for *Burakumin* communities. The Japanese government has spent billions in this effort. The *Burakumin* Liberation League is known for its aggressive tactics, threatening boycotts or violence against people and organizations it believes are guilty of discrimination.

Koreans are another group Japanese generally consider inferior, ironic considering Japan's substantial cultural debt to Korea. Large numbers of Koreans began coming to Japan after the Japanese annexed Korea in 1910. Prejudice against them placed them at constant risk of mistreatment, and even violence. After a 1923 earthquake in the Tokyo area, rumours circulated that Koreans were taking advantage of the disaster to loot businesses and assault Japanese. In response, Japanese mobs went on a murderous rampage against the Korean community, killing thousands.

Around 650,000 ethnic Koreans remain in Japan, most of them second- or third-generation. Many are completely assimilated and could pass for Japanese if not for family registry records. Nevertheless, most Japanese still consider Koreans outsiders with undesirable characteristics, and there is a clear pattern of discrimination against them. In a 1998 court case, for example, a Korean family sued the owner of the condominium where they lived because the owner had told the family not to tell neighbours they were Korean and to avoid wearing traditional Korean clothing in public. The family lost its case in district court, but a higher court ordered the condominium owner to pay them damages. Few high-status occupations are available to Koreans. It is all but impossible, for example, for a even a highly qualified Korean-Japanese to land a high-level executive position in a major Japanese corporation. Koreans in Japan suffer relatively high unemployment and commit a disproportionate share of Japan's crime. (In contrast, Koreans in Korea are noted for their hard work, and crime rates are relatively low.)

After years of complaints from the Japanese Korean community and from Seoul, the Japanese government recently dropped the requirement that resident aliens be fingerprinted, but still requires them to carry an alien registration certificate. New legislation also gives Koreans access to public housing, loans and even some positions in local government. Typically, however, these anti-discrimination laws do not prescribe penalties for violators.

Foreigners with five years of continuous residency in Japan are eligible to apply for citizenship. Most Korean residents, however, choose not to apply, seeing the acquisition of Japanese citizenship (and, as part of the requirements, a Japanese name) as a betrayal of their ethnic heritage. Others apply but are refused, prompting complaints from Koreans that the process is biased against them. Stigmatization may continue to follow even those ethnic Koreans who obtain Japanese citizenship; they will never be 'natural' Japanese in their eyes of many of their countrymen, and their background can be discovered through family records.

To make matters worse for the Korean community, their political power is weakened by internal disunity. In a manifestation of the diplomatic and military conflict between North and South Korea, two rival political organizations vie for the loyalty of Korean expatriates in Japan. Chongryon (General Federation of Koreans in Japan) is sympathetic to the Pyongyang regime, facilitating emigration and the transfer of money to North Korea. Mindan, the Korean Resident Association in Japan, supports South Korea and has tended to encourage the assimilation of Koreans into Japanese society, reflecting the postwar accommodation between Seoul and Tokyo.

SEXUAL DISCRIMINATION

The feudal and Confucian society of pre-modern Japan kept women in a thoroughly subordinate position. Their lot was to serve and obey their fathers, husbands and sons, to be 'good wives and wise mothers'. A double standard toward extra-marital sex also developed, one that persists today, although it shows signs of weakening. Throughout the years of Japan's 'modernization', attitudes towards women remained backward. In Robert J. Smith's words, 'women were thought to be less intelligent than men, more emotional and so less rational, less reliable, vindictive, potentially dangerous if not rigorously disciplined, and worst of all, silly'.[24]

Until the postwar era, only men attended college. Today, colleges and universities freely admit women, but their employment opportunities are still limited. While women make up some 40 per cent of the Japanese workforce, few make it to the highest levels of business, government, law, medicine, science or academia. Most Japanese firms will not hire females for technical or management positions. Instead, women find jobs as unskilled factory workers, elementary school teachers, secretaries, nurses, shop clerks and 'office ladies'. The average female worker earns about half as much as the average male worker, and females often have less job security because they are considered likely to quit after a few years to concentrate on homemaking.

In addition to the constitutional guarantee of legal equality of the sexes, a 1986 Equal Employment Opportunity Law specifically addressed the problem of sexual discrimination in the workplace. This law, however, is weakly worded; while spelling out various forms of potential discrimination, it says only that 'employers should endeavour' to prevent these problems.

The concept of sexual harassment (transliterated in Japan as *seku hara*) has helped sensitize the Japanese public to deep-seated patterns of mistreatment. In recent years, several Japanese women have successfully sued their offending male bosses for damages.

Despite their clear disadvantages in the workplace, and, says Ardath W. Burks, 'to the despair of visiting feminists, most Japanese women really are content'.[25] The reason seems to be the satisfaction women find in their domestic roles as wives and mothers. With their husbands away at work from early in the morning until well into the evening, housewives develop strong bonds with the children and effectively run the household, often including control of the family's finances.

The Japanese government drew criticism from both disabled people's and women's rights groups when it acknowledged in 1997 that between 1949 and 1992, the state oversaw the sterilization of some 16,500 handicapped women without their consent. The government added that it was not obligated to pay compensation in these cases because these sterilizations were legal under the Eugenic Protection Law (repealed in 1996) at the time they were performed.

HUMAN RIGHTS AND JAPAN'S FOREIGN RELATIONS

For many people in the region, the most important human rights issue connected with Japan involves the Pacific War. Throughout the postwar decades, Japan's neighbours felt the Japanese government had not adequately atoned for the atrocities committed by its troops. Anti-Japan sentiments were periodically rekindled by the controversies over sanitized versions of the Pacific War in Japanese textbooks and by offensive comments from the Japanese right wing, such as politician Shintaro Ishihara's claim that the wartime Nanking Massacre was a 'fabrication'.

In recent years, however, the Japanese government has taken unprecedented steps to smooth over bad feelings in the region, including explicitly apologizing for Japan's wartime aggression, admitting to exploitative policies such as the importation of Chinese slave labourers (thousands of whom died in Japan) and offering financial compensation to surviving 'comfort women'.

Despite all this, Tokyo has hardly turned into a human rights crusader. To call Japan's record 'pragmatic' would be kind.

Japan is only beginning to exercise an independent foreign policy. From the end of the Second World War through to the end of the Cold War, Japan generally either supported Washington's goals and policies or kept a low profile. In harmony with US wishes, Japan signed the International Covenant on Economic, Social, and Cultural Rights and the International Covenant on Civil and Political Rights in 1979. Tokyo also agreed in 1991 to make human rights a consideration in its allotment of foreign aid, of which Japan has in recent years become the world's largest donor.

But Japan's expressed interest in promoting human rights internationally seems mainly intended to mollify powerful liberal friends. Despite its 1991 promise, the Japanese government signed the 1993 Bangkok Declaration on human rights, key points of which were that aid from developed to developing countries should *not* be linked with human rights and that no country should impose its values upon another government. In practice, the promotion of human rights has not been much of a factor in Japan's overseas development assistance.

The Japanese government went along reluctantly with Tiananmen massacre sanctions against Beijing, then broke ranks with the West and resumed economic aid to China after barely a year. Numerous Chinese nationals who applied for political asylum or tried to extend their visas in Japan were refused. Worse, Japanese officials have been accused of abetting and even aiding Chinese diplomatic staff in the harassment and intimidation of Chinese dissidents in Japan.[26]

Japan's reaction to Tiananmen fit the pattern visible in its relations with Southeast Asian states as well. The Burmese military slaughtered several hundred pro-democracy demonstrators in September 1988. The Japanese suspended economic aid to Burma, but restored it in February 1989, despite continued sanctions by the western nations. Japan recognized the military government and worked to delay and later to soften a condemnatory UN resolution. In 1992, the Japanese ambassador to Burma said Tokyo was 'satisfied' with the performance of the Burmese government. Similarly, massacres of unarmed demonstrators in Dili, East Timor and Bangkok in 1991 brought no interruptions in Japanese economic aid to Indonesia or Thailand.[27]

All told, Japan's most significant international impact on human rights may be in its emerging role as a mediator between East Asia and the West. Here, Tokyo's main contribution is helping protect illiberal Asian governments from western pressure to democratize and protect human rights.[28]

CONCLUSIONS

Postwar Japan has the best human rights record in East Asia. There is, of course, ample room for improvement. While discrimination against women, Koreans, *Burakumin* and other socially disadvantaged groups cannot be blamed solely on the government, public officials could do more to promote a more favourable environment for these groups, including tougher enforcement of laws forbidding discrimination. Internationally, while Japanese officials have been known to appeal privately to foreign governments for the release of certain political prisoners, Japan's commitment to promoting the protection of human rights have disappointed observers in the West. (In their own defence, Japanese officials have wielded the constructive engagement argument, adding that public scolding and sanctions of offending regimes are counterproductive.)

The Japanese have largely transcended the political versus socio-economic rights trade-off that has been so central to the politics of other Asian countries. Remarkably, postwar Japan has produced a comparatively humane political and social system that has achieved a high degree of prosperity and public safety without resorting to heavy official intrusion or draconian punishments. Traditional Japanese social mores have played an influential role, making the state's task relatively easy. Japan is therefore an example, but not an exemplar; a success story whose methods could not be replicated anywhere else.

Legal concepts are usually adapted to fit Japan's social context, and not the reverse. Like many other western observers, Edwin O. Reischauer argues that 'the Japanese on the whole think less in terms of abstract ethical principles than do Westerners and more in terms of concrete situations and complex human relationships'.[29] Yet

Japan has rather nicely managed the potential conflict between the rights of individuals and the rights of society as a whole. On one hand, certain political liberties have less leeway than they are given in some western countries. The Japanese Supreme Court has held, for example, that obscenity endangers the public welfare and is therefore not protected by the freedom of speech. On the other hand, the postwar governments have avoided anything like the political oppression in contemporary China, recent South Korea or wartime Japan. If the Japanese government has sought to protect social harmony rather than individual rights per se, they have done so in a way that accords individuals considerable protection.

Notes

CHAPTER 1

1. See *The Economist* , 27 April 1994, p. 5. This was from a lecture in 1992 in the Philippines berating their system of democracy.
2. Cited in the *New Straits Times* (Kuala Lumpur) 2 July 1991, p. 1.
3. See *Joint Communiqué of the Twenty-Sixth ASEAN Ministerial Meeting,* Singapore, 23–24 July 1993, p. 8.
4. See David Kelly, 'Freedom – A Eurasian Mosaic', in David Kelly and Anthony Reid (eds), *Asian Freedoms: The Idea of Freedom in East and Southeast Asia* (Cambridge: Cambridge University Press, 1998), p. 3.
5. See S. P. Huntington, *The Third Wave: Democratization in the Late Twentieth Century* (London: University of Oklahoma Press, 1991).
6. See Bikhu Parekh, 'The Cultural Particularity of Liberal Democracy', in David Held (ed.), *Prospects for Democracy: North, South, East, West* (Cambridge: Polity Press, 1993), p. 156.
7. Ibid.
8. See Joanne R. Bauer and Daniel A. Bell (eds), *The East Asian Challenge for Human Rights* (Cambridge: Cambridge University Press, 1999), p. 3.
9. Denny Roy, 'Singapore, China, and the `Soft Authoritarian' Challenge', *Asian Survey*, vol. 34, no. 3 (March 1994), pp. 231–42.
10. Madeleine Albright made this statement on 17 October 1995, while she was US Representative to the United Nations. Symposium on Human Rights and the Lessons of the Holocaust, Senator Thomas J. Dodd Research Center, Storrs, Connecticut. Shattuck's comment is from the introduction to the US State Department's 1996 *Annual Reports on Human Rights Practices*, Washington, DC, 30 January 1997.
11. This example is drawn from the Council of Europe's Convention for Protection of Human Rights and Fundamental Freedoms, signed in Rome in 1950.
12. See J. Hsiung, *Human Rights in East Asia: A Cultural Perspective* (New York: Paragon, 1985), p. 25.
13. See 'The Rule of Law', *Asiaweek*, 25 March 1994, p. 26. Among articles regarding Asian values and their relationship to human rights concerns see Diane K. Mauzy, 'The Human Rights and "Asian Values" Debate in Southeast Asia: Trying to Clarify the Key Issues', in *The Pacific Review*, vol. 10, no. 2 (1997), pp. 210–37; Michael Freeman, 'Human Rights, Asian Values and the Clash of Civilizations', in *Issues and Studies* vol. 34, no. 10 (October 1998), pp. 48–78; Alan Dupont, 'Is There an "Asian Way"?', in *Survival*, vol. 38, no. 2 (summer 1996), pp. 13–33; and the special edition of *Sojourn* covering 'Asian Ways: Asian Values Revisited', in *Sojourn*, vol. 14, no. 2 (October 1999).

14. See 'The Democracy Debate – SM', *Straits Times* (Singapore), 17 June 1993.

15. See Asian Cultural Forum on development, *Our Voice: Bangkok NGO Declaration on Human Rights* Report on the Asia-Pacific NGO Forum on Human Rights, Bangkok, 25–28 March 1993, article 8.

16. See Michael Freeman, 'Human Rights and Real Cultures: Towards a Dialogue on "Asian Values"', in the *Netherlands Quarterly of Human Rights*, vol. 16(1) (1998), p. 26.

17. See Hsiung, *Human Rights in East Asia*, p. 2.

18. Denny Roy argues succinctly that this challenge to the West begins 'much like the West's traditional Orientalist scholarship, with the premise that Asia and the West are fundamentally different. But this time Asia turns the tables by making the West its Other, contrasting favourable "Asian" traits such as industriousness, filial piety, selflessness, and chastity, with caricatures of negative "Western" culture.' See D. Roy, 'Singapore, China and the "Soft Authoritarian" Challenge', *Asian Survey*, vol. XXXIV, no. 3 (1994).

19. This view has been expressed quite clearly by Christopher Lingle, formerly a senior Fellow at the National University of Singapore. See 'Asia's "White Peril" Just a Red Herring', *Australian*, 10 October 1994. For a useful critique of 'Asian values', see D. Jones and D. Brown, 'Singapore and the Myth of the Liberalizing Middle Class', *The Pacific Review* vol. 7, no. 1 (1994), pp. 79–87. They argue that 'the government has been quite explicit in stating that its deployment of "Asian values" as a political rhetoric is necessary precisely to counteract the allegedly fissiparous implications of the rapid social changes experienced by Singaporeans' (p. 83).

20. See 'Asia's New Jobless', in *The Economist*, 28 March 1998, which highlights the dilemma of illegal immigrants who were seen by some governments in the region as a threat to 'national security'.

21. Cited in Adam Schwartz, *A Nation in Waiting: Indonesia in the 1990s* (Boulder, Col.: Westview Press, 1994), p. 255.

22. See 'East Timor: Adrift and Violent', *The Economist*, 10 April 1999, p. 56.

23. See Hsiung, *Human Rights in East Asia*, p. 23.

24. In fact, Samuel Huntington argues that the change to democracy is most prominent in the middle-income countries; 'in poor countries democratization is unlikely, in rich countries it has already occurred. In between there is a political transition zone; countries in that particular economic stratum are most likely to transit to democracy and most countries that transit to democracy will be in that stratum.' See S. P. Huntington, *The Third Wave: Democratization in the Late Twentieth Century* (London: University of Oklahoma Press, 1991), pp. 60–3. This is based on the three classifications of countries into low-, middle- and high-income countries by the World Bank.

25. Huntington, *The Third Wave*, p. 37.

26. A useful overview of this can be found in the Introduction to R. E. Howard and J. Donnelly (eds), *International Handbook of Human Rights* (New York: Greenwood Press, 1987), p. 15.

27. See the White Paper, *Shared Values* (Singapore: Singapore National Printers, 1991), p. 1.
28. See Garry Rodan, 'Singapore's Leadership Transition: Erosion or Refinement of Authoritarian Rule?', in *Bulletin of Concerned Asian Scholars*, vol. 24, no. 1 (January–March 1992), p. 10.
29. See Michael Vatkiosis, *Political Change in Southeast Asia: Trimming the Banyan Tree* (London: Routledge, 1996), p. 122.
30. Daniel Bell et al., *Towards Illiberal Democracy in Pacific Asia* (Oxford and New York: St Antony's College, Oxford and St Martin's Press, 1995), pp. 27–8.
31. See David Martin Jones and David Brown. 'Singapore and the Myth of the Liberalizing Middle Class', in the *Pacific Review*, vol. 7, no. 1 (1995), p. 82.
32. See IMF, *World Economic Outlook: Interim Assessment (Crisis in Asia: Regional and Global Implications)* (Washington, DC: IMF, 1997).
33. Lipset, K. R. Seong and J. C. Torres, 'A Comparative Analysis of the Social Requisites of Democracy', in *International Social Science Journal*, vol. 45, no. 2 (1993), pp. 156–7.
34. C. B. McPherson, *The Real World of Democracy* (Oxford: Clarendon Press, 1966), pp. 33–6.
35. Lipset, K. R. Seong and J. C. Torres, 'A Comparative Analysis of the Social Responsibilities of Democracy', *International Social Sciences Journal*, vol. 45, no. 2 (1993), pp. 156–7.
36. See Joanne R. Bauer and Daniel A. Bell (eds), *The East Asian Challenge For Human Rights* (Cambridge: Cambridge University Press, 1999), p. 4.

CHAPTER 2

1. See Chandran Jeshrun, 'Malaysia: A Backgrounder'. Paper presented at conference on Trends in Malaysia. Singapore, 3 November 1994.
2. See Jomo K. Sundaram, 'A Nationalist Corporatist Alternative for Malaysian Development: Lessons from Singapore'. Paper presented at the Fourth Malaysia–Singapore Forum, Faculty of Arts and Sciences, University of Malaya, 8–11 December 1994.
3. Ibid., p. 6.
4. See 'Hard Labour for Hard Drugs', *The Economist*, 3 September 1994, p. 27.
5. See R. S. Milne and Diane K. Mauzy, *Malaysian Politics under Mahathir* (London: Routledge), pp. 75–6 for a succinct analysis of this problem.
6. See 'Malaysia Police Seize Anwar after Anti- Mahathir protest', *International Herald Tribune* 21 September 1998, p. 1.
7. See '4 Opposition Men Arrested in KL Dragnet', *Straits Times* (Singapore Interactive Web Site) <http://straitstimes.asia1.com/reg/ma11–0921.htr> (21 September 1999).
8. For a fuller account of the Anwar saga, see 'Malaysia' in *HRW Report 1999: Malaysia: Human Rights Developments*, in <http://www.hrw.org/hrw/worldreport99/asia/malaysia.htn>. 1999 had in fact seen a series of developments which finally led to the arrest of Anwar, including the

publication of a book in May 1999 called *50 Dalil Kenapa Anwar Tidak Boleh Jali PM* (50 Reasons Why Anwar Cannot Become PM), which contained graphic sexual allegations against the Deputy Prime Minister and was circulated at UMNO meetings.

9. See Vitit Muntarbhorn, 'Current Challenges of Human Rights in Asia', in D. M. Hill (ed.), *Human Rights and Foreign Policy: Principles and Practice* (London: Macmillan 1989).

10. See L. K. Siang, 'Human Rights in Malaysia' (DAP Human Rights Committee Publication: Kuala Lumpur, 1985).

11. See 'Al-Arqam Ban "in Public Interest"', *Straits Times* (Singapore), 28 August 1994, p. 19.

12. See Leah Makabenta, 'Malaysia: Politics behind Ban on Muslim sect?' (Interpress News Agency, Manila, Malaysia, 8 July 1994).

13. See James Chin, 'Malaysia in 1997: Mahathir's Annus Horribilis', *Asian Survey*, vol. XXXVIII, no. 2 (February 1998), p. 184.

14. See 'Malaysia', *HRW World Report 1999: Malaysia: Human Rights Developments*, in <http://www.hrw.org/hrw/worldreport99/asia/malaysia.htn>. The report noted that 'in mid-March [1998], the government intervened to settle a conflict between Muslims and Hindus in Penang, where Hindus had tried to build a temple within twenty meters of a mosque. Over 180 people were arrested when the conflict was at its height, but most were questioned and released; some 40 remained in detention in the weeks immediately following.'

15. See 'End of an Era', *Asiaweek,* 30 March 1994, pp. 24–30.

16. See Amnesty International, *Malaysia, 'Operation Lallang': Detention without trial under the internal security act* (London: Amnesty International, 1988, ASA 28/18/88).

17. See Lim Kit Siang, 'Human Rights – An Overview', *Human Rights in Malaysia* (Petaling Jaya: Human Rights Committee, 1986).

18. See Amnesty International, *Malaysia: Death of an Innocent?: Death Penalty Accused Presumed Guilty* (June 1993, AI Index: ASA 28/01/93). Official estimates suggest that there may be as many as 100,000 drug addicts among the 19 million people of Malaysia; see the 'Hard Labour for Hard Drugs' in *The Economist,* 3 September 1994, p. 27.

19. See C. Espiritu, *Law and Human Rights in the Development of ASEAN* (Singapore: Friedrich-Naumann-Stiftung, 1986), pp. 23–7.

20. See 'Malaysia Expels Correspondent for "Security" Reasons', *Jakarta Post*, 5 April 1994, p. 11.

21. See Amnesty International, *When the State Kills* (New York: Amnesty International, 1989), p. 171.

22. See Amnesty International, *Malaysia: The Cane to Claim More Victims* (December 1993, AI Index: ASA 28/08/93). One prisoner described his experience as akin to the pain he imagined would result from branding with a red-hot iron.

23. This was reported in 'Confucius or Convenience?', *Bangkok Post,* 22 March 1993, p. 5.

24. See Boo Tion Kwa, 'Righteous Talk', *Far Eastern Economic Review,* 17 June 1993.

25. See Philip Eldridge, 'Human Rights and Democracy in Indonesia and Malaysia: Emerging Contexts and Discourse', *Contemporary Southeast Asia,* vol. 18, no. 3 (December 1996), pp. 311–12.

26. See 'Mahathir Slams Western Press for Inciting Instability in Asia', *Business Times* (Singapore), 4 August 1993, p. 3.

27. See *Far Eastern Economic Review,* 17 June 1993.

28. See Chandra Muzaffar, *Dominance of the West over the Rest* (Penang: Just World Trust, 1995), pp. 100–3.

29. See Philip Eldridge, 'Human Rights and Democracy in Indonesia and Malaysia', *Contemporary Southeast Asia,* vol. 18, no. 3 (December 1996), p. 312.

30. See the *Far Eastern Economic Review,* 23 January 1992, p. 14.

31. See 'Trade with Malaysia: Grovelling Failure', *The Economist,* 27 August 1994, p. 47.

32. See 'Mahathir Cautions against Being Slaves of Democracy', *Business Times* (Singapore), 31 May 1993, p. 1.

33. See Caesar Espiritu, *Law and Human Rights in the Development of ASEAN* (Friedrich-Naumann-Stiftung: Singapore, 1986), p. 25 from where this quote is taken.

34. See Bridget Welsh, 'Attitudes towards Democracy in Malaysia: Challenges to the Regime?', *Asian Survey,* vol. XXXVI, no. 9 (September 1996), p. 884.

35. See 'Dr M Starts to Get Desperate', *Independent on Sunday,* 6 September 1998, p. 19.

36. See M. Leifer, *The Dictionary of Modern Politics of Southeast Asia* (London: Routledge, 1995), p. 29.

37. See G. Rodan, 'Preserving the One-party State in Contemporary Singapore', in K. Hewison, R. Robison and G. Rodan (eds), *Southeast Asia in the 1990's: Authoritarianism, Democracy and Capitalism* (St Leonards: Allen and Unwin, 1993), p. 77.

38. See Michael Vatkiosis, *Political Change in Southeast Asia: Trimming the Banyan Tree* (London: Routledge, 1996), p. 122. In the late 1980s the Singaporean government decided to formulate a national ideology to reinforce important 'Asian' values in the face of westernization. These were (1) Nation before Community and Society before Self. (2) Family as the basic unit of society. (3) Community support and respect for the individual. (4) Consensus, not conflict. (5) Racial and religious harmony. It was only after some public debate that the third value was added to the list because of complaints of the lack of any reference to the individual.

39. See 'No Holds Barred', *Asiaweek,* 17 January 1997, p. 16.

40. See Garry Rodan, 'Singapore in 1997: Living with the neighbours', *Asian Survey,* vol. XXXVIII, no. 2 (February 1998), p. 179.

41. Lee Kuan Yew has sued 13 people for libel. See Stan Sesser, 'A Reporter at Large (Singapore)', *New Yorker,* 13 January 1992, p. 64. Sometimes these damages go into the hundreds of thousands of Singapore dollars with the aim of bankrupting the opposition politician.

42. See Sheila McNulty, 'Singapore: Rising above its Troubled Neighbours', *Financial Times Survey,* 30 March 1999, p. 1. See also 'Singapore's Speech

Maker', *The Economist,* 6 February 1999, p. 60, and 'Shocking Conduct in Singapore', *The Economist,* 9 January 1999, p. 54.

43. In his sweeping electoral victory in January 1997, Goh Chock Tong declared '[the voters] have rejected Western style liberal democracy and freedom [and] putting individual rights over that of society'. See 'No Holds Barred', p. 16.

44. See Harry M. Scoble and Laurie S. Wiseberg, *Access To Justice: Human Rights Struggles in Southeast Asia* (London: Zed Books, 1985), p. 49.

45. See Amitav Acharya and M. Ramesh, 'Economic Foundations of Singapore's Security: From Globalism to Regionalism?', in G. Rodan (ed.) *Singapore Changes Guard* (New York: St. Martin's Press, 1993), p. 141.

46. See K. Jayasurai, 'Singapore – the Politics of Regional Definition'. Unpublished paper, National University of Singapore, 1994.

47. See M. Chew, 'Human Rights in Singapore: Perceptions and Problems'. Unpublished paper, Department of Political Science, NUS, Singapore, 1994.

48. See Lee Lai To, 'Singapore in 1998: The Most Serious Challenge since Independence', *Asian Survey,* vol. XXXIX, no. 1 (January/February 1999), p. 73.

49. This quote is from Lee Kuan Yew, in Alex Josey, *Lee Kuan Yew* (Singapore: Donald Moore Press, 1968), p. 373.

50. See *Asiaweek,* 15 June 1985, p. 20.

51. See Amnesty International, 'Singapore: Detentions without Trial under the Internal Security Act' (New York: Amnesty International, October 1987).

52. See T. F. Har, 'The Experience of Detention under the Internal Security Act in Singapore', in *The Rule of Law and Human Rights in Malaysia and Singapore.* A report of the conference held at the European Parliament, Brussels, 9–10 March 1989 (KEHMA-S/GRAEL: European Parliament, 1990).

53. See F. Seow, *To Catch a Tartar* (New Haven: Yale University Press 1994), p. 142.

54. See P. Bowring, 'In Singapore, Unusual Law Doesn't Bring about Unusual Order', *International Herald Tribune* (1994). Bowring is making the point that despite all the tough restrictions and laws in Singapore, the crime rates and drug rates are not necessarily all that much lower than other countries and that they clearly fail to act as a deterrent.

55. See 'A Singapore Saga', *The Economist,* 7 August 1993, and 'No Love Lost in Singapore', *The Economist,* 11 August 1990, p. 29.

56. See 'Why PAP is Afraid to Debate SDP Publicly on Important Issues', in the Forum Page, *Straits Times* (Singapore), 18 October 1994.

57. See H. F. Kwang, 'What the Voters Were Saying', *Straits Times* (Singapore), 7 September 1991, p. 30.

58. See *The Sunday Times* (Singapore), 1 September 1994, for this speech. Figures and explanations for the electoral decline can be found in Rodan, 'Preserving the One-Party State in Contemporary Singapore', pp. 75–109, and G. Rodan, 'The Growth of Singapore's Middle Class and its Political

Significance', in G. Rodan (ed.), *Singapore Changes Guard* (New York: Longman Cheshire, 1993), pp. 52–72.

59. See 'No Holds Barred', p. 16.

60. See G. C. Tong, 'Why We Had No Choice but to React', *Straits Times* (Singapore), 1 June 1988, p. 4.

61. See J. M. David, 'Don't Count on Me Singapore', *National Review,* 16 May 1994, pp. 59–61.

62. See McNulty, 'Singapore: Rising above its Troubled Neighbours', p. 1.

63. The article was entitled 'The Smoke over Parts of Asia Obscures Some Profound Concerns', *International Herald Tribune,* 7 October 1994, which was framed as a rebuttal to an article by Kishore Mahbubani, a Permanent Secretary in Singapore's Foreign Ministry entitled 'You May Not Like It, Europe, But This Asian Medicine Could Help', *International Herald Tribune*, 1–2 October 1994. Apparently, the authorities took exception to Lingle's statement that regimes in the region relied on 'a compliant judiciary to bankrupt opposition politicians'. Despite no charges being filed at the time, police confiscated materials and documents from the lecturer who shortly thereafter resigned his position. Also see 'Singapore's Philosophers', *Asian Wall Street Journal,* 19 October 1994. Lingle was subsequently charged with 'contempt of court'.

64. See Lingle, 'The Smoke over Parts of Asia Obscures Some Profound Concerns'.

65. See W. Fernandez, 'Judge: Enough Evidence for Case against Lingle, Four Others', *Straits Times,* 10 January 1995, p. 2.

66. See United Nations, *I Human Rights International Instrument (Chart of ratification as at 31 January 1993)* UN, ST/HR/4/Rev. 7.

67. See Asia Watch, *Silencing All Critics: Human Rights Violations in Singapore* (New York: Asia Watch, 1990). A more recent account of one victim of human rights abuses in Singapore is by Francis T. Seow, *To Catch a Tartar: A Dissident in Lee Kuan Yew's Prison* (East Asian Legal Studies: Harvard Law School, 1994).

68. See 'In Caning Case, Doubts about Confession', *International Herald Tribune,* 18 April 1994.

69. See A. Osman, 'US Embassy Here Echoes Stand by State Dept.', *Straits Times* (Singapore), 12 May 1994, p. 21.

70. See F. Seow, 'S'pore's Brutal Charade: The Pain and the Punishment', *Bangkok Post*, 26 May 1994, p. 4.

71. See 'Our Way of Keeping Streets Safe', *Straits Times* (Singapore), 21 April 1994.

72. See Amnesty International, 'Singapore: Cruel Punishment' (London: Amnesty International, August 1991).

73. Ibid.

74. See Amnesty International, *When the State Kills* (New York; Amnesty International, 1989), p. 202.

75. See G. Rodan, 'Singapore's Leadership Transition: Erosion or Refinement of Authoritarian Rule?', *Bulletin of Concerned Asian Scholars,* vol. 24, no. 1 (January–March 1992), p. 10.

76. See 'The Democracy Debate – SM', *Straits Times* (Singapore), 17 June 1993.
77. See Patrice de Beer, 'Democracy, Asia's Major Export from the West', *Guardian Weekly*, 25 July 1993.
78. See Kishore Mahbubani, 'An Asian View of Human Rights and Freedom of the Press'. Paper presented at a conference on Asian and American perspectives on Capitalism and Democracy, Singapore, 1993.
79. A useful overview of this can be found in R. E. Howard and J. Donnelly, 'Introduction' in Donnelly and Howard (eds) *International Handbook of Human Rights* (New York: Greenwood Press, 1987), p. 15.
80. See the White Paper, *Shared Values* (Singapore: Singapore National Printers, 1991), p. 1.
81. See W. Safire, 'Singapore's Assertion of a Right to Torture is Intolerable', *International Herald Tribune*, 8 April 1994, for one of the strongest criticisms of this policy.
82. See 'The Appeal of Singapore's Style', *The Economist*, 5 November 1988.
83. See Lee Lai To, 'Singapore in 1998: The Most Serious Challenge since Independence', *Asian Survey*, vol. XXXIX, no. 1 (January/February 1999).
84. See J. Son, 'Media – Indonesia: Cloudy Forecast for Press Freedom' (Interpress News Agency, 22 November 1994) (IPS/HR/IP/BM/MF/94).
85. See 'How Free a Press?', *Asiaweek*, 14 December 1994, p. 40.
86. US Secretary of State Christopher Warren made these remarks at the opening of the ASEAN post-ministerial conference. This was quoted in the *Straits Times*, 27 July 1993.
87. See F. Fukuyama, 'The End of History', *National Interest* (Summer 1989), pp. 3–4.
88. See Mahbubani, 'An Asian Perspective on Human Rights and Freedom of the Press'.
89. See V. Muntarbhorn, 'ASEAN and Human Rights: Between Particularities and Peculiarities'. Paper presented at an International Seminar on Human Rights, Jakarta, Indonesia, 1993.
90. See R. J. Vincent, 'Human Rights and Foreign Policy', in D. M. Hill (ed.) *Human Rights and Foreign Policy* (Basingstoke: Macmillan, 1989).
91. See J. Wanandi, 'Human Rights and Democracy in the ASEAN Nations: The Next 25 Years', *Indonesian Quarterly*, vol. XXI, no. 1 (1993), p. 18.
92. See V. Muntarbhorn, 'Burma and the Case of Thai Tonsillitis',*Bangkok Post,* 23 September 1993.
93. See Lingle, 'The Smoke over Parts of Asia Obscures some Profound Concerns'.
94. Ibid.
95. See Radhika Coomaraswamy, 'Comments', in Asbjorn Eide and Bernt Hagtvet (eds), *Human Rights In Perspective* (Oxford: Basil Blackwell, 1992).
96. See Muntarbhorn, 'ASEAN and Human Rights: Between Particularities and Peculiarities'.
97. See Carolina Hernandez, 'ASEAN Perspectives on Human Rights and Democracy in International Relations: Problems and Prospects', working

paper, no. 1 (University of Toronto: Centre for International Studies, 1995) p. 13.

CHAPTER 3

1. This was said by Kyaw Sann, the Junta's official spokesman, in September 1989 as an attempt to justify the massacre of pro-democracy supporters. See B. Lintner, 'The Generals' New Clothes', *Far Eastern Economic Review*, 25 November 1994, p. 30.
2. The name of the country was changed to the Union of Myanmar on the 18 June 1989, in the aftermath of the pro-democracy demonstrations. The British ruled Burma between 1896 and 1948 when it became independent.
3. It is said that as many as 3,000 demonstrators were gunned down on the streets in 1988. See *New York Times International*, 2 January 1993, p. 5.
4. Myanmar had roughly 34 million acres of rainforest, which contained 80 per cent of the world's teak reserves as well as oil, gas, natural minerals. Unfortunately, the rainforests are fast disappearing.
5. For some useful overviews of Burmese history and politics, see Aung Cin Win Aung, *Burma: From Monarchy to Dictatorship* (Bloomington, Indiana: Eastern Press, 1994); Maurg Gyi, *Burmese Political Values: The Sociopolitical Roots of Authoritarianism* (New York: Praeger, 1993); Josef Silverstein, *Burmese Politics: The Dilemma of National Unity* (New Brunswick, NJ: Rutgers University Press, 1980) and Shwe Lu Maung, *Burma, Nationalism and Ideology: An Analysis of Society, Culture and Politics* (Dhaka: University Press, 1989), among others.
6. The Burmese Way to Socialism was an ideology based on bringing together Marxist and Buddhist tenets in support of the military government. Myanmar's economy would be self-reliant according to these views.
7. See IPS, 'Burma – Human Rights: Suu Kyi, Five Years in Detention' (Interpress News Agency, 10 July 1994).
8. See 'Burma – Rights: Ethnic Minorities Still Face Persecution' (Interpress news Agency, 1 December 1994).
9. For a good overview of this, see Mikael Gravers, *Nationalism as Political Paranoia: An Essay on the Historical Practice of Power* (Richmond: Curzon, 1998).
10. See Omar Farouk 'A New, Post-Socialist Burma', *Sunday Post* (Bangkok) 5 June 1994.
11. See Amnesty International, *Myanmar* (New York: Amnesty International, ASA 16 September 1990), p. 7.
12. See Andrew Deutz, 'United States' Human Rights Policy towards Burma, 1988–1991', *Contemporary Southeast Asia,* vol. 13, no. 2 (September 1991).
13. See Holly Burkhalter, Committee of Foreign affairs, House of Representatives. 'The Crackdown in Suppression: Suppression of the Democratic Movement and Violation of Human Rights', *Hearing and Markup before*

the Subcommittee on Human Rights and International Organizations and on Asian and Pacific Affairs, 15 September 1989, pp. 83–115 (Asia Watch).

14. See Amnesty International, *Myanmar* (New York: Amnesty International, 1990), p. 11.

15. See IPS 'Human Rights – Burma: Amnesty Protests Across World' (InterPress Service, 20 July 1994).

16. See 'Burma: Human Rights Developments' in *Human Rights Watch World Report 1999,* in
    <http://www.hrw.org/hrw/worldreport99/asia/Myanmar.htn>.

17. See 'Silencing the Democracy Movement', in Amnesty International, *Myanmar*, p. 5.

18. See 'Burma Softens Hard Line on Dissident', *International Herald Tribune,* 12 July 1994, p. 1.

19. See Donald M. Seekins, 'Burma in 1998: Little to Celebrate', *Asian Survey,* vol. XXXIX, no. 1 (January/February 1999), p. 15.

20. See Freedom in the World 1998–1999: *Burma.* <http://freedom house.org/survey99/country/myanmar.html>.

21. See Ron Corben 'Thailand–Burma: Fear of Chaos Prompts Bangkok to Back Junta' (Bangkok, IPS: Interpress Service, 25 May 1994).

22. Ibid.

23. See 'Forced Labour on the SLORC Railway', *Bangkok Post,* 22 May 1994, p. 18.

24. See IPS 'Human Rights – Burma: Amnesty Protests across World' (Interpress Service, 20 July 1994).

25. See L. Makabenta, 'Burma: Refugees Become Pawns of "Constructive Engagement"' (Interpress News Agency, 13 August 1994).

26. See V. Muntarbhorn, 'A Nobel Cause for Burma', *Bangkok Post,* 17 February 1993, p. 5.

27. See 'Rebels Say Thais Fear Junta will Terminate Franchises' (p. 3) and 'National Interest Must Prevail over Loggers', *Bangkok Post,* 29 April 1993, pp. 3 and 4.

28. The most comprehensive and well-written account of ethnic politics in Myanmar is Martin Smith, *Burma: Insurgency and the Politics of Ethnicity* (London: Zed Books, 1991).

29. See 'Burmese Recount Tales of Terror at Hands of Troops', *Washington Post,* 16 February 1992), pp. 51–2.

30. See 'Flagging Enlistment Forces Burmese Army to Conscript Youths', *Bangkok Post,* 26 March 1993, p. 8.

31. See IPS 'Burma – Human Rights: Slave Labour in Ancient City' (Interpress Services, 20 July 1994).

32. See Maung Ye Kyaw, 'Burma's Mad System', *Asia Inc.,* December 1993, p. 6.

33. See Amnesty International, *Myanmar: Atrocities in the Shan State* (London: Amnesty International, 1998).

34. See the US Department of State, *Annual Country Reports on Human Rights Practices for 1993* (section on Burma, introduction).

35. See Andrew M. Deutz, 'United States Human Rights Policy towards Burma', in *Contemporary Southeast Asia,* vol. 13, no. 12 (September 1991), p. 172.

36. See S. Cohen, 'Punish the Butchers in Burma', *New York Times*, 28 March 1992, p. 3.
37. See IPS Bob Maunder 'Burma–Europe: EU Appears to Change Stance on Relations with Rangoon' (Interprets Agency, 27 July 1994).
38. See 'Policy of Pressure and not Dialogue Has Failed: Evans', *Straits Times*, 25 July 1994.
39. This quote is from Mya Maung, Professor of Finance at Boston College. See L. Makabenta, 'Burma: Gaining Friends Despite Continued Rights Abuses' (Interpress News Agency, 8 July 1994).
40. See Amnesty International, *Myanmar: The Climate of Fear Continues* (October 1993: AI Index: ASA 16 June 1993).
41. Ibid., p. 4.
42. See 'Protest as Burma Addresses Rights Meet', *Bangkok Post*, 19 June 1993, p. 11.
43. See D. Gray, 'Burma Policy Quandary: Isolate or Boost Dialogue?', *Bangkok Post*, 19 February 1994, p. 5. The activist's name is Maureen Aung-Thwin.
44. See 'US is Criticized on Burmese Policy', *New York Times International*, 21 June 1993, p. 11.
45. See the *Far Eastern Economic Review*, 17 July 1993, p. 5.
46. This was quoted in Mikael Gravers, *Nationalism as Political Paranoia: An Essay on the Historical Practice of Power* (Richmond: Curzon, 1998), p. 139.
47. See Bruce Matthews, 'The Present Fortune of Tradition-bound Authoritarianism in Myanmar', *Pacific Affairs*, vol. 71, no. 1 (Spring 1998).
48. See David I. Steinberg, 'Stagnation in Burma?', *Bangkok Post*, 17 August 1997.
49. See M. Smith, *Burma: Insurgency and the Politics of Ethnicity* (London: Zed Books, 1991), p. 415. This quote was from an interview with the former head of the Tatmadaw's northeast command, Colonel Aye Myint.
50. See P. Shenon, 'Burmese Loosen Up: Outsiders are Skeptical', *New York Times*, 21 January 1993, p. 5.
51. Quoted in Freedom in the World, 1998–99, *Burma*. <http://freedomhouse.org/survey99/country/myanmar.html>.
52. See M. Parenti, *The Sword and the Dollar* (New York: St Martin's Press, 1989) p. 44.
53. See Melanie Beresford, 'The Political Economy of Dismantling the "Bureaucratic Centralism And Subsidy System" In Vietnam', in Hewison et al., *Southeast Asia in the 1990's* (St Leonards: Allen and Unwin, 1993).
54. See R. Matthews, 'Vietnam Takes a Socialist Road to Profit', *Straits Times* (Singapore), 18 January 1990.
55. See Ramesh Jaura, 'Vietnam – Development: Hanoi Poised to Become "Asian Tiger" economy' (Interpress Service, 20 August, 1994).
56. See S. Sivaranam, 'Vietnam – Outlook: Growth Pains in 1995' (Interprets News Agency, IPS/SS/CB/94).
57. Ibid.
58. Ibid.
59. See T. Fawthrop, 'Vietnam Economy: "Doi Moi" Leaving the Poor Behind?' (Interpress News Agency, IPS/TF/CB/KD/94).

60. See Gabriel Kolko, *Vietnam: Anatomy of a Peace* (London: Routledge, 1997).
61. See 'Vietnam', *HRW World Report 1999: Vietnam: Human Rights Developments*. <http://www.hrw.org/hrw/worldreport99/asia/vietnam.htn>. For instance, 'Sporadic incidents of rural unrest surfaced in Thai Binh province, the site of the most severe unrest in 1997; Long Binh in southern Dong Nai province, where farmers protested evictions by the military in January; Ha tay Province near Hanoi, the site of ongoing dissatisfaction over land rights and corruption; as well as Ha Nam, Nam Dinh, Thanh Hoa, Quang Ngai, and Bac Ninh Province. In March [1998], at least nine local people were convicted for disturbing public order during the January clashes in Dong Nai. In July, the People's Court in Thai Binh sentenced more than thirty local people, whom the government termed 'extremists to prison terms for inciting people to disrupt public order during uprisings in the province in November 1997.'
62. See Amnesty International, *Socialist Republic of Vietnam: Continuing Concerns* (AI Index: ASA 41/06/93).
63. See Mark Sidel, 'Vietnam in 1998: Reform Confronts the Regional Crisis', *Asian Survey,* vol. XXXIX, no. 1 (January/February 1999), pp. 92–3.
64. See Human Rights Watch, *World Report 1990* (HRW) (1991).
65. See 'Forced Repatriation Sparks New Concerns', *Washington Post,* 10 November 1991, A46.
66. See Clark D. Neher and Ross Marlay, *Democracy and Development in Southeast Asia: The Winds of Change* (Colorado: Westview Press, 1995), pp. 157–8.
67. See S. Kanwerayetin, 'VN Activist Sentenced to 20 Years in Prison', *Bangkok Post,* 1 April 1993, p. 10, and 'VN Dissident Declared Guilty Even Before Trial', *Bangkok Post,* 2 April 1993, p. 8.
68. See the 'Vietnam Government Tightens Media Control', *Bangkok Post,* 27 July 1993, p. 7.
69. See Leah Makabenta 'Human Rights: Time to Turn up the Heat on Hanoi' (Interpress Services, 3 August 1994).
70. See 'Vietnam', *HRW World Report 1999: Vietnam: Human Rights Developments*. <http://www.hrw.org/hrw/worldreport99/asia/vietnam.htn>.
71. See Amnesty International, *Socialist Republic of Vietnam: Buddhist Monks in Detention* (AI Index: ASA 41/05/94, May 1994).
72. See 'Buddhist Unrest Spreads to Southern VN', *Sunday Post* (Bangkok), 25 July 1993.
73. See Amnesty International, *Socialist Republic of Vietnam: Buddhist Monks in Detention* (AI Index: ASA 41/05/94. May 1994).
74. Reports of these violations are from 'Buddhist Dissidents Accused of Plotting to Overthrow the Communist Party', *Foreign Broadcast Monitor,* 10 August 1993, pp. 7–8; 'VN Buddhist Dissident under Government Pressure', *Bangkok Post,* 19 August 1993, p. 8; and 'Dissident Buddhist Monks Get Jail in VN', *Bangkok Post,* 16 November 1993, p. 10
75. See Mark Sidel, 'Vietnam in 1998: Reform Confronts the Regional Crisis', *Asian Survey,* vol. XXXIX, no. 1 (January/February 1999), p. 93.
76. See Mark Sidel, 'Vietnam in 1997: A Year of Challenges', *Asian Survey,* vol. XXXVIII, no. 1 (January 1998), pp. 86–7, for these figures and others.

77. See the *Universal Declaration* of 1948 and the *International Covenant on Economic, Social and Cultural Rights* of 1966 as examples of material that mention these rights.
78. See Russell H. H. Khng, 'The 1992 Revised Constitution of Vietnam: Background and Scope of Changes', *Contemporary Southeast Asia*, vol. 14, no. 3 (1992), pp. 221–30.
79. See David G. Marr and Carlyle A. Thayer (eds), *Vietnam and the Rule of Law*, Political and Social Change Monograph No. 19 (Canberra, Department of Political and Social Change, Research School of Pacific Studies, ANU, 1993).
80. See Amnesty International, *When The State Kills: The Death Penalty: A Human Rights Issue* (New York: Amnesty International, 1989), p. 231.
81. See Amnesty International, *Socialist Republic of Vietnam: Continuing Concerns* (London: Amnesty International, October 1993).
82. See Mark Sidel, 'Vietnam in 1998: Reform Confronts the Regional Crisis', *Asian Survey*, vol. XXXIX, no. 1 (January/February 1999), p. 94.
83. Ibid.
84. These issues were reported in 'Are Human Rights a Major Factor in Normalization of Vietnam–US Ties?', *Foreign Broadcast Monitor*, 12 January 1994, pp. 5–6.
85. See 'Human Rights a Thorn in Viet–U.S. Ties', *Jakarta Post*, 26 March 1994, p. 4.
86. See Gabriel Kolko, *Vietnam*, pp. 125–6.

CHAPTER 4

1. See 'The Extended Family', *The Economist*, 15 August 1987.
2. Ibid.
3. Despite the diversity of Indonesia, nearly 90 per cent of the population are Muslims, which in effect makes the country the largest Muslim country in the world. However, this is clearly one of the most secular versions of Islam in existence.
4. See Todung Nulya Lubis, *In Search of Human Rights: Legal-Political Dilemmas of Indonesia's New Order 1966–1990* (Jakarta: PT Gramedia Pustaka Utama, 1993), p. 295.
5. See Clark D. Neher and Ross Marlay, *Democracy and Development in Southeast Asia: The Winds of Change* (Colorado: Westview Press, 1995), p. 77.
6. See Adnan Buyung Nasution, 'Defending Human Rights in Indonesia', *Journal of Democracy*, vol. 5, no. 3 (July 1994).
7. See Judith Bird, 'Indonesia in 1997: the Tinderbox Year', *Asian Survey*, vol. XXXVIII, no. 2, February 1998, p. 175.
8. See 'Indonesia', *International Herald Tribune*, November 1994, p. 3.
9. See the World Bank Economics Department, *Social Indicators of Development* (London: Johns Hopkins University Press, April 1993).
10. See 'Southeast Asian Economies', *The Economist*, 20 March 1993.
11. See Y. Ismartono, 'Rich–Poor Gap Threatens Economic Gains' (Inter-Press News Agency, 30 August 1994).

12. Richard Robison, 'Indonesia: Tensions in State and Regime', in Kevin Hewison, Richard Robison and Garry Rodan (eds), *Southeast Asia in the 1990's: Authoritarianism, Democracy and Capitalism* (St Leonards: Allen and Unwin, 1993), p. 55. Robison's figures come from the World Bank, *Indonesia: Developing Private Enterprise* (Washington, DC, 1991); H. Soesastro, 'The Political Economy of De-regulation in Indonesia', *Asian Survey* vol. 39, no. 9 (1989), pp. 853–69; and Mari Pangestu, 'The Role of the Private Sector in Indonesia', *Indonesian Quarterly*, vol. 19, no. 1 (1991), pp. 27–51.

13. See 'Indonesia', *International Herald Tribune*, November 1994, p. 2.

14. See S. Tripathi, 'The Anxious Archipelago', *Asia Inc.*, May 1994, p. 61.

15. See C. Rossett, 'Indonesia Vote Marks Development Crossroad', *Wall Street Journal*, 20 April 1987. For an excellent guide to capital formation and the nature of ownership in Indonesia, see R. Robison, *Indonesia: The Rise of Capital* (Sydney, Australia: Allen and Unwin, 1986).

16. See 'New Jobless and Newly Angry Threaten Indonesia's Stability'. <http://www.nytimes.com/library/financial/012998indonesia-workers.html> (29 January 1998).

17. See Antara Yogyakarta, 11 April 1999, as reported in *Indonesia-L*, 11 April 1999.

18. See Bob Mantiri 'Labour – Indonesia: ICFTU Presses Jakarta to Release Union Leader' (Interpress News Agency, 16 August 1994).

19. See Bob Mantiri 'Labour – Indonesia: Jakarta Told to Stop Jailing Trade Unionists' (Interpress News Agency, 18 August 1994).

20. See Jeffrey Ballinger, 'The New Free-Trade Heel', *Harpers*, August 1992, pp. 46–7.

21. Ibid.

22. See Human Rights Watch/Asia, *The Limits of Openness* (New York: Human Rights Watch, 1994), p. 52.

23. See Graham Hancock, *The Lords of Poverty* (London: Macmillan, 1989) pp. 133–8. Hancock drew on World Bank reports as well as local newspapers for his excellent exposé of this as well as other World Bank disasters in the Third World.

24. See B. Nietschmann, 'Economic Development by Invasion of Indigenous Nations', *Cultural Survival Quarterly*, vol. 10, no. 2 (1986).

25. See US State Department Annual Country Report on Human Rights Practices for 1993 Section on Indonesia: 'Denial of Fair Trial' (Washington: US Government Printing Office, 1993).

26. See A. B. Nasution, 'Defending Human Rights in Indonesia', *Journal of Democracy*, vol. 5, no. 3 (July 1994).

27. See Amnesty International, *When the State Kills* (New York: Amnesty International, 1989), p. 148.

28. Tapol is a contraction of 'tahanan politik' which means political detainee.

29. See R. Bonner, 'The New Order – 1', *The New Yorker*, 6 June 1988.

30. See Human Rights Watch/Asia (1994) 'Killings at the Nipah Dam', in *The Limits of Openness* (1994), pp. 109–22.

31. See 'Jakarta under Pressure to Stop Widespread Banning of Books', *Foreign Broadcast Monitor*, 6 April 1994, pp. 1–2.

32. See 'No News Is Bad News', *The Economist,* 25 June 1994.

33. See Human Rights Watch/Asia, *The Limits of Openness* (New York: Human Rights Watch/Asia, 1994), p. 20.

34. See 'Indonesian Government Bans Three Top Magazines', *Straits Times,* 22 June 1994, p. 1.

35. See Johanna Son, 'Media-Indonesia: Cloudy Forecast for Press Freedom' (Interpress Third World News Agency, 22 November 1994).

36. See 'Human Rights Activist Brought to Trial on Defamation Charges', *Jakarta Post,* 6 January 1994, p. 2, and 'Human Rights Activist Nuku gets Four-Year Prison Term', *Jakarta Post,* 25 February 1994, p. 1. Soleiman was also accused of calling Suharto the 'mastermind of all disasters'.

37. See J. Dunn, *Timor: A People Betrayed* (Australia: Jacaranda Press, 1983), p. 313.

38. See J. G. Taylor, *Indonesia's Forgotten War: The Hidden History of East Timor* (London: Zed Books, 1991) p. 68.

39. See N. Chomsky, 'Introduction', in R. Horta, *The Unfinished Saga of East Timor* (Trenton, NJ: Red Sea Press, 1987), p. iii.

40. Fretilin is an acronym which comes from Frente Revolucionaria do Timor Leste Independence which is Portugal's term for the Revolutionary Front for an Independent East Timor.

41. See Asia Watch, 'East Timor: The November 12 massacre and its Aftermath', *Indonesia Issues* 17–18 (December 1991).

42. See Joint Standing Committee on Foreign Affairs, Defence and Trade, Australia's Relations with Indonesia (Australian Government Publishing Service, Canberra, 1993), p. 96.

43. This was quoted in the *Guardian,* 15 April 1994, and *Sydney Morning Herald,* 15 April 1994.

44. Ibid., p. 31. For an alternative view on East Timor, see 'The World Should Accept that East Timor is Part of Indonesia', *Asiaweek,* 23 March 1994.

45. See John Pilger, 'Horror behind the West's Big Wink', *Guardian Weekly,* 27 February 1994. Pilger also notes the way in which language is changed in an Orwellian sense; the description for instance of the Dili massacre in November 1991 as an 'incident'. He argues: 'This is the same description used by the Jakarta regime and promoted by the American public relations giant Burson Marsteller, which the regime hired following the massacre in the Santa Cruz cemetery on November 12.' See John Pilger, 'London Complicity in Asian Genocide', *Sunday Morning Post* (South China Morning Post, 15 May 1994), p. 15.

46. See 'East Timor's Past Won't Stay Buried', *The Economist,* 23 April 1994.

47. This was quoted from *Tapol Bulletin,* no. 99 (June 1990), p. 2, by M. G. Williams, 'Funu-Liberation War Continues in East Timor', *Bulletin of Concerned Asian Scholars,* vol. 22, no. 3 (1990), p. 24.

48. For reports on the anarchy that prevailed in East Timor just before and after the elections, see 'East Timor in Turmoil: Why Doesn't Anyone Stop it?' <http://www.independent.co.uk/atp/independent/foreign-news P33S1.html>, 'East Timor in Turmoil: UN Security Council to Act as 150,000 Flee Timor Massacres'. <http://www.independent.co.uk/ frontpage/P1S5.html>, and 'East Timor in Turmoil: This is a Controlled

Carnage, Directed by the Local Police?' <http://www.independent.co.uk/ atp/independent/foreign-news/P3S3.html>, among others.

49. See 'Proof of Systematic Killings in Timor'. <http://www.independent. co.uk/news/world/pacific.rim/timor091299.shtml> (9 December 1999). See also 'Mass Graves Found in East Timor'. <http://www.independent. co.uk/news/world pacific-rim/apeasttimor201299.shmtl>.

50. See Amnesty International,*"Shock Therapy' Restoring Order in Aceh, 1989–1993* (AI Index: ASA 21 July 1993).

51. Ibid., p. 56.

52. See 'Indonesia: Fraying at the Edges?', *The Economist,* 21 August 1999, p. 47.

53. Ibid., p. 48.

54. See 'Dozens Injured in Independence Protest in Irian Jaya. <http://www. independent.co.uk/news/world/pacific-Rim/jaya021299.shtml> (2 February 1999).

55. See Asia Watch, *Human Rights in Indonesia and East Timor* (New York: Asia Watch, 1989), p. 7.

56. Ibid., pp. 125–7.

57. See *Straits Times* (Singapore), 16 June 1993, p. 1.

58. See 'Stop Protests over East Timor, Alatas Urges Australia', *Straits Times* (Singapore), 25 August 1984, p. 14.

59. See Y. Ismartono, "Amnesty Report Gets Thumbs Down' (Interpress News Agency, 30 September 1994).

60. See 'Human Rights Activist Sceptical about Effectiveness of Government – Initiated Body to Guard Human Rights', *Foreign Broadcast Monitor,* 11 December 1993, pp. 4–6.

61. See 'Activist Casts Doubt in Human Rights Commission's Ability to Establish Rule of Law', *Foreign Broadcast Monitor,* 6 April 1994.

62. See Larry Niksch, 'Indonesia–US Relations and Impact of East Timor Issue', US Report for Congress, Library of Congress, 15 December 1992.

63. See A. B. Nasution, 'Defending Human Rights in Indonesia', *Journal of Democracy*, vol. 5, no. 3 (July 1994).

64. In a curious twist to the calls for stopping aid, in October 1994, an American lawyer pushed to make aid to Indonesia contingent on payment of a $14 million dollar award to a New Zealander whose son was killed in the Dili incident in November 1991. The award was made under the US Torture Victim Protection Act.

65. See 'Timor's Pain', *Asiaweek,* 7 December 1994, p. 21.

66. See M. Dujisin, 'East Timor: Human Rights Forgotten in Race for Trade?' (Interpress News Agency, 16 November 1994); J. Son, 'Indonesia–East Timor: Unwelcome Guest at Suharto's Party' (Interpress News Agency, 17 November 1994).

67. See John Pilger, 'Horror behind the West's Big Wink', *Guardian Weekly,* 27 February 1994.

68. See M. Dujisin, 'Portugal Condemns Repression in University' (Interpress News Agency, 14 July 1994).

69. See 'Beating a Retreat: Ramos Caves in to Jakarta's Pressure on Timor Forum', *Far Eastern Economic Review,* 2 June 1994. Perhaps a more salient reason why Ramos took the position was that joint economic ventures

would have been threatened in the Philippines if he had not made concessions.

70. See Ramon Isberto, 'Philippines: East Timor Fiasco Hurts Democratic Image' (Interpress Third World News Agency, 1 June 1994) (IPS/RI/LNH/94).

71. See Human Rights Watch/Asia, *The Limits of Openness* (New York: Human Rights Watch/Asia, 1994), p. 1.

72. See 'Timor's Pain', *Asiaweek*, p. 69.

CHAPTER 5

1. See Benedict R. Anderson, 'Elections and Participation in Three Southeast Asian Countries', in R. H. Taylor, *The Politics of Elections in Southeast Asia* (New York: Woodrow Wilson Press Center and Cambridge University Press, 1996), p. 33.

2. See Anek Laothamatas, 'A Tale of Two Democracies: Conflicting Perceptions of Elections and Democracy in Thailand', in ibid., pp. 210–12.

3. See 'Coup in Thailand Follows Old Pattern', *New York Times*, 24 February 1991, p. 14.

4. See 'Rainbow Coalition', *Far Eastern Economic Review*, 4 June 1992. To qualify this the writer makes the point that protesters came from all walks of life. See also 'Mobile Phones Primed, Affluent Thais Join Fray', *New York Times International*, 20 May 1992, p. 10.

5. See 'A Tale of Two Systems', *The Economist*, 9 July 1994.

6. See 'ASEAN Investment Anxiety', *Far Eastern Economic Review*, 4 June 1992, pp. 12–13.

7. See Kevin Hewison et al. (eds), *Southeast Asia in the 1990's: Authoritarianism, Democracy and Capitalism* (St Leonards: Allen and Unwin 1993), p. 182. This was a statement made by a group of academic petitioners against the coup and was originally cited in the *Journal of Contemporary Asia*, vol. 21, no. 4 (1991).

8. See Suchtra Punyaratabandhu, 'Thailand in 1998: A False Sense of Recovery', *Asian Survey*, vol. XXXIX, no. 1 (January/February 1999), p. 83.

9. See Peter Warr, 'Thailand', in Ross H. Mcleod and Ross Garnet (eds), *East Asia in Crisis: From Being a Miracle to Needing One?* (London: Routledge, 1998), p. 63.

10. See *Country Reports on Human Rights Practices for 1993*, Report submitted to the committee on FA (US House of Representatives) and the Committee on FR (US Senate). Department of State (Washington: US Government Printing Office, 1994).

11. See 'Are Police Abusing Rights of the Accused?', *Sunday Post*, 28 March 1993; 'Chuan Govt. Must Put an End to Violations of Our Privacy Rights', *Sunday Post*, 14 November 1993, and 'Probe Pledged after Prison Barbarity Claims', *Bangkok Post*, 22 April 1994, among other reports indicating the ability of newspapers to pursue allegations of corruption and dirty tricks.

12. See 'MP's Favour Limit on Police Power', *Bangkok Post*, 26 January 1993.

13. See 'Are Police Abusing Rights of the Accused?', *Sunday Post* (Bangkok), 28 March 1993, p. 24. CGRS is an NGO that works to protect human rights, including the rights of prisoners and suspects under police custody.

14. See 'Police Death Squad Uncovered', *Bangkok Post*, 29 January 1994, p. 1.

15. For these reports see *Bangkok Post*, 8 July, 1993, p. 8; *Bangkok Post,* 1 February 1993, p. 3; *Sunday Post* (Bangkok), 14 February, 1993, p. 24; *Far Eastern Economic Review*, 15 July 1993; and *New York Times,* 18 April 1990, p. A3.

16. See 'Burmese Army's Success Produces a New Flood of Refugees for Thailand', *New York Times*, 18 April 1990.

17. See 'Thailand', *HRW World Report 1999: Thailand: Human Rights Developments*. <http://www.hrw.org/hrw/worldreport99/asia/thailand.htn>.

18. See C. Espiritu, *Law and Human Rights in the Development of ASEAN* (Singapore: Friedrich-Naumann-Stiftung, 1986), p. 29.

19. Ibid., p. 29.

20. See Wanjiku Kaime-Atterhog and Orathai ard-am, 'Children without Childhood', Paper presented at the 22nd International Conference on World Peace, Bangkok, 1–5 December 1993.

21. See 'Thailand: Dirty Business', *Far Eastern Economic Review,* 13 January 1994, p. 23.

22. Ibid.

23. See 'Thailand – Aids: Vaccine Tests to Continue despite Fears' (Interpress News Agency, IPS/LM/KD/94, 4 July 1994).

24. See L. Makabenta, 'Children – Thailand: AIDS is also a Legal Disease' (Interpress News Agency, 31 August 1994, IPS/LM/LNH/94).

25. See Amnesty International, *When the State Kills: The Death Penalty: A Human Rights Issue* (New York: Amnesty International, 1989).

26. See *Far Eastern Economic Review*, 15 April 1993.

27. Quoted in Leonard R. Sussman, 'The Essential Role of Human Rights', in *The World and I,* July 1993, p. 41.

28. See 'Human Rights – A Down to Earth Practice, but a Touchy Issue', *Sunday Post*, 31 January 1993, p. 22.

29. See 'Peace Mission May Have Soured Govt–Military Ties', *Sunday Post,* 21 January 1993, p. 20.

30. See Leah Makabenta, 'Southeast Asia: Democracies Bullied by Powerful Neighbours' (Interpress Third World News Agency, 7 September 1994, IPS/LM/LNH/94).

31. See *Bangkok Post*, 6 July 1993, p. 6.

32. See R. Ehrlich, 'Thailand: Upset by US Aid' (Interpress News Agency, IPS/RE/MU).

33. See 'Has the Coup Had its Day?', *Asiaweek*, 20 January 1995, p. 27.

34. This was a personal communication I received in response to a paper I gave entitled 'Human Rights in Southeast Asia and Globalization' at an international symposium at Thammasat University, Bangkok, 14–15 June 1999. The respondent was a commentator on my paper.

35. See Dr H. E. Surin Pitsuwan, 'Thailand's Foreign Policy during the Economic and Social Crisis' (keynote address delivered at a seminar in commemoration of the 49th anniversary of the Faculty of Political

Science, Thammasat University, June 1998). From the internet: <http://www.mfa.go.th/policy/fm02.htm>.

36. For a useful introduction to the history and culture of the Philippines, see D. G. Timberman, *A Changeless Land: Continuity and Change in Philippine Politics* (New York: M. E. Sharpe, 1991), Chapter 1.

37. See Benedict Anderson, 'Cacique Democracy in the Philippines: Origin and Dreams', *New Left Review*, no. 169 (May–June 1998), pp. 3–31.

38. See Richard Pierre Claude, *Educating for Human Rights: The Philippines and Beyond* (Quezon City: University of the Philippines Press, 1996).

39. See Jon Moran, 'Patterns of Corruption and Development in East Asia', *Third World Quarterly*, vol. 20, no. 3 (1999), pp. 569–87.

40. See Surin Maisrikrod, 'Changing Forms of Democracy in Asia? Some Observations on the Thai and Philippine Constitutions', *Asian Studies Review*, vol. 23, no. 3 (September 1999), pp. 360–1.

41. See F. Ramos, 'Catalyst for Change' in *Asiaweek*, 20 January 1995.

42. See Maisrikrod, 'Changing Forms of Democracy in Asia?', p. 357.

43. See Johanno Son, 'Philippines – Economy: Finally Some Praise from the IMF' (Interpress News Agency, 20 October 1994).

44. See Richard P. Claude, 'The Philippines', in Jack Donnelly and Rhoda E. Howard, *International Handbook of Human Rights* (New York: Greenwood Press, 1987), p. 286.

45. The poverty line has been defined as 'that income level below which people cannot buy for their families recommended nutrient requirements, cannot provide two changes of garments, cannot provide grade six schooling for their children and cannot pay for food and rent.' See A. F. Santos and L. F. Lee, *The Debt Crisis: A Treadmill of Poverty for Filipino Women* (Manila: Kalayaan, 1989) p. 22.

46. See Son, 'Philippine – Economy'.

47. See Jonathan Rigg (1997) *Southeast Asia: The Human Landscape of Modernization and Development* (London: Routledge, 1997), p. 135.

48. See D. Lacson Jr, 'The Philippines: Yesterday, Today and Tomorrow; Political and Socio-Economic Developments' (IPS: Times Academic Press, 1991), p. 15.

49. See A. Doronila, 'Issues on Democracy and Development: Ramos Political Will', Seminar presented at Department of Political and Social Change, Research School for Pacific and Asian Studies, ANU, Canberra, 18 March 1994.

50. See Gabriella R. Montinola, 'The Philippines in 1998: Opportunity and Crisis', *Asian Survey*, vol. XXXIX, no. 1 (January/February 1999), p. 68.

51. See Espiritu, *Law and Human Rights in the Development of ASEAN*, p. 38.

52. See C. Siljaru, 'State of Human Rights Advancement in the Philippines', *LAWASIA Human Rights Bulletin*, no. 4 (1985), pp. 58–65.

53. See F. Marcos, *The Democratic Revolution in the Philippines* (Manila: The Marcos Foundation, 1977), p. 1.

54. See Richard P. Claude, 'Human Rights in the Philippines and US Responsibility', in Mclean (ed.), *Human Rights and US Foreign Policy* (Massachussetts: Lexington Books. 1979), pp. 237–9. And US House Appropriations Committee, Subcommittee on Foreign Operations, 'Foreign Assistance', 95th Congress, 1st session, 2 March 1977, p. 48.

55. See Claude, 'The Philippines', p. 285.
56. See James Putzel, 'Survival of an Imperfect Democracy in the Philippines', *Democratization*, vol. 6, no. 1 (1999), p. 210.
57. See The Lawyers Committee for Human Rights, *'Salvaging' Democracy: Human Rights in the Philippines* (December 1985), p. 201.
58. See 'Amnesty for Philippine Communists', *South China Morning Post*, 1 August 1992, p. 12, and 'Ramos Vows to Destroy Guerrillas', *South China Morning Post*, 4 August 1992, p. 12.
59. See Amnesty International, *Philippines: Disappearances in the Context of Counter-insurgency* (AI Index: ASA 35, May 1991).
60. See Asia Watch, *The Philippines: Violations of the Wars by Both Sides* (New York: Asia Watch, 1990), p. 47.
61. See B. Mantiri, 'Philippines Politics: Ramos Accused of Imposing Martial Law Tactics' (Interpress News Agency, 14 September 1994).
62. See 'The Ultimate Price', *Asiaweek*, 16 March 1994.
63. See *The Philippines*. <http://freedomhouse.org/survey99/country/philip. htn>, p. 2.
64. This speech in 1992 was quoted in Doronila, 'Issues on Democracy'.
65. See *Time*, 14 June 1993.
66. This quote was by Michel Camdessus, the managing director of the IMF. See J. Son, 'Philippines: A Model for Development-friendly Democracy?' (Interpress News Agency, 1 November 1994).
67. See Amartya Sen, 'Human Rights and Economic Achievements', Paper presented at the workshop on *Changing Conceptions of Human Rights in a Growing East Asia,* sponsored by Carnegie Council on Ethics and International Affairs, Hakone, Japan, 23–25 June 1995.
68. See Segundo E. Romero, 'The Philippines in 1997: Weathering Political and Economic Turmoil', *Asian Survey*, vol. XXXVIII, no. 2 (February 1998), p. 199.
69. See 'The Philippines', *Economist Intelligence Unit Country Report*, 4th Quarter 1999, p. 11.
70. See D. Timberman, *A Changeless Land* (New York: M. E. Sharpe, ISEAS, 1991), p. 385.
71. See J. W. Bakker, 'Human Rights Discourse in the Philippines: Fragmentation and Politicization', *Pioom Newsletter and Progress Report*, vol. 6, no. 1 (Summer 1994), pp. 30–3.
72. See James Putzel, 'Survival of an Imperfect Democracy in the Philippines', *Democratization*, vol. 6, no. 1 (1999) p. 214.
73. Gabriella Montinola has argued that 'Most notable among the rehabilitated cronies is Eduardo "Danding" Cojuangco, whose control over the coconut industry when Marcos was in power resulted in the immiserization of millions of coconut farmers and their families. In 1986, a substantial amount of Cojuangco's assets were impounded by the administration of then-President Corazon Aquino on the grounds that Cojuanco had obtained them illegally through his relationship with Marcos.' See Gabriella Montinola, 'The Philippines in 1998: Opportunity amid Crisis', *Asian Survey,* vol. XXXIX, no. 1 (January/February 1999), pp. 70–1.

74. See 'Filipinos Join Protest over "Crony State"'.
    <http//:www.independent.co.uk/atp> (21 August 1999).
75. See Claude, *Educating for Human Rights*, p. 52.

CHAPTER 6

1. This was a quote by Prince Norodom Ranariddh, President of FUNCINPEC, from the *Phnom Penh Post* on 25 August 1995 and cited in Joakim Ojendal and Hans Antlov, 'Asian values and its political consequences: is Cambodia the first domino?', *Pacific Review*, vol. 11, no. 4 (1998), p. 532.
2. In fact, Cambodia, along with countries like Bosnia and Somalia, have been regarded as crisis societies by the United Nations because of the seemingly intractable nature of the conflict.
3. This was quoted in Carlyle A. Thayer, 'The UN Transitional Authority in Cambodia', in Ramesh Thakur and Carlyle A. Thayer (eds), *A Crisis of Expectations: UN Peacekeeping in the 1990's* (Colorado: Westview Press, 1995), p. 122.
4. This is sometimes referred to as the *Pretikar* which is 'the event' (the events surrounding this period 5–6 July 1997). See Joakim Ojendal and Hans Antlov, 'Asian Values and its Political Consequences: Is Cambodia the First Domino?', *The Pacific Review*, vol. 11, no. 4 (1998), p. 531.
5. One writer has argued that the July events must be considered a coup: 'CPP troop involvement in the summary executions and torture of several Funcinpec officials has been well documented. According to a United nations report, a large number of corpses were incinerated; in addition, somewhere between 41 and 60 people were found to have been executed in custody.' See Sorpong Peou, 'Cambodia in 1997, Back to Square One?', *Asian Survey*, vol. XXXVIII, no. 1 (January 1998), p. 71.
6. John Pilger wrote that during 'one six month period in 1973 B-52s dropped more bombs in 3,695 raids on the populated heartland of Cambodia than were dropped on Japan during all of the Second World War: the equivalent, in tons of bombs, of five Hiroshimas'. See John Pilger, *Heroes* (London: Pan, 1989), p. 387.
7. There were a quarter of a million bombs dropped in Cambodia between February and August 1973 alone. See Marilyn B. Young, *The Vietnam War, 1945–1990* (New York: HarperCollins, 1991), p. 280.
8. See Charles H. Twining, 'The Economy', in Karl D. Jackson, *Cambodia 1975–1978: Rendezvous with Death* (Princeton: Princeton University Press. 1989).
9. John Pilger argued that the landscape was barely discernible when he arrived in August 1979: 'On the edge of towns this grass would follow straight lines, as though planned. Fertilised by human compost, by the remains of thousands upon thousands of men, women and children, these lines marked common graves in a nation where perhaps as many as two million people, or between a third and a quarter of the population, were "missing".' Pilger, *Heroes*, p. 385. For other accounts of the Pol Pot regime, see Karl D. Jackson (ed.), *Cambodia 1975–1978:*

Rendezvous with Death (Princeton, NJ: Princeton University Press, 1989); John Barron and Anthony Paul, *Murder of a Gentle Land* (New York: Reader's Digest Press, 1977); William Shawcross, *The Quality of Mercy: Cambodia, Holocaust and Modern Conscience* (Glasgow: Collins, 1985).

10. See David Chandler, *Facing the Cambodian Past* (St Leonards: Allen and Unwin, 1996), p. 207.
11. United Nations, *Agreements on a Comprehensive Political Settlement of the Cambodia Conflict* (Paris, 23 October 1991), p. 48.
12. Pang Meth, 'The United Nations Peace Plan, The Cambodian Conflict, and the Future of Cambodia', in *Contemporary Southeast Asia*, vol. 14 (June 1992), p. 33.
13. See Kate G. Frieson, 'The Cambodian Elections of 1993: A Case of Power to the People?', in R. H. Taylor (ed.), *The Politics of Elections in Southeast Asia* (New York: Woodrow Wilson Center Press and Cambridge University Press, 1996), p. 224.
14. See 'Cambodia', in *Human Rights Dialogue,* vol. 6 (September 1996), p. 5.
15. Samuel Huntington has argued that electoral democracy in Asian societies is more likely to be designed to produce consensus than choice and will not be accompanied by the liberal practices of western democracy. See Samuel Huntington, 'The Erosion of American National Interests', *Foreign Affairs*, vol. 76(5) (1997), pp. 10–11.
16. See David Chandler, 'Normative Poems (CHBAP) and Pre-Colonial Cambodian Society', *Journal of Southeast Asian Studies,* vol. XV, no. 2 (September 1984).
17. See 'Cambodia', *Human Rights Watch World Report 1999: Cambodia: Human Rights Developments.* <http://www.hrw.org/hrw/worldreport99/asia/cambodia.htn>.
18. See *Cambodia Times,* 4–10 August 1997, p. 12.
19. Sorpong Peou, 'Cambodia in 1998: From Despair to Hope?', in *Asian Survey,* vol. XXXIX, no. 1 (January/February 1999), p. 23.
20. Ibid. Sorpong Peou notes that 'although forest exploitation had the potential to generate US$100 million per year, the government managed to collect only US$15 million on average. Meanwhile the environmental damage caused by deforestation continued to affect agricultural production' (p. 23).
21. See Peou, 'Cambodia in 1997: Back to Square One?', p. 73.
22. This is quoted in Peou, 'Cambodia in 1998: From Despair to Hope?', p. 24.
23. See Milan Kundera, *The Book of Laughing and Forgetting* (London: Faber and Faber, 1982), p. 7.
24. They noted that Yam Mouern, a 29-year-old labourer, was kidnapped by soldiers of the S-91 unit of the army in Battambang Province. He was beaten, threatened with death and forced to watch the execution of another prisoner in 1993. He was also conscripted against his will, losing both arms and sight in one eye when he was forced to lay landmines. See *Kingdom of Cambodia – Human Rights and theNnew Government* (AI index: ASA 23 February 1995).
25. As one writer has argued: 'What makes Cambodian politics particularly grim, and complex, is that it is not a black-and-white struggle of good guys versus bad guys. There is a huge band of gray. When they were in government, many of Ranariddh's people were just as corrupt and

abusive as Hun Sen's people. It is not clear that Cambodia would be any better off today if FUNCINPEC had been able to take a greater share of power after the 1993 election.' See Peter Eng, 'Cambodian Democracy: In a Bleak Landscape, Strong Signs of Hope', *Washington Quarterly*, vol. 21, no. 3 (1998), p. 74.

26. See Amnesty International, *Kingdom of Cambodia: Human Rights and the New Government* (London: ASA 23 February 1995), p. 8.

27. Ibid., p. 16.

28. See US Department of State, *Cambodia Report on Human Rights Practices for 1996* (1997).

29. Ibid.

30. See Peter Eng, 'The Democracy Boom', *Development Dialogue* (1998), p. 2.

31. See Huntington, 'The Erosion of American National Interests', p. 25.

32. See 'Cambodia', in *HRW World Report 1999: Cambodia: Human Rights Developments,* in <http://www.hrw.org/hrw/worldreport99/asia/cambodia.htn>. Prior to and after the return of Prince Ranariddh on 3 March 1998, several high-ranking FUNCINPEC officials had been assassinated in Phnom Penh, including Lt. Col. Moung Sameth on 3 March, General Thacj Kim Sang on 4 March and Lt. Col. Chea Vutha on 28 March, in addition to the targeting of local activists in the countryside.

33. See Eng, 'Cambodian Democracy: In a Bleak Landscape, Strong Signs of Hope', pp. 71–91 for a good overview of these developments.

CHAPTER 7

1. Edgar Snow, *The Other Side of the River* (New York: Random House, 1970), p. 350.

2. Agence France Presse, 22 June 1999. <uschina@listbox.com>.

3. Tang Boqiao, *Anthems of Defeat: Crackdown in Hunan Province 1989–1992* (New York and Washington: Human Rights Watch, 1992), p. 75.

4. Hongda Harry Wu, pp. 15, 21; James Walsh, 'The Human Rights Game', *Time*, 31 January 1994, p. 29.

5. Even reported executions sometimes exceed 60 in a single day. 'Canton Executes 65 in One Day', *Shih-chieh Jih-pao*, 7 September 1990, p. 16; 'Beijing executes 64 in one day', *Straits Times*, 26 September 1994, p. 2.

6. 'Phone Code Stealers in Guangdong "May Face Death"', *Straits Times*, 10 January 1995, p. 33.

7. 'Chinese Censors Destroy Hundreds of Thousands of Publications', Agence France Presse, 22 June 1999. <uschina@listbox.com>.

8. The quotations are from the regime-approved Tibetan scholar Li Yan, in 'No Religious Freedom for Tibetans?', *Beijing Review*, 22–28 February 1993, pp. 19–20.

9. John Pomfret, 'Chinese Crime Rate Soars as Economic Problems Grow', Washington Post Foreign Service, 21 January 1999, p. A19; Reuters report, 10 February 1999. <uschina@listbox.com>.

10. *China News Digest*, internet edition, 11 November 1994, p. 10; 5 June 1994, p. 5.

CHAPTER 8

1. Gregory Henderson, *Korea: The Politics of the Vortex* (Cambridge, Mass.: Harvard University Press, 1968).
2. Jerome Alan Cohen and Edward J. Baker, 'U.S. Foreign Policy and Human Rights in South Korea', in William Shaw (ed.), *Human Rights in Korea* (Cambridge, Mass.: Harvard University Press, 1991), p. 223.
3. Quoted in Ed Paisley, 'Rights of the Accused', *Far Eastern Economic Review*, 31 March 1994, p. 16.
4. Statistics are from Chong-Sik Lee, 'South Korea: The Challenge of Democracy', in Steven M. Goldstein (ed.), *Minidragons: Fragile Economic Miracles in the Pacific* (Boulder, Col.: Westview Press, 1991); 'The Bottom Line', *Asiaweek*, 13 July 1994, p. 45; and 'Vital Signs', *Asiaweek*, 13 July 1994, p. 46.
5. Chungmoo Choi, 'Korean Women in a Culture of Inequality', in Donald N. Clark (ed.), *Korea Briefing, 1992* (Boulder, Col.: Westview Press and the Asia Society, 1992), pp. 97–116.
6. William Shaw, 'Between Class and Nation: The Equalization Society of the 1920s,' in Shaw (ed.), *Human Rights in Korea*, pp. 95–8.
7. Cohen and Baker, 'US Foreign Policy', p. 181.
8. Donald S. MacDonald, 'U.S. Human-Rights Objectives and Korean Realities,' in Shaw (ed.), *Human Rights in Korea*, p. 258.
9. Vipan Chandra, 'Korean Human-Rights Consciousness in an Era of Transition: A Survey of Late-Nineteenth-Century Developments,' in Shaw (ed.), *Human Rights in Korea*, p. 49.
10. Bruce Cumings, *The Two Koreas* (New York: Foreign Policy Association, 1984), p. 42.
11. Lee Tae Yon, 'Human Rights Violations in the Democratic People's Republic of (North) Korea', *East Asian Review*, vol. 5, no. 4 (Winter 1993), p. 66.
12. Amnesty International, 'North Korea: Summary of Amnesty International's Concerns' (October 1993, ASA 24/03/93), p. 1.
13. Ibid., p. 11.
14. Letter from Permanent Representative of the Democratic People's Republic of Korea in the United Nations to Amnesty International, p. 2, in appendix, Amnesty International, NORTH KOREA: Government Replies to Amnesty International Report (October 1993, ASA 24/06/93).
15. 'Koreans Tell of Rights Bbuses by Pyongyang', *Bangkok Post*, 11 November 1993, p. 10.
16. An example of this theory is Kenichi Ohmae, 'The Rise of the Region State', *Foreign Affairs*, vol. 72, no. 2 (Spring 1993), pp. 85–6.
17. Ed Vulliamy, 'Deadly Games with a Secret Foe', *Observer*, 12 June 1994, p. 15.

CHAPTER 9

1. The title of Ruth Benedict's famous book on Japan (New York: The World Publishing Co., 1967).

2. Takie S. Lebra, *Japanese Patterns of Behavior* (Honolulu: University of Hawaii Press, 1976), p. 111; Bowen, in Peter Schwab and Adamantia Pollis (eds), *Toward a Human Rights Framework* (New York: Praeger, 1982), p. 144. The quotation is Bowen's.

3. Roger W. Bowen, 'Human Rights in Japan', in Schwab and Pollis (eds), *Toward a Human Rights Framework* , pp. 146, 147.

4. Saburo Ienaga, *The Pacific War, 1931–1945: A Critical Perspective on Japan's Role in World War II* (New York: Pantheon Books, 1978), p. 19.

5. Quoted in ibid., p. 116.

6. The atrocities perpetrated by Japanese troops against conquered peoples during the Pacific War are well known. But Japanese soldiers also killed or forced many Japanese to commit suicide civilians on Okinawa, Saipan and other islands as they were attacked by US troops – in effect, forcing these civilians to abide by the Japanese military code forbidding surrender. Ibid., pp. 51, 53, 185.

7. See, for example, Karel van Wolferen, *The Enigma of Japanese Power: People and Politics in a Stateless Nation* (New York: Alfred A. Knopf, 1989).

8. Robert Garran, 'Police Hit Streets in Thousands to Contain Yakuza War', *The Australian*, 10 September 1997, p. 9.

9. Amnesty International, 'Japan: The "Substitute Prison" System: A Source of Human Rights Violations' (ASA 22/10/93, October 1993).

10. Frank Gibney Jr and Hiroko Tashiro, 'Hard Time', *Time*, 28 October 1996, pp. 36–40.

11. John O. Haley, 'Sheathing the Sword of Justice in Japan: An Essay on Law Without Sanctions', *Journal of Japanese Studies*, vol. 8 (1982), p. 269.

12. Bowen, 'Human Rights in Japan', p. 134.

13. Taichi Sakaiya, *What is Japan? Contradictions and Transformations* (New York and Tokyo: Kodansha International, 1993), p. 7.

14. Kwan Weng Kin, 'Japan's safe image shot down by illegal arms,' *Sunday Times*, 25 December 1994, p. 5.

15. Louis D. Hayes, *Introduction to Japanese Politics* (New York: Paragon House, 1992), p. 203.

16. Horio Teruhisa, *Education Thought and Ideology in Modern Japan: State Authority and Intellectual Freedom* (Tokyo: University of Tokyo Press, 1988), p. 15.

17. Hayes, *Introduction to Japanese Politics*, p. 139.

18. United States Department of State, 'Japan Report on Human Rights Practices for 1996', 30 January 1997. <http://www.usis.usemb.se/human/japan.html>, p. 3.

19. Amnesty International, 'Japan: Inadequate protection for refugees and asylum-seekers' (ASA 22/01/93, March 1993); and Amnesty International, 'Japan: Asylum-seekers still at risk' (ASA 22/01/94, January 1994).

20. Joe Joseph, *The Japanese* (London: Viking, 1993), pp. 148, 149.

21. Edwin M. Reingold, *Chrysanthemums and Thorns: The Untold Story of Modern Japan* (New York: St. Martin's Press, 1992), pp. 160–1.

22. Ibid., p. 163.

23. Joseph, *The Japanese*, pp. 155–8.

24. Robert J. Smith, 'Gender Inequality in Contemporary Japan', *The Journal of Japanese Studies*, vol. 13 (Winter 1987), p. 9.

25. Ardath W. Burks, 'Japan: The Bellwether of East Asian Human Rights?' in James C. Hsiung (ed.), *Human Rights in East Asia* (New York: Paragon House, 1988), p. 39.
26. Asia Watch, 'Japan: Harassment of Chinese Dissidents', *News from Asia Watch*, 4 October 1990, p. 9.
27. David Arase, 'Japanese Policy toward Democracy and Human Rights in Asia', *Asian Survey*, vol. 33, no. 10 (October 1993), pp. 946–8.
28. Ibid., p. 938.
29. Edwin O. Reischauer, *The Japanese Today: Change and Continuity* (Cambridge, Mass.: Harvard University Press, 1988), p. 142.

Index